AFRICAN POLITICAL PHILOSOPHY

Edited By

Prof. Godfrey O. Ozumba
&
Elijah Okon John, Ph.D.

AFRICAN POLITICAL PHILOSOPHY

© Copyright 2017 G. O. Ozumba & Elijah O. John

All rights reserved. No part of this publication may be reproduced or stored in a retrieval system or transmitted in any form or by any means, electronic, mechanical, photocopying, recording or otherwise, without the prior written permission of the publisher.

Typeset in Nigeria by El-johns Services
+234 (0) 70322878735, (0) 8028322626

Publisher
Edioms Research and Innovation Centre (E-RIC), UK
Website: www.ediomsric.com
Email: helpdesk@ediomsric.com

Distribution
Edioms Research and Innovation Centre (E-RIC), Nigeria
&
Edioms Media and Publishing, Nigeria
Email: helpdesk@ediomsric.com

Printed by: Lulu Press Inc. USA

DEDICATION

This book is graciously dedicated to our intellectual descendants in African political philosophy both at home and in the Diaspora.

ACKNOWLEDGEMENTS

We acknowledge the unbounded help we received from the Omnipotent God who bestowed us with health and quickness of intellect throughout the period of this research. We are indepted in no small measure to all the contributors who responded with speed and accuracy in making their contributions to reach us on time, we remain grateful to Professor Udobafa Onunwa for the powerful foreword which bears true testimony of the merit of the work. To you, our erudite professor, we say many thanks

We remember many individuals for making themselves available as members of the editorial team and also and some as contributors to this work. We remain indebted to the secretariat staff of *El-johns Publishers,* Nigeria for the wonderful work of type setting this book. We cannot forget the many authors, from whom the contributors have drawn to enrich the quality of this look.

What we have done is to articulate some of the loose ideas on African philosophy to give it the necessary academic ornamentation for the purposes of documentation and purveyance to enrich our African intellectual heritage. Ideas as floating mass constitute no intellectual value unless they are systematized, synthesized and tied down or moored to the anchor of documentation through the tradition of writing. The false view that Africa had no history; no science and philosophy are attributable to this lacuna created by undocumentation. We have become wiser now, hence the resolve of these erudite philosophers never again to allow western ethnographers to commit the second sin against Africa by denigrating her as a continent without achievement. We are on the vanguard to ensure that the negative events of history do not undermine our identity and sovereignty.

This book is therefore a must read for all, those who wish to update their knowledge on how Africa has faired as a people of destiny. A reconstruction and resystematization of our history and philosophy is the only way we can chart a way forward and position Africa and Africans to play their role as the cradle of civilization and the worthy agents of positive change. We are on a threshold of reversal of history for Africa's advantage. We must not allow this moment of opportunity to impact on the global community momentously and expeditiously. Europe and the whole west have led us but not well, it is now our chance to provide leadership through a corrective optical vision that has enjoyed the benefits of hindsight and "present sight". With better spiritual, moral and cultural binoculars, it is our firm belief that Africa will provide more equitable and just leadership in the years ahead. We have worn the shoe of all human woes in the history of mankind and it is our determination that these woes cannot continue. In the spirit of integrative humanism, we are poised to weave a world where all will have a sense of belonging and have access to a fair share of all that providence has provided mankind to enjoy with no room for injustice, subordination, subjugation, exploitation marginalization and expropriation. Man's inhumanity to man which have characterized the era of western imperialism will be a thing of the past. Justice will banish terrorism and make our world a safe place for all.

Prof. G. O. Ozumba
Dr. Elijah Okon John

FOREWORD

This new book, *African Political Philosophy*, is both timely and auspicious. At a time when many African countries are suffering from poor leadership styles and management, poor ideological principles, poor methods of implementation of policies, when mediocre are occupying leadership positions which they are neither intellectually nor morally equipped to handle, therefore, a book of this nature is both challenging and refreshing. The chapters are current research results carried out by both established and budding scholars in different disciplines including philosophy, linguistics, communication studies, public administration, political science, history and international studies. There is an exegetical and analytical presentation of current research results giving new meanings and in-depth interpretations to *African Political Philosophy, African Identity, Colonialism in Africa, Pan-Africanism, African Nationalism, African Socialism, African Cultural Values, The Church and African Politics, Ethnicity in African Politics, and Women Participation in African Politics,* among others. A critical look at the chapters confirms a new approach and results which had hitherto been unrevealed about a repository of mine of wisdom and knowledge in traditional African philosophical thought and action. They are African scholars writing from their own African experiences. The work is simply written with coherent logic, clarity and systematic presentation of ideas.

The first thirteen chapters which form Section One of the book treat various aspects of traditional and modern African thought and wisdom in a most stimulating way. The last four chapters which incidentally fall into Section Two of the book, give a resume of the works of five outstanding African philosopher-kings, writers, thinkers and nationalists like Leopold Senghor, Fanon, King, Achebe and Iroegbu whose thought and ideas of Africa still challenge modern African scholars, politicians, leaders and nationalists. These four great men left indelible marks of African sands to time.

This book will be of immense value to various people including lecturers in tertiary institutions students of African studies, international diplomats, administrators, political office holders, policy makers, *practicing politicians,* traditional leaders and all who are interested in seeing peaceful, democratic, just and progressive governments in Africa. More so, those who understand and expect a pattern of servant leadership that ushers growth and development in any given society would be challenged and encouraged by the sort of African political philosophical principles espoused in the various chapters of this book. Leadership in African traditional society was not a business of the small minds but for wise and great philosophical minds. Today that is not a case. That is why *African Political Philosophy* must be a standard hand book and guide for any one in Africa aspiring to take up any political office or serve in public institutions. Those already occupying seats of power in governments need to study the chapters meticulously to help them understand some principles of leadership and service.

Finally, *African Political Philosophy* has come to dismiss the bogey myth of non-existence of the great and noble ideas of African philosophy, African theology and African history. It has rather come to justify the reality and existence of African philosophy espoused in the early 1970s by people like Professor Innocent Onyewuenyi who propounded the notion of Egyptian–African origin of Greek philosophy. This has also added to its academic merit and market potential. It is indeed a necessary addition to the growing volumes of brilliant books by a number of indigenous African scholars and writers.

Professor Udobata R. Onunwa, Fnas
Fellow of New York Academy of Sciences
Birmingham, UK
September 23, 2011

LIST OF CONTRIBUTORS

G. O. Ozumba, Ph.D., Professor, Editor and Head, Department of Philosophy, University of Calabar, Calabar, Nigeria.

Elijah Okon John, Ph.D., Editor and Senior Lecturer, Department of Philosophy, University of Uyo, Uyo, Nigeria.

Nwachukwu M. Anyim, Senior Lecturer, Department of Philosophy, University of Uyo, Uyo, Nigeria.

IKS J. Nwankwor, Ph.D., Senior Lecturer, Department of Philosophy, University of Uyo, Uyo, Nigeria.

David Lishilinimle Imbua, Ph.D., Lecturer, Department of History and International Studies, University of Calabar, Calabar, Nigeria.

Etim O. Frank, Ph.D., Lecturer, Department of Political Science and Public Administration, University of Uyo, Uyo, Nigeria.

Gabriel E. Idang, Ph.D., Lecturer, Department of Philosophy, University of Uyo, Uyo, Nigeria.

Iniobong Umotong, Ph.D., Senior Lecturer, Department of Philosophy, University of Uyo, Uyo, Nigeria.

Udeme U. Afia, Lecturer, Department of Zoology, University of Uyo, Uyo, Nigeria

Sylvester M. Eka, Ph.D., Senior Lecturer, Department of History and International Studies, University of Uyo, Uyo, Nigeria.

Enyimba Maduka, Lecturer, Department of Philosophy, University of Calabar, Calabar, Nigeria.

Ephraim A. Ikegbu, Ph.D. Lecturer, Department of Philosophy, University of Calabar, Calabar, Nigeria.

Emmanuel E. Etta, Ph.D. Lecturer, Department of Philosophy, University of Calabar, Calabar, Nigeria.

Solomon Kingsley Christopher, Post-Graduate Candidate, Department of Philosophy, University of Calabar, Calabar, Nigeria.

Dennis E. Igwe, Lecturer, Department of Philosophy, University of Uyo, Uyo, Akwa Ibom State and Doctoral Candidate, Department of Philosophy, University of Calabar, Nigeria.

Oduora Okpokam Asuo, Doctoral Candidate, Department of Philosophy, University of Calabar, Calabar, Nigeria.

Okeke Jonathan Chima, Doctoral Candidate, Department of Philosophy, University of Calabar, Calabar, Nigeria.

Godwin C. S. Iwuchukwu, Ph.D., Lecturer, Department of Linguistics and Communicaton Studies, University of Calabar, Calabar, Nigeria.

CONTENTS

Dedication iii
Acknowledgements iv
Foreword vi
List of contributors viii

SECTION ONE 1
Chapter 1
The Meaning of African Political Philosophy 2
Chapter 2
African Identity 11
Chapter 3
Colonialism In Africa 26
Chapter 4
Pan-Africanism 55
Chapter 5
African Nationalism 69
Chapter 6
Post-Colonial Africa: Problems and Prospects 84
Chapter 7
African Socialism 92
Chapter 8
Towards An Ideology For Africa: An Integrative Humanist
Approach 104
Chapter 9
African Cultural Values 130
Chapter 10
Ethnicity And African Political Philosophy 149
Chapter 11
Religious Factor In African Politics 172
Chapter 12
Women Participation In African Politics 182
Chapter 13
The Church And African Political Development 197
Chapter 14
Africa's Restoration: Rediscovering The Place Of African Cultural
Values In An *Ichabodded* History 216

SECTION TWO 240
Chapter 15 241

Senghor's Negritude 241
Chapter 16 256
Nkrumah'S Ideology For Africa 256
Chapter 17 271
Fanon's Philosophy Of Decolonization 271
Chapter 18 282
King's Pan-African Vision 282
Chapter 19 291
ACHEBE'S CONCEPT OF AN AFRICAN PHILOSOPHER 291
Chapter 20 306
Iroegbu's Ohacratic Philosophy 306

SECTION ONE

CHAPTER 1

THE MEANING OF AFRICAN POLITICAL PHILOSOPHY

By
PROF. G. O. OZUMBA
&
ELIJAH OKON JOHN, Ph.D.

Introduction

Philosophy does not flourish in a vacuum. It is watered by the social, religious, political, economic and cultural experiences of a people. Philosophy that is not grounded in the foregoing will be vacuous and blind. It will be an abstract weaving of metaphysical nonsense. This is not to say that metaphysics is no longer one of the life-giving arteries to the philosophical enterprise. What we are saying is that metaphysics that is devoid of the moorings of the existential facts of human existence will both be irrelevant and procrustean as humans may be handled as being the same with animals, plants and stones. The difference between man and other creatures is that man has a type of consciousness which is creative and transcending within the framework of reason and logic. It is this consciousness which compel man to take judicious, sociological and philosophic notice of his existence by asking the how, the what, and the why of the incidentals to his earthly existence.

It is on the note of the foregoing that it has become necessary to articulate and document the philosophical underpinnings of the African people's experience. In this work, we are concerned with what we have called African political philosophy. The question that should immediately come to mind is what do we mean by African political philosophy? We can still hear a reverberation of the prejudice of the western mind-set querying why not African political thought instead of African political philosophy? The obvious reason is that the west still sees philosophy as their birth-right and an exclusive reserve of issues that are centreed on western discourse and insight. For us Africans, political philosophy is very much fecund, alive and viable. There are many issues that are scattered in the body of extant literature. Our singular assignment is to see how to collate, systematize and put the breath of philosophy into a forlorn, prosaic and jejune account of the African experiences and documented historiography of the African people as were presented by western ethnographers and historians.

What is African Political Philosophy?

Before we delve into the rigorous issue of the meaning of African political philosophy, we shall first of all seek to understand the meaning of African philosophy as well as political philosophy. These two areas of study unarguably constitute the foundation of African political philosophy. Thus, defining them becomes very necessary if we must clearly understand what African political philosophy is all about. We have taken this position because, for philosophers, the pursuit of truth travels on precise definition. However, defining a term, concept or movement has never been an easy task. This problem of definition becomes even more pronounced and complicated when it involves a core area of philosophy like this one, which is inextricably wrapped up in the age-long controversy and inveterate prejudices. This problem of perennialism in definition notwithstanding, African philosophy can be defined as that area of investigation which is predominantly a socio-political philosophy. This assertion implies that African philosophy reflects mainly on the socio-political atmosphere of its time and place (John, 2009:208). According to Iroegbu (116), African philosophy is that aspect of reflective inquiry that burrows into the marvels and problems that confronts man in the African world with a view to producing systematic explanation and sustained responses. Similarly, Okolo (11), states that African philosophy is that enterprise which seeks to understand the African person and systematically and coherently articulate his experience of reality.

In this chapter, we shall, however, conceive the study of African philosophy as that peculiar discipline that reacts and demonstrates the spirit of universal philosophy to be relevant and convenient for the African experience of politics and culture. This view-point on African philosophy has, in the present, become what some thinkers like Momoh (xiv) refer to as African doctrines on the universe, its creator, its socio-political and economic challenges and the things and elements in t. We now move into the definition of political philosophy. According to John, political philosophy is:

> that area of philosophy which consistently and constantly seeks to use the tools of logic, epistemology, ethics and metaphysics to discover the proper nature and ideal form of society and how a justifiable government ought to be (John, 1999:52).

According to Joseph Omoregbe (2007:vi), socio-political philosophy is the philosophical investigation on how best a society can be organized in order to provide man with what he needs, in order to develop himself and live a happy life. In this respect, socio-political philosophy seeks to evaluate society and its many sub-units: the family, the church, the various unions and major political forms like socialism, communism, democracy, welfarism and other forms of governance. A socio-political philosophy deals directly with the issue of ideal social organization. It does not venture unto the art and science of capturing power and keeping office. Rather, it evaluates and discusses critically the problems of how an ideal state should be organized. It studies social and political phenomena and relationships among people, particularly those relations which exist in a state (Blocker and Steward, 449).

Furthermore, it investigates into and tackles the issue of man's social behaviour from the view-point of ethics, law, religion and politics. That is, it focuses on how society is arranged and accordingly deals with how the needs of individuals and that of the state could properly be satisfied. Basically, therefore, socio-political philosophy deals with such issues as the origin, functions, powers and limitations of the state as well as its relationship with the individuals and sub-groups, which make up the society. Broadly speaking, however, socio-political philosophy as a serious enterprise that controls the affairs of men in the society, mainly deals with two basic issues, namely; the substantive and the conceptual problems in political matters. The substantive matters relate to issues such as the true nature of the state, the origin of the state, the grounds for the justification of the state, that is, the purpose and ultimate reason for the existence of the state. In a proper political parlance, the summary of the above issues is: why does the state xist? (John, 2009:37).

Closely linked to the substantive crust of socio-political theory are the problems of proper relationship between individuals and that state. That is to ask, does the state exist on its own right over and above the citizen's rights? Or, is there no right of the state besides those of the citizens? Socio-political philosophy further asks: are there some conditions under which citizens are justified to seek for the dissolution of the state if the citizens are obsessed with it? Is civic disobedience always or even justified? Aside from the substantive matters, some of the conceptual problems tackled by socio-political philosophy relate to issues like "justice", "power", "authority", "the state of nature", "liberty", "majority rule", "the general will", political institutions like "democracy", "socialism", "communism", "fascism", among others. It is proper to say at this point that socio-political philosophers raise and tackle the substantive and the conceptual matters from different area perspectives and they, accordingly, draw different conclusions. Some socio-political thinkers even concentrate much of their time and energy to ascertain problems in certain areas of interest.

Having attempted some definitions of African philosophy as well as political philosophy, we now move unto the meaning of African political philosophy. By way of definition, African political philosophy is a sub-set of political philosophy that researches into, conforms and domesticates everything that is ascribed to the universal political philosophy. That is, it has everything in common with global political thought except its Africanness. In other words, it addresses the unique problems and nature of African societies. This may be the probable reason why Falaiye defines African political philosophy as:
> A response to the different experiences of slavery, colonialism, radicalism, and neo-colonialism having made the African ready and capable of evolving a

peculiar political philosophy. Such political philosophy is intended to capture the Africanness of his thought, system and experience (1997:33).

This view shows that African political philosophy is the systematization, the logicization and the rational articulation of the African experience as it relates to the pre-colonial, colonial and post-colonial politics. It involves the analyses of political concepts from the point of view of African experience within or outside the shores of Africa. It may also include critical analysis of the political actions or inactions of non-Africans and their direct or indirect reflections on the African life and system of government.

The best way of understanding the African people is through their history. And their history is nothing but their experiences comprising of events, actions and inactions. This makes it imperative to take a historical approach in the understanding of the political philosophy of the African. African nations had their political systems ranging from what we call primitive heroic rulership to organized kingship systems to some forms of primitive communal democracyto some forms of republicanism and then to modern-Athenian-like form of direct democracy. It depends on where we begin to trace the forms of governance that had been in vogue over the years. Democracy is therefore not alien to the African people. We have always been a strong advocate of the view that humans in all climes have similar capacities; the differences we see among men are merely circumstantial or situational. Men over the years have always been concerned on how to improve their lots in terns of social and political harmony. It is this understanding that necessitated the movement from the Hobbesian state of nature where life was nasty, short, poor and brutish to modern democracy where there is hope for security. There is the inherent instinct to move away from a barbaric and unjust system to a more just and fair system. Africans and the African society are not left out of this evolution of political ideas and systems.

The above definitions point to the fact that African socio-political philosophy, as a discipline, has its roots in the different experiences that are reflected in the thought system of the African. And this actually started between 18th and the middle of the 20th centuries.

This was the period that African continent suffered severe form of colonialism from European nations such as Britain, France, Portugal, Belgium, Germany, Italy and Spain. As at that time, these European countries were more developed scientifically, technologically, economically and politically than African nation-states. To a large extent, what is regarded today as African political philosophy sprang from the desire to find solutions to the adversarial consequences of colonialism on the continent.

The European invaders had as their paramount interest, in many forms and shades, the discovery and acquisition of cheap labour and raw materials for their new farms, industries as well as markets for their finished products: this interest, predictably, led to what has been described as the scramble for and partitioning of Africa. By the end of the 1890s the partition among the European colonizers earlier mentioned was complete. This incident brought about the unfortunate lumping together of several linguistic independent nations into various entities called countries with artificial boundaries. Mbiti (1967), George James (1954), Walter Rodney (1977), Diop (1978) and Onyewuenyi (1993) have vividly exposed the impact of colonialism with all its attendant vices.

We have therefore tried to showcase the different strands of perspectives on African experience starting from the primordial times to the times of supplantation of the African consciousness and life patterns in virtually all areas of their endeavour. We have had some critical experiences like Christianization, islamization, slavery, colonization, neo-colonization, imperialism, manipulation and "underdogization". All these experiences have come to intimately characterize our perception of ourselves and in relation to others. It is akin to what Simone de Beauvoir has said that man's perception of the woman has led him to see her as the second sex and as an underdog meant only to be used, manipulated and exploited. The story of women vis-à-vis men is the story of Africa vis-à-vis the colonizers.

Our construction of African political philosophy is not a vengeance mission but a corrective vision to help us heal the wounds of the past and provide enabling intellectual environment for a reconstruction of a world view that makes for peaceful coexistence and harmony. This is what Ozumba (2010) calls the philosophy of integrative humanism.

African political philosophy should be concerned with how Africans in a pragmatic fashion could cause a re-engineering of their world-views, ways of doing things, system of values, objectives and life-ideals. A nation that has no system of ideals that will direct it endeavours is bound to steer off the path of nobility. Today, we are forced back to the practice of democracy. The question is: what are the cardinal indices for a democratically compliant nation? The canons of democracy include equal participation, justice, separation of powers, independence of the judiciary and the legislature, equitable distribution of resources, people-oriented leadership, accountability, freedom of speech, right to vote and be voted for, due process, etc.

In our peculiar Nigerian situation, we are talking about zoning and federal character in order to avoid domination of one section over others. But how do we articulate a zoning system that is fair and equitable? This is the crux of the matter. How do we live and deal in sincerity one with another? If one obeys the principle of zoning, how is he sure that the next one will respect the principle when it is his turn? How do we redress past injustices and lopsided leadership that had been endemic in Nigeria before the present political dispensation? Justice is a holistic thing. Reparations, restitutions and just balancing must be done before we can inaugurate a new and authentic zoning policy in Nigeria.

African political philosophy must therefore be concerned with creativity, adaptation and rational weaving of ideologies to meet the hopes and aspirations of the African people. We are not to excavate, re-invent and recorgitate anachronistic ways of the past to become a dominant paradigm for the present. Those aspects of our past that are glorious and positive can be re-invented and re-engineered to suit the present realities that abound in the African soils. We must address issues that relate to election rigging, sit-tightism, administrative infantilism, executive lawlessness, corruption (in its many facets), poverty, disease, lack of vision, highhandedness, self-centredness of leadership, lack of people-oriented programmes, having square pegs in round holes (choice of leaders), clientellism, godfatherism, political thuggery, unemployment, lack of prioritization of policies and their implementations.

We must put in place adequate mechanism for reward and punishment. Evil and corrupt men cannot continue to walk our streets unpunished while petty thieves are clobbered down as culprits of our system. A credible electoral system that allows people's choice to prevail and a subsequent possibility to change non-performers must be installed. The political scenario in most African nations is indicative of an evolving scenario that promises positive things in the near future. People are becoming not just aware of their rights but showing equal willingness to defend same. We must visualize and work towards a future for Africans where sanity will reign and it will not be business as usual.

Our socio-political education should be made more practical, issue based, critical and creative. With this, we are then going to set ourselves on a steady progress to the actualization of our political ideals.

WORKS CITED

Diop, Anta C. *African Origin of Western Civilization: Myth or Reality?* Westport, Connecticut: Lawrence Hill, 1974.

Falaiye, O. A. "Democracy in Africa: Problems and Prospects" in *Journal for the Advancement of Africans and Blacks in the Diaspora*. Vol.2, No.1, 1997.

Iroegbu, Pantaleon. *Enwisdomization and African Philosophy*. Owerri: International University Press, 1994.

James, George G. M. *The Stolen Legacy*. San Francisco: Julian Richardson Publishers, 1954.

John, Elijah Okon. "Social and Political Philosophy" in Udo Etuk (Ed). *Introduction to Philosophy and Logic*. Uyo: Afahaide Publishers, 1999.

John, Elijah Okon. "African Socio-Political Philosophy" in Andrew F. Uduigwomen (Ed). *From Footmarks to Landmarks in African Philosophy*. Lagos: Obaroh and Ogbinaka Publishers, 2009.

Mbiti, John S. *African Religions and Philosophy*. London: Heinemann Books, 1969.

Momoh, C. S. *The Substance of African Philosophy*. Auchi: African Philosophy Projects Publication, 2000.

Okolo, C. B. *What is African Philosophy?* Enugu: Freeman's Press, 1987.

Onyewuenyi, Innocent C. *The African Origin of Greek Philosophy: An Exercise in Afrocentricism*. Nsukka: University of Nigeria Press, 1993.

Ozumba, G. O. *Philosophy and Method of Integrative Humanism*. Calabar: Jochrisam Publishers, 2010.

Rodney, Walter. Africa. Tanzania Publishing House, 1972.

CHAPTER 2

AFRICAN IDENTITY

By
ELIJAH OKON JOHN, Ph.D.
&
DENNIS E. IGWE

Introduction

The origin of the search for an African identity dates back to the latter part of the 19th and first half of the 20th-century. In other words, Africans in the first half of this century began the attempt at determining the identity of the African. By making the said search, Africans must have believed that they had lost their identity or had been denied of it. Though such belief is difficult to prove, such thinking however, must have been influenced by three major factors, namely, slavery, colonialism, and racism. Quite regrettably, the problem of African identity was made worse by colonialism, which had made the African to lose the things that make him a real African. Simply put, the African has been influenced by the Euro-Christian tradition, the Afro-Islamic culture, and the traditional African heritage. Consequently, he is neither a real European nor a real African. The gravity of this problem prompted scholars and political thinkers in the 1960s to suggest the adoption of a peculiar African political philosophy, which is commonly referred to as African socialism. But does African socialism constitute African identity? In this chapter, we are concerned with African identity. In doing this, we shall treat the notions of 'identity' and 'Africa', as well as consider thinkers' views on African identity; thereafter; we shall undertake a critical analysis of the issues involved.

Identity

Sociologically, identity is a term used to describe a person's conception and expression of his individuality or group affiliation (e.g. cultural identity, and national identity). It is also used with respect to place of identity. Psychologically, identity relates to self-image, self-esteem, and individuality. In other words, it has to do with a person's mental mode of himself or herself. Gender identity is an important instance of identity in psychology, as it dictates significantly how an individual views himself in nature (Leary and Tangney, 3). Philosophers have also reflected on the concept of identity. Philosophical discourse on identity which predated psychological discourse began with Rene Descartes. Descartes' famous dictum, 'I think, therefore I am' has made thinkers to seriously inquire what exactly 'I' is, and if indeed 'I-ness' can be derived from doubt. Viewed generally, identity is what identifies somebody or something. In other words, it is the name or essential character that identifies somebody or something. It is called 'essential self', the set of character that somebody recognizes as belonging uniquely to himself or herself and constantly his or her individual personality for life. Furthermore, identity could be said to mean sameness, the fact or condition of being the same or exactly alike.

Africa

Africa is the world's second largest and second most populous continent after Asia, occupying an area of about 30,221,532km^2 and having a population of about 1,022,234,000 (Barnard and Spencer, 23). It is bounded by the Atlantic Ocean on the west, the Indian Ocean and the Red sea on the east and the Mediterranean sea on the north. The continent has fifty-four sovereign states and various island groups. It is commonly divided along the lines of Sahara, the world's largest desert, which cuts a huge swath through the northern half of the continent. The countries north of the Sahara make up the region of North Africa, while the region south of the desert is known as sub-Saharan Africa. North Africa consists of the countries of Algeria, Egypt, Libya, Morocco, Sudan, and Tunisia. Sub-Saharan Africa is generally subdivided into the regions of West Africa, East Africa, Central Africa and Southern Africa. Well over a thousand languages are spoken in Africa, making it the most multi-lingual continent in the world. Most are of African origin, though, some are of European and Asian origin.

Africa is considered by most pale-oanthropologists to be the oldest inhabited territory on earth, with the human species originating from the continent (Newman, 23). Africa, after many centuries became increasingly dominated by European traders and colonies. Millions of Africans were sent to work as slaves on colonial plantations in North America, South America and the Caribbean by European traders. Europeans also sought Africa's wealth of raw materials to fuel their industries. In the late 19th century, Euro-powers seized and colonized virtually all of Africa. However, through slow reform and violent struggle, most of Africa won independence in the 1950s and 60s. Sadly, independent Africa inherited from colonization, a weak position in the global economy, underdeveloped communication and transportation systems, and arbitrarily drawn boundaries. The citizens of these new nations generally had little in terms of history or culture to bind them together.

The culture of Africa encompasses and includes all cultures which were ever in the continent of Africa. Some aspects of traditional African cultures have become less practiced in recent years as a result of years of neglect and suppression by colonial and post-colonial regimes. In the 1960s and 70s, the notion of a "Pan-African" culture which was discussed earnestly in the context of the *Negritude* movement, tends to have fallen out of fashion in African studies. At present, there is resurgence in the attempts to rediscover and revitalize African traditional cultures, under such movements as the African Renaissance led by Thabo Mbeki, Afrocentricism, led by a group of scholars including Molefi Asante, as well as the increasing recognition of traditional spiritualism.

African Identity

According to Colin Legum, the term African identity or personality was first initiated by Edward Blyden in his presidential address on the occasion of the opening of the Liberian College, Liberia in 1981. In the said address entitled: "The Idea of African Personality" Blyden calls for the reasonableness of the African in order to advance by the methods of his own… to find out his own phase and work, develop his peculiar gifts and powers; and the training for the Negro youth upon the basis of their own idiosyncrasies with a sense of race individuality, self-respect and liberty (21-22).

Provoked by the untrammeled trespassing Africa's history, personality and economy by the imperialist nations in addition to other negative influence of the colonial situation in Africa, Nkrumah echoed the need for the articulation of a peculiar African personality and identity thus:

> For so long in our history, Africa has spoken through the voices of others. Now, what I have called an African personality in international affairs will have a chance of making its proper impact and let the world know it through the voices of Africa's own sons (1961: 125).

The search for an African identity intensified after the independence of most African nations. The dismantling of the colonial empires built by the colonial masters or imperialists provided the driving force. In an attempt to provide a solution to the problems encountered by Africans as a result of colonization, many Africans embraced African socialism as the remedy for a true African identity. Such socialism must reflect on the problems and mysteries of the Negroid race if it is to be truly African by nature. Most importantly, it must encapsulate the Africanness of the Negroid people. African socialism is a belief in sharing economic resources in a "traditional" African way, as distinct from classical socialism. Many African leaders and politicians of the 1950s and 1960s upheld African socialism, although definitions and interpretations of this term varied considerably. Following the wars of independence, most African nations quickly embraced socialism. At its base, African socialism is all about *Africanness* (all things Africa), or more precisely, an afrocentric notion of knowledge (epistemology) premised on a legacy of connection to the history of suffering or the physical location of Africa as a focal point. Friedland and Rosberg (34) summarize the three main characteristics of African socialism thus: no private ownership of land; no social classes; and no shirking of responsibility to cooperate (work).

We will discuss some of the ideologies postulated by some of the most famous African leaders. For example, there was Leopold Senghor who devised the philosophy of *Negritude*, Mobutu Sese Seko who came up with *Mobutism*, Kenneth Kaunda who subscribed to a philosophy of *Humanism*, Julius Nyerere who came up with the concept of *Ujamaa*, and Kwame Nkrumah reputed as the father of *African socialism*.

Leopold Senghor: Senghor (1906-2001) was the president of Senegal. His famous philosophy, negritude, is based on the idea that the history of Black Africa includes the ancient Egypt and that blackness is an aesthetic matter of beauty and pride (a kind of anti-racist racism). His concept of *négritude* which owes a great deal to its French intellectual origin has been used widely after the Second World War. It embraces the revolt against colonial values, glorification of the African past, and nostalgia for the beauty and harmony of traditional African society. Senghor defined the concept in contradistinction to Europe and gave it more positive meaning. According to Senghor, it is "the sum total of the values of the civilization of the African world" – not an antithesis but a fundamentally different culture (12). Senghor argues that African mode of experience is far from irrational; the experience that proceeds from intuition which is fuller and more comprehensive than that derived from a discursive approach. Senghor sees "negritude" as a way of identifying with "Blackness" without having to draw upon culture, language, or nationality. In this way, Senghor believes people of African descent could transcend their differences and unite on the basis of a shared collective experience and sensibility. He perceives Blacks as unique people with special contributions to make to the world. Negritude therefore is an ideological attempt to re-discover African identity. According to its Patron Saints, Senghor, negritude represents the black man's history, pride, strength, culture, economy, politics, philosophy, religion, and destiny (Markowitz, 65).

Mobutu Sese Seko: Sese Seko (1930-1997) was the leader of Zaire. His philosophy, technically called Mobutism, is also known as authenticity, which was similar to negritude but also involved the call for Africans everywhere to drop their European names and adopt African names, clothing, hats, and attire. Mobutu pursued a national, cultural revival program in Zaire called *Authenticité* which began in 1967 and sought to purge colonial or European culture from Zaire and restore local culture, by forbidding Christian names and culture while promoting local African names and culture as well as forbidding western suits and creating a state-authorized uniform called the *abacost* (Young and Turner, 70). The ideology survives today in such organizations as Nzanga Mobutu's Union of Mobutuist Democrats.

As president, Mobutu sought to foster a cult of personality revolving around his stature as a hero and a leader. He emphasized the need to "return to African authenticity". As a result, Mobutu renamed the country, Zaire in 1971, after an old, local name for the Congo River. He changed his name to *Mobutu Sese Seko Kuku Ngbendu wa za Banga* (officially translated as 'the all-powerful warrior who, because of his endurance and inflexible will to win, will go from conquest to conquest leaving fire in his wake'). He banned European names and dress, and began to wear his leopard-skin signature hat. Credited with developing a sense of unity among the diverse ethnic groups, Mobutu promoted the use of four African languages (Lingala, Swahili, Kikongo, and Tshiluba) to complement the official language, French. Under the 1973 'Zairianization' policy, his government seized about 2000 foreign-owned businesses. Most were distributed within Mobutu's inner circle (Fegley, 4).

Kenneth Kaunda: Kaunda (1924 till date) was the leader of Zambia and an important figure in the Non-Aligned Movement (an organization of States who chose not to align with any Cold War blocs). He invested heavily in the country's educational system, engaged in central economic planning, and nationalized several corporations. His political rule has been described as a "one-party participatory democracy" which amounts to a one-party state with a written document that can only loosely be called a constitution. He founded a left nationalist-socialist ideology called Zambian Humanism which emphasized the importance of modern central planning/state control with basic African values such as mutual aid, trust, and loyalty. Kaunda stated that in traditional African society, inter-dependence among members was a common feature. The poor, the lame, the sick and the old relied upon stronger members of the society for care and support. Traditional African society, thus, was premised on communal living.

Julius Nyerere: Nyerere (1922-1999) was the leader of Tanzania. As president, he established one-party rule, redistributed wealth from the rich to the poor, and created a socialist economy which involved collectivization of the country's agricultural system (cooperative and community farms). His philosophy was known as *Ujamaa,* or *familyhood* which is usually taken as a reference to the traditional African extended family system. The extended family according to Nyerere is the foundation and the objective of African socialism. The true African socialist does not look on one class of men as his brethren and another as his natural enemies. He rather regards all men as his brethren, as members of his ever extending family. Nyerere in this direction affirms the first article of TANU's creed: "*Binadamu wote ni ndugu zangu, na Afrika ni moja.*" Meaning: "I believe in human brotherhood and the unity of Africa." "*Ujamaa,*" then, or "familyhood," describes African socialism. It is opposed to capitalism, which seeks to build a happy society on the basis of the exploitation of man by man; and it is equally opposed to doctrinaire socialism which seeks to build its happy society on a philosophy of inevitable conflict between man and man (Nyerere, 17).

Kwame Nkrumah: Nkrumah (1909-1972) was the leader of Ghana, and under his rule, Ghana adopted the trademark African socialism, including a welfare system, an educational system, and various community programmes. He described his philosophy as "consciencism" which refers to an ethics of practicing good will and dignity (Nkrumah, 1964). Philosophical consciencism was his discursive attempt to forge a new harmony between the re-Africanized identity of the post-colonial state and the conflicting subjectivities that emerged from the forced mixing of indigenous African, Islamic and Euro-Christian traditions during the colonial period. His strategy was to see the modern socialism of Marx as the fulfillment of the communalism and redistributive policies of pre-colonial chieftaincies, and as the suppression of Islamic feudalism and Christian liberal capitalism. Nkrumah's hope was that, in spite of neo-colonial pressures, socialists in post-colonial states would be able to contain the above "schimatic tendencies" before they were ripe (Thomson, 104).

Critical Analysis

The concept of African socialism contended by many African thinkers to represent African identity is believed to follow three basic directions: the search for an African identity; the crisis of economic development; and the dilemma of control and class formation. Obviously, African identity and African socialism are related to each other, both in origin and in objective. Both were reactions to colonialism. After independence, most African leaders became very antagonistic to all forms of colonial tendencies. They showed distinguishing differences between the colonialists and Africans with regard to culture, skin colour, traditional socio-political experience, and so forth. A new philosophy became very expedient which was geared toward purging Africans of colonial contaminations. This metamorphosed into African identity and African socialism. Friedland and Rosberg (41) corroborated this view when they said that African socialism had become both a reaction against Europe and a search for a unifying doctrine. Thus, for Africans to be united and mobilized towards sustained economic development, the common factors binding them together must have to be emphasized. It was strongly believed that the common factor was the 'Africanness'. In an attempt to propagate the Africanness of the people, African leaders and scholars developed and propounded the idea of African socialism. African orthodox socialists changed and became African socialists. African leaders and scholars had the desire to make their type of socialism to be radically different from that of Europe. The main purpose of this attempt was to prove that African identity was distinct. This distinct identity depended on what was meant or supposed to be an indigenous, egalitarian, classless and communal society.

However, it is expedient to note that the relationship between African socialism and African identity is neither causal nor logical. African socialism tends to have produced an imaginary traditional communalism spread through every part of Africa. Communalism and socialism do not have any necessary or scientific nexus. Thus, it cannot be the case that socialism must surely develop ultimately wherever communalism existed. It is wrong to assume that African identity can only be found by a return to that communal African past. The issue of split personality in Africa and cross personality created by the effect of foreign cultures must not be overlooked. Africa's socio-political experience in contemporary times shows a hybrid of confusing cultures and values. The traditional identity has been lost in most cases. The rate at which the African is being converted into a European and an American has continued to increase. Western influences have seriously marred African heritage and values.

African socialism has the problem of trying to prove African identity by all means. This attempt in our opinion cannot achieve the desired goal. African identity must not be seen from the perspective of African socialism. Socialism must not be confused with communalism. There can still be African identity in African democracy or any other theory. Having a particular identity for the African is pretty difficult. Africa has divergent cultures, hence, different conceptions and perceptions of life. There is no one theory that can be equated with African identity. Having different cultures, arts, languages, leadership, and so on, makes it almost impossible to have a theory that could constitute African identity. However, it must be stressed that most African nations, historically, have appreciable values such as communal living, respect for elders, fear of God and gods, morals, diligence and so on. These values cannot be seen only from the searchlight of African socialism, for such values can also be viewed from other perspectives such as African democracy, African capitalism, and African theocracy and so on, depending on the analysis and explanation. Falaiye in this direction postulated that African socialism as developed especially by Nyerere and Senghor is a poor attempt at creating a special world for the African (91-101).

The crisis of economic development and the East-West polarization of the world also contributed to the quest for an African identity and the inevitable development of African socialism. It is, as well, true to say that the need for a redefinition of African identity arose from the lopsidedness of the colonial economy. It made the exploitation of African economies easy; because Africans had no industries for the processing of raw materials, they had no entrepreneurs during the colonial era. Many African leaders had argued or asserted that economic development has to rely, to a large extent, on the public sector or on the joint control of both the public and private sectors. The Russian federation, it was believed, found its identity by developing a different and distinct mode of production. Economically and scientifically, former USSR achieved a lot within forty years and was able to catch up with (and overtook in some respects), the rest of Europe via the public control of the means of production and distribution.

Many African leaders were/are of the view that African socialism will solve the economic problem of Africa and reshape African identity if it is carefully planned and coordinated. But how can this be planned in the face of multi-cultural, multi-religious, and multi-linguistic disposition of Africa? Must Africa's economic development be achieved only through socialism as propounded by some African thinkers? Surprisingly, capitalist nations are thriving more, economically, than socialist nations. How then could Africa align with socialism?

Lastly, let us look at the dilemma of control and class formation. During the colonial rule, it was very essential for the colonialists to try hard to get the respect of the Africans. For this reason, the leaders of independent African nations inherited followers who were disinterested. They had to start mobilizing. The followership was made to know the necessity of having a strong control so as to affect a strong and joint effort to make Africa, a force to be reckoned with. The employment of coercion and intimidation gave way to the general will, the will of the people as put forward by Rousseau. Unity and harmony were necessary in achieving the general will. The division of people into classes, which the colonialists introduced, was discarded. African socialism was believed to be capable of putting an end to the unnecessary class and group antagonisms.

While we denounce conscious class formation, we disagree that African socialism is the solution to the problem. Humans by nature are not the same, hence, are not equal. And since they are not equal, class distinction is bound to exist. We do not think there is any system of government that can erase class distinction. The existence of government alone is a sufficient prove that class distinction is unavoidable. And of course, no rational being will opt for anarchy. Viewing African identity from the perspective of African socialism is not acceptable to us. It cannot discard class distinction as believed by some thinkers. We are however, against exploitation and dehumanization of any form. It is unjust. Class can exist, yet, devoid of exploitation and dehumanization.

Indeed, the experiences of Africans during the colonial era were very disheartening. The conscious, artificial class distinction that existed between the colonialists and the colonized (Africans) was evil. The colonialists saw Africans as nonentities and humans of very low esteem; lower creatures that could be called cannibals; people without any known achievements. Many negative things were and are propagated by the Western press against Africa and many Africans are made to believe that there is nothing positive about them. David Hume had stated that the Negroes, and in general, all the other species of men are naturally inferior to whites. For him, there never was a civilized nation of any complexion than the white. His European brother, Hegel a great philosopher of the German idealist tradition excludes the black as people with full consciousness and he concludes that Africans have no history because they lack full development of their consciousness and are ignorant of their freedom and as such have made no contribution to human development. However, it is on record that Africa of antiquity has been the centre of attraction for many. The great civilizations of the world began in Africa. This was the reason many ancient philosophers and scholars visited Africa to develop their philosophical doctrines. Onyeocha (32-34), John (147,148), Onyewuenyi (1994), James (1954), Diop (1974) and Rodney (1972) write that Africa was an intellectual Mecca to European scholars in antiquity.

Thales of Miletus and Democritus who were Ionian philosophers as well as the first luminaries of Greek science, made their most important discoveries in astronomy and mathematics after their visit to Egypt and Mesopotamia. They also write that Pythagoras who developed one of the most famous mathematical formulas spent twenty years studying in Egypt. Also, Socrates, Plato, Aristotle and many others visited Egypt, studied there and freely referred to Egyptian writers. According to Homer, the great poet and scholar, in terms of the knowledge of medicine, Africa left the rest of the world behind (70). This can be further attested to, by a historical research carried out by Mary Motley. Her result was that the first physician of antiquity of any fame was the black Egyptian, Imhotep, who lived about 2980BC during the third dynasty. He cured physical and mental sicknesses (42).

Walter Rodney from his researches offers us a lot about the glorious years of Africa, the years before slave trade and colonialism. He discovered that Africans of five centuries ago were producing high quality products that attracted the attention of the whole world. According to him, through North Africa, Europeans became aware of a superior brand of red leather from Africa, which was given the name "Moroccan leather". This leather, it is said, was tanned and dyed by the Hausa and Mandinga specialists in northern Nigeria and Mali. This was also the case with cloths. As soon as the Portuguese reached the old kingdom of Kongo, they sent back words on the high quality cloths made there that were comparable to velvet. Before the Europeans arrived Africa, Africans were widely manufacturing the best cotton cloth. Even to the last century, local cottons from the Guinea coast were stronger than those from Manchester. Also in Katanga and Zambia, local copper continued to be preferred to the imported ones because of the quality. The same holds true for iron in Sierra Leone (50). The summary of what we are saying here is that Africa has a unique identity, though the west and the rest of the world have tried to corrupt it. African identity is the basis and foundation of our humanism, aspirations and freedom. Africans must therefore give expression to what they perceive and identify themselves in the context of the world situation and of the problems of mankind.

Conclusion

Africa indeed, has a glorious past and greatly relevant in global matters, hence, cannot be ignored. All humans share same essence irrespective of race. The notion of superiority and inferiority therefore, need not arise. Such is absurd. African socialism as propounded by many African leaders and scholars as a solution to the problem of African identity is unacceptable. Developing African socialism out of African communal living is wrong. Any other theory can as well be traced to pre-colonial African communal living. Africa is multifaceted, hence cannot be aligned with any particular theory. African identity, ultimately, remains unique as it is evident in many African values: cultures, traditions, morals, folklores, religious practices, songs, dances, leadership, and so on. It is on this note that we agree with Okadigbo that inspite of the seeming contradictions that envelop it, African identity is that which defines the ideological, psychological, territorial and paternalistic boundaries of Africans within the system of direct religious and colonial domination, and it represents the aspiration of contemporary Africans to speak and act like Africans with honour and dignity (21).

WORKS CITED

Barnard, A. and Spencer, J. (Eds). *Encyclopedia of Social and Cultural Anthropology*. London: Routledge, 1996.

Diop, Anta C. *African Origin of Westrn Civilization: Myth or Reality?* Westport, Connecticut: Lawrence Hill Publishers, 1974.

Falaiye, O. A. "African Socialism and the Dilemma of African Identity" in *Journal for the Advancement of Africans and Blacks in the Diaspora*. Vol. 1, No. 1, 1996.

Fegley, Randall Arlin. "Mobutu Sese Seko" in *Microsoft Encarta*. Redmond, WA: Microsoft Corporation, 2008.

Friedland, W. and Rosberg, C. (Eds.). *African Socialism*. Stanford: Hoover Institution, 1992.

Homer. *The Odyssey*. Trans. E. V. Rieu. Harmondsworth: Penguin Books, 1946.

James, George G. M. *The Stolen Legacy.* San Francisco: Julian Richardson Publishers, 1954.

John, Elijah Okon. *Man and the State: Issues in Socio-political Philosophy.* Uyo: Afahaide, 2009.

Leary, M. R and J. P. Tangney. *Handbook of Self And Identity.* New York:Guilford Press, 2003.

Legum, Colin. *Pan-Africanism.* New York: Frederick A. Praeger, 1962.

Markowitz, I. L. *Leopold Sedar Senghor and the Polictics of Negritude.* New York: Atheneum, 1969.

Motley, Mary. *Africa: Its Empires and People.* Detroit: Wayne State University Press, 1969.

Newman, James, et al. "Africa" in *Microsoft Encarta.* Washington: Microsoft Corporation, 2008.

Nkrumah, Kwame. *Consciencism.* New York: Monthly Review Press, 1964.

Nyerere, Julius. *Ujamaa: Essays on Socialism.* Oxford: Oxford University Press, 1968.

Okadigbo, Chuba. *Consciencism in African Polictical Philosophy.* Enugu: Fourth Dimension Publishers, 1985.

Onyeocha, Izu. *Africa: The Question of Identity.* Washington: The Council of Research in Values and Philosophy, 1997.

Onyewuenyi, Innocent C. *The African Origin of Greek Pilosophy: An Exercise in Afrocentrism.* Nsukka: University of Nigeria, 1994.

Rodney, Walter. *How Europe Underdeveloped Africa.* Howard: Howard University Press, 1981.

Senghor, Leopold. *The Concept of Negritude.* New York: New York Athenium, 1969.

Thomson, A. An Introduction to African Politics. NY: Routledge, 2010.

Young, Crawford and Thomas, Turner. *The Rise and Decline of the Zairian State.* Wisconsin: University of Wisconsin Press, 1985.

CHAPTER 3

COLONIALISM IN AFRICA

By

ELIJAH OKON JOHN, Ph.D.

Introduction and Background

Students of history are familiar with the argument that prior to colonialism in Africa the traditional African society had enjoyed a glorious and enviable past in its entire ramification. The implication of this assertion is that African civilization before the emergence of colonialism had reached a kind of apogee in the fourteenth and fifteenth centuries earlier in areas around Benin. Writer such as Dumont (34), have shown that African blacksmiths knew how to work gold, copper, bronze and even iron; the latter as early as the time of Christ. Thus, African civilizations surpassed the Oceanic, and like those of pre-Columbian American, in technical development. The system of civilization practiced at the time, that is, working the earth with hoes after clearing it with fire, and rotation of fallow lands, is still used today in Africa with rare modifications. Agricultural progress was great in the traditional African society.

The pre-colonial civilization was also characterized by the absence of private landed property. However, Dumont (35) has lamented the fact that no one knows where African civilization would have been today if it had been able to follow a normal development, perhaps in peaceful contact with European techniques. But these potentialities for development were brusquely arrested, and Africans are still paying for the crimes of their white masters, who believed that they were free to do anything since they were endowed as they claimed, with "innate superiority". This paper does not intend to go into the argument either for or against the glorious past. However, we must admit as a truism that there was African art, clearly distinguished from all other alien forms of art, and sharing the same characteristic distortion of form and soft symmetries of lifelike art. This distortion of forms, according to Okadigbo (4), was an attempt to avoid the impression of the superiority of force and an immediate expression of a general attitude of non-violence.

Also, in traditional African society there was a viable and fruitful political system that was built on a uniquely African sense of communalism, founded on kinship or extended families, in a proportion unequalled and unrivalled elsewhere outside Africa. To show how strong and enviable African nations had been before they allowed themselves to be deceived and consequently colonized by the West and East, we shall briefly consider Ethiopia as a case study here. Firstly, Ethiopia goes into record as the only nation in Africa that was never colonized.

Secondly, it must be observed that Ethiopia's combined effort with other African nations like Egypt, Libya, etc made Africa a formidable race and a super-power of a sort which created the desired impact in the field of commerce, arts, mathematics, warfare, engineering, medicine, agriculture, etc. The Holy Bible also speaks unequivocally in support of these historical facts concerning Africa's mental and physical strength (Jeremiah 46: 9; 1 Kings 4: 30; Acts 7: 22; Proverbs 7: 16; 2 Chronicles 1: 16, 17). In addition to these Biblical testimonies, great European writers such as Thomas Sowell in his *Race and Culture: A World-View* attests to the strength and wisdom of the ancient Black race. Sowell, in particular, states among other things that the "ancient Europe was more underdeveloped than Africa" (193).

Thirdly, Ethiopia is also on record as the only nation that has had 3, 000 years of uninterrupted monarchical system of government which lasted till the reign of Haille Sellassie (Ashimolowo, 35). Fourthly, in military might, ancient Ethiopia was known to be ferocious in its warfares. Thus, Ethiopia was highly respected in the comity of nations for keeping a winning edge in matters of the powers of government, war and conquest. Instances abound to support this claim, for example, in 332 BC; Ethiopia single-handedly fought and forced the dreaded Alexander the Great to retreat. In that case, Alexander the Great foolishly underestimated the strength of Ethiopia's might and thus assumed that he could overrun her as he did to Egypt but he was shamefully disgraced by Ethiopia.

In the same vein, Augustus Caesar, in 25 BC ignorantly tested his military might by fighting Ethiopia, but was brutally defeated by the Ethiopian army. During the era of colonial madness in the 19th century in Africa, Ethiopia stood out as one nation that comprehensively fought and resisted Italy from colonizing her. By that wonderful act of conquest, Ethiopia has become the only country in the contemporary society that has defeated a European nation. That also explains why Ethiopia was never colonized. However, in 1935, Benito Mussolini of Italy became mad having recalled with regret the disgrace, humiliation and the attendant embarrassment that followed that great defeat; thus in his political cum military inanity, Mussolini re-launched a surprise offensive to capture Ethiopia. Though the Italians had an edge over Ethiopians in that invasion, but Italy could not still colonize Ethiopia. The reprehensible act already exhibited by Mussolini greatly polarized the League of Nations and ultimately led to its dissolution that dovetailed into the Second World War in 1945, which Italy supported Germany.

The above is a brief overview of Africa that was, that is, before it became dislocated by colonialism. In other words, Africa's real and meaningful predicament all began in the 1880s when Belgiun saw the need to invade the rich continent of Africa. This untoward idea came soon after the abolition of slave trade. That means, instead of the West taking people to Europe for slavery, she rather decided to come and effectively made Africans slaves in their own countries.

Although it was Belgium that initiated the idea of African colonization but she was not strong enough to control and dominate the entire continent of Africa. Consequently, the King of Belgium, Leopold II, in his political craftiness, extended the invitation to six other European powers, namely: Britain, France, Portugal, Germany, Italy and Spain to divide and rule Africa among themselves. Thus,

African countries fell under these European nations. It must be noted that though the Portuguese were the first to have had a contact with Africa, but they did not at that material time nurse any intention of colonizing Africa; the Portuguese at that time were only interested in ordinary explorational trade contact, though in most cases, the business in question was very obnoxious.

The point here is that the intention to colonize Africa actually came as a result of the evil-prompting from King Leopold II of Belgium to exploit the wealth of Africa. This also explains why the Portuguese did not colonize any African territory at the first instance in 1488 when they established trade link with some parts of Africa like the old Mid-Western and South-Eastern regions of Nigeria probably because their eyes were not opened to Africa's enormous wealth at that time.

It is on account of the incontrovertible wealth of Africa that European invaders even fought among themselves, and history refers to the fight as the Boer War which took place between 1899 and 1902. This was the war in which the British fought the Dutch invaders over who owned what in Africa (Ashimolowo, 58). And one of the forces behind Apartheid regime in South Africa for 300 years was nothing more than the economic interest that is, digging of "free" diamonds by European occupation in South African soil.

Ancient Colonization

Colonialism in Africa has a pretty long history; a history that spanned many centuries and phases. In the light of this consideration, the most famous history as far as colonialism is concerned is the European colonization of Africa, which took place between the late 19th and 20th century. However, in the ancient period, North Africa experienced colonization from Greece and Phoenics (West Asia). This explains why a Greek mercantile colony was established at Naucratis (in Egypt) during the reign of Pharoah Amasis (Boardman, 114).

Greece also colonized Cyrene and Carthage (Tunisia) and established colonies there in 513 BC. It was during this colonization period that Alexander the Great (356 - 323 BC) founded Alexandria, which eventually became one of the cities of Hellenistic and Roman times (Boardman, 151 – 208). According to Scullard (216), once the strength of Greece under Alexander the Great was seriously weakened by Ethiopia, Carthage became a free empire but only to be colonized again by Rome, which made her the capital of the Roman province of Africa. In the 7th century, the whole of Roman-Byzantine North Africa eventually fell to the Arab world, which introduced the Islamic religion and Arabic language to the continent of Africa.

From the 7th-century up, Arab trade with sub-Saharan Africa led to a gradual colonization of East Africa, especially areas around Zanziba (in today's Tanzania) and other areas. Again, it is a truism that trans-Saharan trade led to a small number of West African cities developing Arab quarters, though these cities were not regarded as colonies.

What this labourious tracing is portraying is that the later part of the 19th century witnessed the beginning of the down-ward trend in the development process of the African race through the instrument of colonialism. In particular, African continent was segmented into spheres of influence and colonies of the European powers for the sole purpose of exploitation, subjugation and domination. While the Africans themselves became slaves to the European invaders, the Europeans became masters of the continent and owners of virtually everything in Africa that was of any value.

Various schools have written on this forceful subjugation, exploitation and domination of Africa. It was during this period that the reins of exalted traditional government and institution were compulsively seized from African bona fide rulers by the European colonialists who became self-appointed master. Africans who dared to resist the European infiltration and inhumanity were ruthlessly dealt with. That is to say that some rulers and outstanding African personalities were deposed and exiled or in many cases killed (Mbiti, 128). Thus, European colonizers by their inhuman dispositions, tacitly justified Bartholomeo Vanzetti's cynical observation that man is wolf to the man.

Having overpowered African nations through their sophisticated weapons, the colonialists moved into the second stage of their ambition, namely: humiliation – to divide, rule and exploit the Africans to the maximum. It is on record that this process of humiliation started with the undermining of African cultures and values. And all these set the pace for the underdevelopment of the continent. Rodney (52-82) indicates that African civilization, culture, beliefs and values were trodden under the feet. For these European invaders to effectively realize their objectives, they had to establish themselves firmly on the continent of Africa by introducing and imposing on Africans, their religious, political, economic, social, linguistic and administrative systems, thereby upstaging the noble and enviable African institutions.

The important thing to note here, perhaps, is that during this colonial period in Africa, some Africans went abroad and studied political science, history, philosophy, law, etc which were tilted towards one direction, namely: the purported "divine" superiority of the whites over the blacks. But these Africans consciously refused to imbibe this kind of dubious intellectual indoctrination that they were exposed to. Hence, they all gave different interpretations and considerations to the things they were taught. The point here is that colonialism had great significance on Africa: It left a lasting legacy on the African mode of thought and civilization.

What is Colonialism?

Colonialism is one experience that has greatly affected Africa in a number of ways than any other thing. Though many societies of the world had also suffered from colonialism in different senses, but it is African society that was badly hit by colonialism. Colonialism, like a severe wound, though healed but the scar is still there. Beyond this fact, the scar has metamorphosed into a dreaded monster called neo-colonialism. Neo-colonialism, with all its accompanying side effects, has come to stay in Africa.

Though colonialism had since been removed from the continent, but its impact on African mode of reasoning, its effect on African cultures, worldview, identity, languages and history is still felt today. This means, Africans had had an arrangement by which reality was known, transmitted and preserved, and by which traditional societies were organized. But all these were set aside as a strange and difficult situation arose with the experience of colonialism. More than this, African leaders who become the apostles of modern African socio-economic and political philosophies were subjected to colonial rule. Consequently, this experience also contributed greatly to the wrong orientation and permutation, which they meted out to the Africans during the post-colonial era. But what is colonialism? According to Nkrumah, colonialism is:

> The means of the European powers to satisfy the ends, the exploitation of the subject territories for the aggrandizement of the metropolitan countries. They were all rapacious, they all repressed and despoiled, degraded and oppressed (1963: xiii).

From Nkrumah's point of view, it appears that the industrialization of European countries gave rise to the outward drive for the acquisition of new territories. Thus, colonialism is the direct political, social, and economic subjugation of one political entity by another. In this case, it is the domination of Africa by the West, which involves direct exercise of political control through the adoption of certain policies aimed at the structural and economic pauperization of the colonized territories. This understanding may be the probable reason that most Marxists perceive colonialism as the monopoly stage of capitalism. Falaiye, in describing the experience of colonialism in Africa, puts it more vividly when he declares:

> The European aggressive incursion and subsequent imposition of colonial domination on Africa had both traumatic and destructive consequences on the political, social and cultural situation of the continent. Africa did not only lose her political freedom; but more fundamentally, the structures of political power were weakened, retarded and even dismantled in some occasions and replaced with those of the metropolis that were considered more "enlightened" and "sophisticated" without any consideration whatever for the people's worldview (1997:35).

History scholars such as Ali Masrui and Vincent Khapoya subscribe to three interrelated broad reasons for European exploration and subsequent exploitation of Africa, and these are: to increase knowledge, to spread Christianity and to increase national esteem of established empires. According to Khapoya (112, 114), these reasons coincided with the political cum strategic, cultural and economic reasons for colonization.

Decolonization

The main period of decolonization in Africa started soon after the Second World War, that is, while British veterans were handsomely rewarded for their service in serving British empire with generous pensions and offer of free landed properties in choice areas in the colonies, the African soldiers were given mere handshakes and train tickets for the journey back home. African soldiers were also permitted to keep their khaki uniforms as their only testimonies, and nothing more. These ex-servicemen of African origin having felt the manifest gravity of ingratitude, which they received for their selfless efforts in supporting imperialist countries, were willing and more ready than before, after returning home, to use their new skills to assist nationalist movements in fighting for their national freedom that were beginning to take shape in many colonies.

Again, Africans recognized the value of European education in dealing with Europeans in Africa. This assisted them greatly to notice the hypocrisy of the whites and the irreconcilable discrepancies between Christian teachings of universal brotherhood as contained in the Holy Writ and the disgraceful treatment they received from missionaries.

A generation of Africans necessarily benefited from some of the facilities and policies that accompanied colonial incursion. As pointed out earlier, principal among these benefits was the European educational system acquired in those foreign countries, which guaranteed them positions in the colonial administration. According to John (2009: 102, 103), this generation of Africans which also included Africans in the Diaspora such as Stokely Carmicael (Kwame Toure), George Padmore and Henry Sylvester-Williams of Trinidad, Marcus Garvey of Jamaica, Edward Blyden, Huey

Newton, Malcolm X, W. E. B. Du Bois, Casely Hayford and Booker Washington of the United States of America, Haile Selassie of Ethiopia, Frantz Fanon and Aime Cesaire of Martinique, Sekou Toure of Guinea, Keita Modibo of Mali, Patrice Lumumba of Congo, Amilcar Cabral of Guinea Bissau, Kwame Nkrumah of Ghana, Herbert Macaulay, Nnamdi Azikiwe, Effiong Okon Eyo (popularly known as Eyo Uyo), Eyo Ita, Nyong Essien, Obafemi Awolowo, Edidem Uyoata Akpabio III and Sir Udo Udoma of Nigeria, Leopold Sedar Senghor of Senegal, Antonio Augustinho Neto of Angola, Ernest Che Gueverra of Argentina, Julius Nyerere of Tanzania, Nelson Mandela of South Africa, Jomo Kenyatta and Tom Mboya of Kenya, Kenneth Kaunda of Zambia and many more rose to the task of putting an end to colonialism in Africa and the business of establishing African identity and personality. These men were thorough-going African socio-political thinkers, irrespective of their race, condition, religion, etc.

Fanon's *Black Skin, White Mask* and Padmore's *Pan-Africanism* were useful instruments of fighting colonialism. Colin Legum's seminal work: *Pan-Africanism* was and is still very interesting thesis. It intellectualizes the emotions associated with blackness and makes Pan-Africanism a vehicle for the struggle of black people to regain their pride, strength and independence. Although
>black skins were made into the shield for the battle, yet Pan-Africanism only became a race-conscious movement, and not a racialist one (Legume, 60).

In addition to the above observation, Okadigbo (81) has pointed out that there have been assertions of various African currents and schools such as Black Theology, Black Identity, Black Power, Blackism, Conciencism, African Revolution, African Philosophy, *Negritude, Ujamaa,* African Socialism, Black Culture, etc, pioneered differently and at times, collectively by various activists such as Martin Luther King Jr., Malcolm X, Augustinho Neto, Patrice Lumumba, Colin Legum, Amilcar Cabral, Carmichael Stokely, Huey Newton, among others. But it should be noted also that these various schools failed to meet, attain and address the need for the status and impact of a complete ideology which was the expectation.

Some Africans established their own Churches as instruments of decolonization. Other professional Africans such as lawyers, doctors, engineers, educationists, poets, the petite bourgeoisie (clerks, teachers, small scale merchants, cash crop and peasant farmers), urban workers, etc, who equally benefited from Western education, directly or indirectly, established or joined independence movements, indigenous political parties, trade unions and other-initially-non-political associations evolved into political movements; and with pressures from within the imperialist powers and from the United States especially the Atlantic Charter in 1941 and the Soviet criticism of imperialism, all worked for decolonization of Africa.

However, a time came when the process of colonialism in Africa would surely come to an end; "For it is impossible to continue indefinitely to deprive any people of their fundamental rights" (Omoregbe, 1990:31). Thus, having acquired western education, these Africans realized that though absorbed into the colonial administrative set-up, they were not considered properly fit to climb to the top positions which would have meant replacing or displacing the colonial masters.

Again, while schooling in the European, American and Eastern countries, these African scholars became exposed to the revolutionary and other positive changes that were totally different from what they were introduced to and operational in the European invaded African colonies. These experiences revealed to the Africans the truth that African societies were being unjustly exploited, raped and their cultures destroyed. Hence the fight was intensified: firstly, to dislodge the colonial authorities from gaining more ascendancy to African inheritance. And secondly, to liberate African societies from material, political and mental slavery by challenging the decision of the Berlin Conference of 1885 initiated by Chancellor Bismarck, which gave official approval to colonialism in Africa. Though the fight was launched and won but there has actually been little done toward economic and mental decolonization of Africans.

One has to note that all philosophical activities during this time were tilted towards decolonization process. This is because colonialism was the main problem of the day. While the whites were busy entrenching colonialism into African minds, African nationalists both abroad and at home were busy destroying it. They formed unions and associations that demanded for greater African participation in the politics and administration of African society. In other words, while the European colonizers were busy presenting the philosophy of colonialism to the Africans through direct and indirect rule; assimilation and acculturization processes, the Africans on the other hand countered it with the philosophy of decolonization through their outright rejection of capitalism and colonialism through any form and process. This attitude was a reaction to the various cultural, socio-economic and political problems which colonialism brought. For instance, Kwame Nkrumah saw capitalism as a gentleman's method of slavery. He concluded that its furtherance in Africa would be a betrayal of the personality and conscience of Africa. By 1980, virtually the whole of the continent was free from European control.

It is also discovered that immediately after independence, African political thinkers who needed a contemporary political philosophy that would maximize their efforts at nation-building and the challenge of decolonization embraced divergent political philosophies. These philosophies were in response to the challenges which colonialism posed. As earlier observed, what is known and regarded today as African political philosophy sprang from the desire to find lasting solutions to the negative consequences of colonialism in Africa. Perhaps, this accounts for the experiences of the 1960s when most African states which achieved political independence settled for different political philosophies like *negritude, ujamaa*, humanism, welfarism, *communucrautique*, democratic-socialism, African socialism, conciencism, etc. These philosophies, to say the least, were reactionary in nature, revolutionary in method and myopic in scope. Once African states variously embraced their national political philosophies, they were once again faced with another round of trouble. Leslie Stephen puts it clearly when he insightfully asserts:

> Happy is the nation which has no political philosophy for such philosophy is generally the offspring of a recent, or the symptom of an approaching revolution (Wayper, vii).

The truth of the matter is that none of these political philosophies had proposed any viable thesis for a continental unity. What Africa has (as she is still having) was a rather narrow and parochial ethnic and at times national interest. The larger interest of the continent was less considered as paramount. But with the global political wind of change, it appears that other continents of the world are better positioned and equipped in their more sufficient and monopolistic economic and political integration to sideline or play away African continent. The fundamental problem that has existed for quite sometime now is that African political leaders only embraced the form and not the essence of independence. Their political, social, economic and even philosophical desperation at independence attest to this fact. There were no tangible structures to match their philosophical thesis with the development of the continent. The needed political energy that would generate, circulate and sustain the system was lacking.

In this circumstance, we cannot accept the political philosophies that were peddled in the 1960s as they were formulated in error. King David, from a divine background had asked more rhetorically: "If the foundation be faulty, what can the righteous do?" (Psalm 11:3). This means that the conceptual and fundamental errors must be replaced by a scientifically indigenous political system. But, by proper counter-balance, it must be observed that in the heat of that independent euphoria, when everyone was against the colonial spirit in whatever form, the reactionary philosophies were a better alternative in the interim, though not the best political world-view for Africa.

Impact of Colonialism on Africa

African history, right from the traditional Africa to the invaded and colonial Africa, is a long sad story of over eight hundred million people. The experience of the invaded Africa has metamorphosed into our contemporary African society which Okadigbo (1) has described as the battle ground of four contending forces, namely: tradition, Islam, Euro-Christianity and colonialism. These "forces" carried along their respective cultures, ideologies, ideals, agencies, theories, religious beliefs, languages, conceptions, and some other lesser issues.

But before Okadigbo's view, there were other thinkers such as Nkrumah (1964:68) and Ferkiss (149) who saw colonialism as a central force in the crisis. It follows therefore that in their understanding, the crisis was simply a result of colonialism. The impact of colonialism with all its attendant vices is well known to many scholars. However, we shall x-ray few of them as follows:

Linguistic Problem: To begin with, in the traditional African society there were more than one thousand ethnic languages spoken by more than one thousand ethnic groupings. Colonialism also brought along seven different languages, viz; English, French, German, Italian, Spanish, Portuguese and Dutch. As colonial territories, these colonial languages were enforced on African nation-states as their official languages. And language being another divisive rather than unifying factor added to the African multi-faceted lingual problems.

While Africa was still struggling with these official, colonial languages, Islam appeared on the continent. Where its adherents and protagonists lacked political power to enforce it, the Koran written in Arabic, stepped in to escalate lingual and cultural problems, and at once, added to the divisive political problems as prayers and other liturgical practices were "divinely" instructed to be done in Arabic. Apart from Islam, the Euro-Christianity of the Catholic order also contributed to the lingual confusion as all its adherents and protagonists were demanded both in church worship and educational training to use Latin as the God-ordained language for any sacred exercise.

From the above, it can be seen that colonialism did not make room for the development of any African language. The understanding here is that with the imposition of at least nine official languages on the continent, colonialism contributed immensely to the death of many African languages and thereby distorting African facts.

Crisis in Traditional Political Authority: Another problem with colonialism is that it imposed a hybrid and confusing structure on a people who were hitherto used to a different type of relationship. Falaiye (1997:34) reports that the exalted traditional seat of authority, for instance, was wrestled from the traditional rulers. And the traditional contact and understanding which the traditional rulers maintained with their people were replaced by an impersonal bureaucracy whose source of authority was derived from legal pattern of titles, enshrined in the constitution and which did not augur well with traditional African rulers whose powers were derivative of the special ties they possessed with the ancestors, spirits and God, in line with traditional beliefs.

Crisis in African Cultural Values: The colonial period also witnessed crisis in African values. That is, African values suffered tremendous distortion and even destruction in many cases. The colonial and capitalist influences of individualism, domination and exploitation forcefully replaced the African cultural contents of social relations and brotherliness, which had promised a welfare system of communalism, humanism and egalitarianism.

Economic Crisis: The process of colonialism also entailed, concurrently, a systematic and extensive pillage of the natural and human resources of African societies. According to Falaiye (1997:35), this situation jolted the minds of the immediate African political leaders in the post colonial era towards the direction of socialism, which was perceived as a better economic theory.

Furthermore, colonialism gave established empires rights, free of all restraints to exploit African wealth. Thus, colonialism saw massive transfer of wealth from Africa to Europe. This included: acquisition of land, enforced labour, introduction of cash crops, even to the neglect of food crops, halting inter-African trading patterns of pre-colonial times and the continuation of Africa as a source of raw materials for European industry, thereby making Africa a continent not to be industrialized.

Political Misconceptions: To the average African leader shortly after independence, capitalism was seen as an off-shoot of colonial rule. The linkage of capitalism with colonialism inadvertently gave way to an anti-capitalist philosophy in post independent Africa. Perhaps that explains why largely, the post independent African contains an amalgam of philosophies that have close affinity with socialism. This means capitalism and colonialism were seen as a twin-engine of suppression and were defined as anti-African. This was a clear misconception of reality.

Effects on Population and Industries: In order to exploit the rich lands of Africa, from Egypt to South Africa, the "profitable" slave trade was established. Estimates of the number of Africans taken as slaves from the sixteenth to the nineteenth centuries vary from ten to twenty million. Dumont (36) reports that Santo Domingo, which received more African slaves than any other area, took in 2.2 million in less than fifty years. These slaves were badly treated in many ways. Many of these slaves were killed during the raids or the wars the colonialists initiated. Some also died during the long march to the coast, in the camps awaiting transporation, and above all during the long sea voyage. In this consideration, the Asantewa and Asantehe people of Ghana must be mentioned; they were carried away and left to die abroad.

Vincent Khapoya (115), states that over three million people of African descent fought for the Allies in the First and Second World Wars. And a greater number of them lost their lives in the warfronts.

It should be noted that these slaves were able-bodied men and women. These people became the work force in the Newfound Land. The truth here is that African demographic structure was seriously affected. The personnel needed for African industries and commerce was greatly reduced.

It must be noted that the damaging effects of the slave trade went much further. Internal wars became unprofitable and multiplied; thereby blocking political and economic development and the evolution towards large empires, and helping to dismantle those already in existence. If the Europeans had traded with the Africans on equal basis, they would have brought goods, carts, wheels and other materials that could increase production, in exchange for African products. If they had also provided some education and training, the simple art of harnessing oxen, for example, instead of searching for slaves and easy money, the situation in Africa today would certainly be very different (Dumont, 36).

Crisis of African Identity: The crisis of African identity in the post-colonial era was and still is a serious issue; that is to say that Africans had lost their identity or had been denied of it during the colonial period. Busia (286-288) holds that the search for African identity was influenced by three major factors, namely; slavery, colonialism and racism. Quite regrettably, the problem of African identity was made worse by colonialism, which made the African to lose those things such as religion, language and world-view, which made him a real African. This has caused what Falaiye (1996:98) describes as "the triple heritage" of Islamic, Euro-Christian and traditional African experiences. Colonialism tampered not only with African resources but also with African personality and identity.

Colonialism made the Europeans to assume attitudes of superiority and a sense of mission at the detriment of their African counterparts, and thus, African personality and identity were trampled upon. For instance, the French accepted Africans, if and only if Africans gave up their culture, personality and identity and adopted French ways (including marriage with a French person). The British did not fancy full equality even for an African adopting their ways: that is, both culture and lifestyles, and rejected interracial marriage. The Portuguese accepted mixed marriages, but strongly considered full blooded Portuguese as superior. Thus, one was considered civilized if and only if he possessed the knowledge of Portuguese language, culture and abandonment of African ways, culture, identity and personality. In fact, in most cases, the colonialists created artificial borders which did not correspond with traditional territories that identified Africans properly. This is in consonant with one Ibibio proverb which states: *ke ekpuk, ke ekpuk idoho adusat* (family by family is not discriminatory).

The search for an African identity intensified after the gaining of independence. The desire to propagate the "Africanness" of the people lured African leaders and scholars to anchor such and, in most cases, on an ill-conceived and hastily put together concept of African socialism. Accordingly, the outcome was the creation of a hybrid monster. Thus, Africans who were orthodox socialists disappeared only to reappear as African socialists. Writing in a similar direction, Friedland and Rosberg (4) comment: "African socialism has thus become both a reaction against Europe and a search for a unifying doctrine".

Hybrid of Confusing Cultures and Values: It is very clear that African experience of colonialism in contemporary times shows a hybrid of confusing cultures and values. The traditional identity has been lost in most cases. The rate at which the African is being converted into European person has continued to increase. Basic African values have been made dirty or impure by Western influences. For instance, it was Trevor-Roper in his racist and myopic claim who opined that Africa has no history which can be incorporated into the mainstream of historical studies. Momoh (1-4) has carried out a useful exposition on the origin of the denial of African existence, humanity, logical ability, philosophy, thought, history, law, morality, religion, arts, science and technology. Moreover, archaeological and anthropological studies have traced the earliest and oldest artifacts to the African continent, apart from the existing records of the empires of Ghana, Tekrur, Songhai, Mali and Egypt in the year 3,000 BC, to mention but a few.

Educational Problem: Colonial policy made it that Africans received only limited education, which would enable them only to read the Bible, take orders efficiently from the white masters and missionaries, and function, at best, as interpreters, messengers and clerks in the colonial bureaucracy. This explains why in the 1960s, Africa had high illiteracy rate. For example, Zaire, in 1960, could only boast of one ollege (not university) graduate.

The impact of colonialism on Africa cannot and will not be overestimated. This is true because colonialism did unimaginable havoc to Africa. Colonialism in Africa did not only affect our commerce, landscapes, industries, population, culture, religion, science and technology, but everything Africa. More than that, colonialism has created an impossible and a messy order for the African continent. Till date, it is clear that the African has not truly recovered from the colonial shock as it grossly affects its person, mind, science, history, identity, destiny and every other pursuit. Recounting the experience of colonialism in Africa, Ashimolowo, with a wounded voice, declares:

No greater humiliation can come upon a people than to have their power, possessions, and beauty taken away from them (78).

The Problems of Neo-Colonialism

In the present, the emphasis has shifted from colonialism to neo-colonialism. That means Africans are in search of a tenable political thesis that would tackle not only the peculiar multi-faceted African problems, but also position the continent on a sound and surer footing to challenge the rest of the continents. The problems of neo-colonialism, that is, the exploitation of the Africans, corruption, nepotism, economic backwardness, ineffective leadership and sit-tight syndrome of typical African rulers in this contemporary era, are some of the off-shoots of colonialism, which have refused to leave African continent. But incidentally, African leaders have run short of the political will needed to address these off-shoots of colonialism. These multi-faceted colonial problems have become a drag on the African society in the 21st-century.

The contemporary African historians, philosophers and other thinkers should begin to consider ways appropriate in dealing with the colonial spirit which is negatively affecting most Africans. This last comment is made in the hope that African nations like many other nations of the world could still rise above the past colonial influence. It is a challenge to African nations that South Korea, Israel, China, Malaysia, India, Japan, United States of America, etc that suffered from colonialism have become pacesetters in science, art, technology, commerce and politics. In the present, they are commanding global respect in the world of science, technology, politics and commerce. African nations should wake up and device means of becoming strategically important in the comity of nations.

From the foregoing discussions, it will be discovered that African contemporary problem is basically neo-colonialism. By neo-colonialism, it means puppet and irresponsible governments in Africa. It also stands for governments which are used by the western forces in furtherance of the neo-colonial interests by undermining the sovereignty of independent African states. Neo-colonialism can also be described as a government represented by stooges either through fabricated elections or anti-people system, comprados and corrupt civil and military functionaries. The point one is trying to arrive at is that national independence of various African states was expected to transform the continent and fundamentally empower the people. But at independence, such expectations could not be realized as no leader was blessed with proper and adequate vision. Thus, no leader could translate political independence into economic and social freedom. This lack of visionary leader in Africa has remained the number one set-back for the continental development (Nekabari, 182).

In the absence of visionary and courageous leadership, purposeful articulation and execution of people-oriented programmes have continued to remain a mirage. A cryptic investigation into the leadership challenge in Africa shows that African leaders are endangered species and, in many cases, they are being replaced with rulers rather than leaders (John, 2007:133). This may account for the reason that personalized leadership as opposed to collective leadership is very common in Africa. It is the position of this paper that African continental problems of neo-colonialism, inequality, economic and technological backwardness, tribalism and parochial national interest, insecurity of lives and property as well as poverty, disease and illiteracy will remain unabated without a strong recourse to a sound and purposeful leadership; A leadership that will be sincerely patriotic, rationalistic, utilitarian, detribalized and forthright in the pursuit of collective set goals. Ineffective leadership in Africa has in turn given rise to other multiple problems such as discrimination, corruption, social injustice, hunger, insecurity, threats of wars and general backwardness in the contemporary world of progress and civilization.

The Way Forward

As a way forward, African leaders must first and foremost adopt a viable political philosophy for the continent. Elsewhere, I have proposed a confederated democracy as the best political option for the continent of Africa (John, 2006: 216-237). This system, by my humble assessment, will have relationism as its premise. The proposal of mutual interrelatedness of all African states will count for its strength, and interdependence for its attraction. Adequate and relevant criteria of self-control, logical ability and detribalized personality are some of the required qualifications for political appointment. The highest theoretical and philosophical frame of reference is the elevation of humanism and altruism.

Secondly, African leaders must work towards a continent-wide socio-political thesis. This will make possible the full realization and utilization of the African continental body: African Union (AU) formerly Organization of African Unity (OAU). African leaders must begin to emphasize and promote the solidarity of the entire African nation states. People in Africa must strive to build a new Africa where civilization worthy of the African person and a true culture of freedom can thrive. This continental project will perfectly fit our unique African culture which is synergetic, that is, a culture of cooperation, a team or coalition culture rather than the parochial tribal and national interest.

Africa must be challenged by recent global development in certain parts of the world. For instance, with effect from January, 2002 about twelve European nations (Austria, Belgium, Finland, France, Germany, Greece, Ireland, Italy, Luxembourg, Netherlands, Portugal and Spain) have come together to use a common currency (the Euro), believing that it will help strengthen their economy. No one should be deceived; this development in Europe goes beyond economic consideration alone. It has a serious political as well as military undertone.

The idea of Economic Community of West African States (ECOWAS) and its currency, which has remained dormant for so long now should be revisited. Effort should also be directed to seeing the possibility of applying the idea of ECOWAS currency to the entire continent of Africa through the birth of African Union. If Africa succeeds in this way, socio-economic and political activities can once again be on the life-line. So with the formation of our nascent African Union, it is hoped that it will not only be a change in the nomenclature of the erstwhile OAU. The AU should be structurally, administratively, militarily and ideologically different from the moribund and comically OAU in such a way that it would address African problems of cooperation, integration, unity, economy and peace among African states in a more practical terms.

That means the structure should be so placed to match with the ideas in a way that Africa will be taken out of the woods. All that the AU needs now is the political courage to marshal out things that will stop Africa's dependence on the West or East marauders.

Furthermore, if the AU wants to succeed, she must see to it that her economic community, monetary fund and parliament (the pan-African consultative forum) are not killed especially by the West through any fiat and thereby making the continent only an appendage necessary to decorate the world map (John, 2009:159). Africa must therefore give a lucid and laconic definition on and tacit defense to their central interest as a continent. Africans must not stop at their micro-ethnic or macro-national socio-political and economic interests that would become parochial. What Africans and other Africans in the Diaspora should strive at should be for a clear-cut, broad-based and fundamentally pan-African orientation for a new continental order, which will work. This is very crucial in the case of peace and development of the continent as the resurgence of tribal and regional nationalities is posing some serious socio-economic and political problems to Africa. African leaders must drop all backward cultures that promote the abuse and degradation of women and other vices, irrespective of religion, clime, culture and social status.

As a mark of understanding, African leaders should begin to respect human rights. This is because every violation committed by corrupt African governments is sticking to Africa's identity like the leopard's colour to our disadvantage. In addition to this opinion, Africa must also learn to develop detribalized culture in order to eliminate the ridiculous ethnic clashes that keep many African countries divided or in perpetual conflics and backward. This kind of orientation cannot be possible except African governments will take the development of the citizens' mind as paramount. This last observation takes us to the third issue, namely: democratic education as one of the necessary conditions for African development. That means African leaders must domesticate democracy in such a way that it will make provision for reasonable high standard of education available to all. But with poor educational infrastructures and facilities which account for illiteracy and make education inaccessible to people in Africa, the real practice of democracy may be very doubtful. This is where African continent must watch in their attempt to please western super-powers by embracing democracy uncautiously.

From the above observations, two things should be pointed out and taken very seriously at this stage. And these are: poverty and illiteracy. That is to say that Africa voting pattern can be negatively affected by these two factors. In the first place, illiteracy would not allow the very process of election to be fair and free. The understanding here is that owing to illiteracy, the people do not know how to distinguish party symbols and how to vote for ideology. Instead, tribalism has become the main issue or determinant factor in Africa's voting pattern.

The second factor is poverty. That is, the masses are poor. Hence, they usually suspend their rationality and sense of justice during election period because of poverty. This is the case when one considers the role played by money in the voting pattern in Nigerians in the face of poverty and hunger. In other words, the people would not mind mortgaging their conscience for any immediate gain they could grab. As a result, political office is always given to the highest bidder. In fact, this point is a combine effect of poverty and ignorance, which hampers the very democratic due process in Africa. It is on the above score that I strongly agree with Whitehead (125) that "there can be no successful democratic society till general education conveys a philosophic outlook". That means there must be a general education which emphasizes the fundamental issues of human existence, that is, the issues of the nature, meaning and importance of life, truth, goodness, justice, etc.

The message here is that any nation or country in Africa desirous of meaningful development, sound moral principles and social values, must see and adopt the promotion of education along the Platonic curriculum with exclusive respects to full funding, provision of adequate facilities and teaching materials at all levels. In fact, this should take the centre-stage in our political ideology. In this regard, incessant strike actions constantly embarked upon by teachers and lecturers in many educational institutions across the continent could be grossly minimized, if not, completely eradicated, once the sector is made attractive. And a situation when teachers are on strike, students are busy rioting, in most cases, over poor facilities or exorbitant tuition and other sundry fees would cease with the new and emergent concept of education as the chief source of morals and total development. The fourth suggestion is in the area of leadership. African leaders lack the technical know-how. Thus, the continent is yet to produce leaders in the mould of the philosopher-kings who would not be selfish, myopic and embarrassingly disgraceful. Chinua Achebe captures leadership deficiency in Africa very appropriately when he describes the Nigerian nation thus:

> In spite of conventional opinion Nigeria has been less than fortunate in its leadership. A basic element of this misfortune is the seminal absence of intellectual rigour in the political thought of our founding fathers - a tendency to pious materialistic wooliness and self-centred pedestrianism (13).

The problem of leadership in Africa is a serious one. Since the time of African founding fathers till 1990 and right into the 21st century, Africans must blame their leaders for the continental backwardness. No leader in Africa seems to be aware of the problems associated with the call for foreign investors and the need for a kinetic economic energy in Africa. The call, in the first place, is technically wrong. It is so because such a call is an indication of a poor environment. Secondly, sound economic investigation reveals that there is no actual need for African leaders to scout for foreign investors. This is because once the socio-political and economic paradigms are properly structured or restructured to favour mankind; people from all walks of life across the globe will come around to invest in Africa.

In the past, most expatriates and firms from all over the world rushed to Nigeria and other African nations for investment and for other sundry activities. This was the case because the economic situation was very conducive. No one wooed or beckoned on them to come: they all came on their own accord. It is on record that many Indians, Americans, and Europeans, and many others took the lead in the rush to Nigeria. These foreigners occupied almost every sector of Nigeria's economy and education: they established firms and industries. It was also noticed that when the economic environment became un-conducive, all the expatriates left. The mass exodus of these foreigners from Nigeria in the early 80s is still fresh in people's memories. There is an economic pattern which can augur well for Africa if her leaders will be sincere and take it seriously. The matter is aptly demonstrated in the Holy Bible through the story of Noah's ark. In other words, Noah did not have to woo the animals to come into the ark. The truth is that all the animals that Noah needed in the ark came on their own accord because the ark was conducive for them.

But today, because African leaders lack proper foresight, they do not know what to do with leadership. They are blind to reality and have become restless, roaming around the globe in search of foreign investment. In most cases, they have become a laughing stock in America and Europe. What a tragedy of leadership cum development in Africa? The bitter truth is that no foreign investor will respond to the call because the economic atmosphere is not well favourably disposed. One should not think of any foreign investor in a corrupt society. Political analysts hold that it is difficult for an incumbent government in any African nation to fight corruption because almost every government in the continent apart from a few is a product of corruption. And like the Biblical saying: "Like begets like". This is a metaphysical or spiritual principle that is difficult to overcome. In Africa, the problem is dualistic: foundational and lack of men of character.

It appears that leaders in Africa, who are calling on foreign investors have failed to know that every intending foreign investor is getting adequate information from their embassies and high commissions about the moral, political, economic and social climate in Africa. Since such briefs and reports are not favourable, they cannot come. One should take for instance the issue of vigilante groups and private militias in Africa. These are all indications of corrupt and polluted environment, lawlessness and disorder. The increase in the wave of armed robberies, kidnappings and assassinations is a viable threat to the development of the continent as no investor would like to risk his life and assets in such environment. A government that cannot ensure the security of lives and property of its people cannot be said to be a government. In the consideration of Hobbes and Locke, an irresponsible government should be dissolved; that is, when a state fails to offer peace and protection – two basic functions for which it was founded – the legitimacy of the leaders should be queried and resisted or disposed. Socrates, Plato, Aristotle, Hobbes, Locke, Rousseau, Mill and other political philosophers all condemned states that would not ensure security of lives and property of their citizens as irresponsible (John, 2009:188). Therefore, African leaders must consciously work towards creating an enabling environment for the old manufacturers to survive and for the new ones to launch out. It is a truism that the prosperity and success of any nation, to a very large extent, does not depend on the abundance of natural resources and its revenues accruing therefrom, but rather on the number of its cultivated minds and characters. This is where African leaders are deficient.

The worst thing that can happen to any country or continent is to have neophytes entrusted with political powers. Perhaps, Robert Nesta Marley has seen the situation better when he elucidates that "History has taken the slavery chains from the Blackman's feet to his brains" (Okafor, 15). This aptly explains our political situation in the continent. African leaders have failed to know that it is not the quantity of natural resources of the continent that makes its people economically, scientifically, industrially or strategically important, but the mental quality of its people. That is, how much they can translate their potential into economic power. It is on this note that I quite agree with Igwe that

> Genuine development is fundamentally of human being in terms of ideas which imbue in them the capacity to think qualitatively and tackle the problems that emerge out of their living conditions (4).

Moreover, it must be understood that one major reason for sit-tight rulers in Africa is corruption. They do not want other people to investigate high-level corruption that they have enmeshed themselves in. Unrestrained looting of the treasury by African rulers has become a daunting scenario for some decades now, and this has substantially contributed to the present economic straits. African leaders must determine not to submit to any economic set-back, political maneuvering and technological deception of the West. Every attempt to down-grade African identity by turning to the West for help and expertise by African leaders themselves should be resisted.

The above point is made because as long as Africa depends on importation, there is no way the currency of any nation in Africa would not be in free fall. The reason is simple: all manner of imports is done with foreign exchange. But the real question is: why should Africa be a trading continent and not expanding her productive ability? Again, the answer is not far-fetched: about 90 percent of the total population in Africa depends on foreign foods and goods for their sustenance. Hence Africa is spending billions in foreign exchange, importing foodstuffs and other needed items. This contrasts sharply with the earlier days of agricultural glory in Nigeria when, between 1930 and 1960, exports of palm products, cocoa and groundnut doubled, while cotton exports increased by 300 percent and rubber by twenty percent.

Presently, farm holdings are hindered by many factors such as socio-cultural, bio-physiographic, technological, politico- problems. Some of these problems often lead to illness and lessening of body resistance to disease. Added to this abject situation administrative, input-constraining and management is that fact that people do not have access to health facilities, good roads, education and electricity. Unqualified and illegal personnel are already exploiting the situation and thus worsen the already battered conditions of life in Africa. Attempts by few leaders in Africa to proffer solution to the above situation imply their falling back on the West, which is a different problem in itself. But even then, their intention is bad: they are self-driven. This is because more than half of the budgeted expenditure ends up in their private pockets and bank accounts.

This explains why it is not unrealistic or utopian for one to hold that African governments can still put an end to crime. All that is required is a concerted effort on the part of African leaders to bring about some social programmes and justices. Once the effort is matched with proper planning and execution, then Africa will be on the part of breakthrough. The social and political monster hindering development in Africa has to be overcome. In other words, the urgency involved in this exercise cannot be substituted for anything else. But it must be stated that the antidote or panacea for these ills must include patriotism, concretization of citizens and a viable, vigorous, responsible and patriotic press. Others are: a morally sound legislature, uncorrupt judiciary, vigilant and proactive populace, a praying and righteous church, social crusaders and human rights activists. The above suggestions are given in the hope that unless something drastic is done, corruption at high and low places may remain endemic and the hypocritical face-saving pretentious war against it will continue to be a ridiculous one in Africa.

Conclusion

The above specifications have their political, social, and economic dimensions. In the political sphere, it means the ability to allow democracy to bloom through meaningful political participation and the provision of adequate opportunities for the citizens to choose their leaders through free and fair elections. In the social and economic fronts, it means ensuring that the system is equitable and just in the distribution of governmental rewards and punishments. Added to this, it implies that the economic system should be managed in ways that will make for economic modernization, diversification, development and the sustenance of attained economic development over time.

WORKS CITED

Achebe, Chinua. *The Trouble with Nigeria*. Enugu: Fourth Dimension Publishers, 1998.

Ashimolowo, Matthew. *What is Wrong with Being Black?* Shippensburg, PA: Destiny Image Publishers, 2007.

Blocker G. and Steward D. *Fundamentals of Philosophy*. New York: The Macmillan Publishers, 1987.

Boardman, John. *The Greeks Overseas*. Harmondsworth: Penguin Books, 1973.

Busia, K. A. "This Dark Slein" in Gidem-Cyrus M. Mutiso and S. W. Roho (Eds). *African Political Thought*. London: Heinemann Publishers, 1975.

Dumont, Rene. *False Start in Africa*. Trans, Phyllis Nauts Ott. London: Earthscam Publishers, 1862.

Falaiye, O. A. "African Socialism and the Dilemma of African Identity" in *Journal for the Advancement of Africans and Blacks in the Diaspora*. Vol. 1, No.1, 1996.

Falaiye, O. A. "Democracy in African: Problems and Prospects" in *Journal for the Advancement of Africans and Blacks in the Diaspora*. Vol. 2, No.1, 1997.

Ferliss, V. C. *Africa's Search for Identity*. New York: George Braziller publishers, 1966.

Friedland, W. H. and Rosberg, C. S. (Eds). *African Socialism*. Standford, California: Standford University Press, 1981.

Igwe, A. (Ed). *Philosophy and National Development: A Periscope of the Next Millennium*. Uyo: MEF Publishers, 1999.

John, Elijah Okon. *Man and the State: Issues in Socio-Political Philosophy*. Uyo: Afahaide Publishers, 2009.

John, Elijah Okon. "Machiavelli and the Leadership Challenge: The Case of Nigeria" in *Uyo Journal of Humanities*. Vol.12, January, 2007.

John, Elijah Okon. *The Relevance of Machiavelli's Political Philosophy to Contemporary Nigerian Politics*. Unpublished Ph.D. Dissertation: University of Calabar, 2006.

Khapoya, Vincent B. *The Phoenicians*. Harmondsworth: Penguin Books, 1971.

Legum, Colin. *Pan-Africanism*. New York: Frederick A Praeger Publishers, 1962.

Mbiti, John S. *African Religions and Philosophy*. London: Heinemann Books, 1969.

Momoh, C. S. *The Substance of African Philosophy*. Auchi: African Philosophy Projects' Publication, 2000.

Nekabari, J. Nna. *Contemporary Political Analysis: An Introduction*. Port Harcourt: The Blueprint Publishers, 2000.

Nkrumah, Kwame. *Africa Must Unite*. London: Panaf Books, 1963.

Nkrumah, Kwame. *Consciencism: Philosophy and Ideology for Decolonization and Development with Particular Reference to African Revolution*. London: Heinemann Books, 1964.

Okadigbo, Chuba. *Consciencism in African Political Philosophy*. Enugu: Fourth Dimension Publishers, 1985.

Okafor, Basil. "Back to Bob Marley" in *Insider Weekly*. No.2, 2001.

Omoregbe, Joseph. *Knowing Philosophy*. Lagos: Joja Educational Research and Publishers, 1990.

Rodney, Walter. *How Europe Underdeveloped Africa*. Tanzania: Tanzania Publishing House, 1972.

Scullard, H. H. *From the Gracchi to Nero*. London: Methuen Books, 1976.

Sowell, Thomas. *Race and Culture: A World View*. New York: Basic Books, 1994.

Wayper, C. I. *Teach Yourself Political Thought*. London: The English University Press, 1964.

Whitehead, Alfred North. *Adventures of Ideas*. New York: New American Library of World Literature, 1953.

CHAPTER 4

PAN-AFRICANISM
By
DAVID LISHILINIMLE IMBUA, Ph.D.

Introduction

One inspiring and challenging lesson in Africa's chequered and tortured history is the continuous bold attempts by Africans of various walks of life to resist western domination and exploitation as well as rallying among themselves in making the world a better place for Africans and people of African descent. To this end, various people and movements have, with great commitment and devotion rejected the idea that Blacks are inherently inferior to other races. The story of pan-Africanism was and still is the expression of the shared values and common interests of Africa, defined in terms of the shared historical experience of domination and nationalist struggles of people of African descent for their cultural, economic and political liberation. Indeed, pan-Africanist intellectual, cultural, and political movements tend to view all Africans and descendants of Africa as belonging to a single "race" and sharing cultural unity. Pan-Africanism posits a sense of a shared historical fate for Africans in the Americas, West Indies, and, on the continent itself. In general terms, Pan-Africanism is a concept in which the ideas of solidarity and unity of the African continent are crystallized. This concept binds all African people and African states together at a level. By it the African peoples and states emphasize the things that unite them and tend to ignore those things that divide them (Anene, 23). All the states of pan-African Movement, except Ethiopia and Liberia, had at one time or the other suffered under the colonial regime.

Pan-Africanism: Background and Impetus

There is no agreement among historians on who was the first person to express pan-Africanist sentiments. This will forever remain conjectural and controversial even as it is suggested in some quarters that Henry Sylvester Williams was the first person to apply the term "Pan-Africanism" to what had earlier been called "the African Movement" in 1900 during the London Conference. Admitting the difficulty in trying to precisely situate Pan-african consciousness in history, Julius Nyerere said rather prosaically "the Africans looked at the Europeans and looked at themselves and knew that vis-à-vis the Europeans, they were one" (qtd in Akinyemi, 1). This explanation is rather simplistic and has the capacity to sweep important developments in the black world under the carpet. We should always stress that pan-Africanism is a product of the Atlantic slave trade. Enslaved Africans of diverse origins and their descendants found themselves embedded in a system of exploitation where their African origin became a sign of their servile status. Pan-Africanism set aside cultural differences, asserting the principality of these shared experiences to foster solidarity and resistance to exploitation. It is in this sense that Northrup's assertion that forced migration was the father of the black Atlantic becomes self-explanatory. Northrup asserts that torn from their homes in Africa, millions of Africans were discriminated and oppressed and there was the emergence of black leaders in the Atlantic who showed remarkable determination to build institutions that would enable them to fight the racial discrimination that held them all back (8).

Despite the intertwined connection between Atlantic slavery and pan-Africanism, it is inadvisable and perhaps little rewarding for us to recount the brutal, dehumanizing and excruciating experiences of the African slaves whose labour went uncompensated in the Atlantic economy. Doing so would blur the thesis of this chapter. However, there is need to re-echo in passing Okon E. Uya's assertion that "everyday in the life of the slave meant hard work, poor medical attention, the lash and intimate separations" (*Contemporary Issues, 15*). Uya argues further that it was indeed a most agonizing experience for the slaves and he affirms G. W. F. Hegel's verdict that black slavery was, for the enslaved blacks, "a trial by death". By the last quarter of the 18th century, a constellation of humanitarian, economic, and ideological forces combined with the determined resistance of those in slavery to challenge slavery. Acknowledging the inherent evil of this parasitic and unusually lucrative traffic and no longer able to ignore the struggle against bondage, such as that mounted in Haiti between 1793 and 1804, the governments of several Atlantic world nations initiated policies, between 1789 and 1807, to make the slave trade, and later slavery illegal. Unfortunately, in the post-slavery era, the African-Americans contribution to the making of the American civilization and society was omitted, ignored and distorted. Slavery was systematically replaced by U. S. style apartheid called segregation (The "Jim Crow" System) (Alkalimat, 375). African Americans realized with frustration that the expectation that emancipation would end exploitation of blacks and restore their dignity to them was completely misplaced. This is the idea behind the claim that pan-Africanism was born out of "complete alienation, physical exploitation and spiritual torment" (Chime, 121).

In total disregard to their talents and demonstrated abilities, free blacks were compelled to face restrictions to their occupational and social mobility in all societies of the New World. European immigrants or their offspring were often able to overcome prejudice and discrimination, and for most immigrant groups, excluding Blacks, the handicap of ethnic background diminished over time (Taeuber & Taeuber, 17). Pan-Africanism was thus conceived as a liberation movement. In the light of this, there is consensus among historians that the idea of pan-Africanism came out of the Africans in Diaspora. Amongst the great names associated with its development are Edward W. Blyden, Henry Sylvester Williams, Marcus Garvey, W. E. B. Du Bois, Orishatukeh Fadunma, and George Padmore. Esedebe includes Beale Horton and Reverend James Johnson as the foremost precursors to the pan-Africanist movement, who sought "to Africanise Christianity and tended toward the formation of independent African churches" (*The Emergence...* 89). As "a movement of ideas and emotions" (Legum, 443), the Pan-Africanist struggle was in two basic directions – a struggle to end the legacies of slavery; and a struggle to actualize the promise of freedom. In many regards, pan-Africanism was a struggle to end two important phenomena identified by two earlier writers: W. E. B. Du Bois who regarded the history of blacks in the New World as a struggle to end a "double consciousness" and what Ralph Allison, the famous novelist, called a struggle to end the "invisible man status". The visionaries of pan-Africanism had the vision of securing equal rights, self-government, independence and unity for African peoples. Unlike nationalism which is primarily concerned with the political unification of different ethnic groups within a single state, Pan-Africanism concerned itself with achieving large political units, a commonwealth of African states, or a supra-state political unification. On this, W.E.B. Du Bois opined that pan-Africanism aims at an "intellectual understanding and cooperation among all peoples of Negro descent in order to bring about, at the earliest possible time, the industrial and spiritual emancipation of the Negro People" (qtd in *The Emergence... 75*).

Despite the controversy surrounding its origin, it is reasonable to admit that the roots of pan-Africanism are traceable to the late eighteenth-century writings of westernized Africans expressing the pain and resentment of humiliating encounters with slavery, colonialism and white supremacy. In 1787, a group of Africans living in England drafted a letter of appreciation to the British philanthropist, Granville Sharp, for his efforts toward abolition of the international slave trade. One of the drafters, Olaudah Equiano, had traveled widely and eventually published his *Interesting Narrative*, revealing emotional commitments to the universal improvement of the African condition. Ottobah Cugoano, one of Equiano's associates, also issued a book titled *Thoughts and Sentiments on the Evil of Slavery* and significantly addressed it to the "sons of Africa". In the early 1800s, two free African entrepreneurs in the maritime professions, Paul Cuffe, a sea captain, and James Forten, a sail maker, took steps to establish a West African trading company, and actually settled a few people in the British colony of Sierra Leone. In 1820 the slave conspiracy planned in South Carolina by Denmark Vesey, putatively a native of the Danish West Indies, aimed at creating an empire of emancipated Africans throughout the American South and the Caribbean. Vesey's conspiracy influenced another South Carolinian, David Walker, who published his *Appeal, in Four Articles, Together with a Preamble, to the Colored Citizens of the World* (1829). This was a bold example of pan-African sentiment, as its title declares. The Convention of the Free People of color, meeting in 1831, likewise demonstrated a hemispheric pan-Africanism as it declared a plan for a college in New Haven, Connecticut, arguing that a seaport location would facilitate communication with the West Indies. Closely related to the above idea of pan-Africanism is the rather well-known "Back to Africa" movement of Marcus Garvey (1887 – 1940), who is fondly referred to in the literature as the "Black Moses" (Northrup, 80). Famed for his fiery oratory, and insistence on race pride, Marcus Garvey saw pan-Africanism as a battle to link the destiny of the Diaspora and continent forever together (Legum, 449). Pan-Africanists declared without mincing words that "Africa Must Unite" and "Africa for Africans". It is in this context that we could appreciate Uya's incisive analysis that

> One of the most persisting themes in the social, political and intellectual history of Africans abroad, especially those in the Americas and the Caribbeans, has been their consciousness of Africa as a potentially revolutionary force in black liberation; as an ancestral "home" where true dignity, equality and manhood can be expressed; and as a land made wretched by outside invaders crying for attention of Africans abroad especially in areas of education, investment and economic development …it has exploded at various times in such events as the Back to Africa movement, the Marcus Garvey movement and the Roots phenomenon found expression in such intellectual and creative activities as the Negro spirituals, the Harlem Renaissance, Negritude, Soul and Jazz music, and Black English or Ebonics. It has influenced the works of such prominent black intellectuals and publicists like Edward Blyden, George Padmore, W. E. B. Du Bois, Carter G. Woodson, Lorenzo Turner, Edward Braithwaitte, William Leo Hansberry, Chancellor Williams, Franz Fanon, Kwame Nkrumah, Cheik Anta Diop, Nnamdi Azikiwe, Lorraine Hansberry and Tony

Morrison.... Put differently, concretizing the relationship between Africans abroad and those at home in our collective responsibility to meet the challenges of the hostile world we have found ourselves in has been one of the most important issues confronting the black world since the eras of slavery and the slave trade (*Our Future in our Past*... 45).

The major constituent concepts of pan-Africanism are: Africa as the homeland of Africans and persons of African extraction, solidarity among men of African blood, belief in a distinct African personality, rehabilitation of Africa's past, pride in African culture, Africa for Africans in church and state, the love for a united and glorious future Africa; all these permeate the pronouncements and publications of pan-Africans like Du Bois, Garvey, Padmore, Nkrumah and a host of others. As an ideology, pan-Africanism is made up of the most important ideas that have brought the black race thus far in the quest for liberation from racism and for the amelioration of our condition in the world. The ideology of Pan-Africanism promoted racial pride and spoke for all Africans, rather than focusing on a particular ethnic group or nation. This notion of pan-Africanism was beautifully captured by Longston Hugues in the following poetic lines:

> We are related, you and I. You from the West Indies, I from Kentucky. We are related – you and I. You from Africa. I from the States. We are brothers – you and I

We see the same kind of passion in the following spirituals:

> See these poor souls from Africa, transported to America; we are stolen, and sold in Georgia. Working all day, and part of the night; and up before the morning light. When will Jehovah hear our cry and free the sons of Africa? (Berghain, 58).

Undoubtedly, pan-Africanism has been a powerful ideal since its inception which, apart from its inspiration of the brotherhood of Negro blood, African personality and Negritude, has at some times fostered in the minds of its advocates "the racist concept of Black

Zionism, Black Power and Blackism" (McKay, 93). Africans on the continent also shared the views of Diaspora pan-Africanists. The view of Peter Abrahams vividly captures this: "Africa... is the heart of us who are black. Without her we are nothing, while she is not free we are not men. That is why we must free her, or die. That is how it is" (Mckay, 93). Pan-African feelings cut across all classes of the New World Society. There is nothing to suggest that the pan-African sentiment of highly literate intellectuals was disassociated from the consciousness of the masses. The historian, Edwin S. Redeye, found evidence that black peasants in the south were aware of such leadership figures as Blyden. The cultural historian, Miles Mark Fisher, has insisted that folk songs and folklores gave evidence of a continuing identification with Africa among the masses.

The pan-African flag that was designed by Marcus Garvey, The Red, Black, and Green colours, was well celebrated by black people around the world. Expressing pan-African sentiments, the "red" represents the blood that unites all people of African ancestry; "black" stands for the colour of the skin of the people of Africa; and "green" represents the rich land of Africa. It follows that pan-Africanism consciously and deliberately aimed at creating a band of solidarity based upon community of faith imposed by the slave trade and its aftermath. This succinctly informs Esedebe's categorization of the essentials of pan-Africanism in seven major ideas:

> First is the conception of Africa as the home of Africans and persons of African origin. Second is reflective and organic solidarity among all peoples of African descent. Third is collective and individual pride in African culture. Fourth is the pride is belief in a distinct African personality. Fifth is rehabilitation of Africa's past. Sixth is the Africanization of church and state, thus preserving Africa for Africans at political and religious planes. Seven is the hope of emergence of a united and glorious federation of African States ("Pan-Africanism", 4).

One catalyst for the rapid and widespread development of pan-Africanism was the colonization of the continent by European powers in the late 19th century. We should remark here that the growth of pan-African sentiments in the late nineteenth century should be seen as a continuation of "Pan-nationalist" thinking and a reaction to the limits of emancipation for former slaves in the Diaspora and European colonial expansion in Africa rather than the starting point of pan-Africanism, as some scholars have suggested. From 1900, Pan-Africanist scholars increasingly pressed for self-government, and independence for African peoples, which was crystallized into a programme of African "autonomy and independence". There were six pan-African Congresses between 1900 and 1945. The first five were dominated by Negroes from the United States and the West Indies. The pan-African Conferences, including that of 1900 and those organized by Du Bois in 1919, 1921, 1923, and 1927, were the forerunners of another, and held in Manchester, England in 1945, which focused on the promotion of African independence from European colonialism.

In 1944, several African organizations in London joined to form the pan-African federation, which for the first time demanded African "autonomy and independence". The federation convened in 1945 in Manchester the sixth pan-African Congress, which was attended by such future political figures as Jomo Kenyatta (Kenya), Kwame Nkrumah (Gold Coast), S. L. Akintola (Nigeria), Peter Abrahams (South Africa), H. O. Davis (Nigeria), Magnus Williams (Nigeria), Wallace Johnson (Sierra Leone) and Ralph Armattoe (Togo). Du Bois was the only African American present and congressmen eulogized him as "the grand old man of Pan-Africanism" (Thompson, 27). While at the Manchester congress, Nkrumah founded the West African National Secretariat to promote the so-called United States of Africa. It was proposed and agreed in the Manchester Conference that if all other methods failed, force should be used to achieve their aspirations. Participants at the congress were very optimistic that before long the peoples of Asia and Africa would have broken their centuries old chains of colonialism. And as free nations, they would stand united to consolidate and safeguard their liberties and independence from the restoration of western imperialism (Ayandele, et al, 382).

The towering posture of the 1945 Manchester Congress in the flowering of pan-African ideals on the African continent should in no way suggest that the previous congresses achieved nothing important. It was at the first Pan-African Congress, convened in London in 1900 by Henry Sylvester Williams, a Trinidadian lawyer that delegates protested to Queen Victoria against the treatment of Africans in South Africa and Rhodesia. The second Pan-African Congress, which held in Paris (1919) advocated that in colonial Africa, Africans should be given the right to participate in the government "as fast as their development permits" (Anene, 25). The third, fourth and fifth Pan-African Congrsses which met in London and Brussels (1921), London and Lisbon (1923) and in New York (1927) respectively, reiterated and affirmed the principle of African participation in the administration of colonial Africa (25). There could be no doubt that these congresses laid the foundation for the success story of the 1945 Manchester Congress. The 1945 congress came at the heels of the Atlantic Charter's principle of self-determination (1941), which urge colonial powers to prepare their subjects to manage their own affairs without external control.

Pan-Africanism as an inter-governmental movement was launched on the African soil in 1958; in this historic year, Kwame Nkrumah, the first President of Ghana, brought pan-Africanism to Ghana, its real home, after the country had achieved independence in 1957. This was expressed through the Conference of Independent African States in Accra, Ghana in April 1958. Ghana and Liberia were the only sub-Saharan African countries represented, the rest (Ethiopia, Libya, Morocco, Tunisia and Egypt) were Arab and Muslim. In many ways their resolutions anticipated those of the Organization for African Unity (now African Union) five years later. Kwame Nkrumah's political credo was "seek ye first the political kingdom and all else will be added unto you". What had began essentially as a social and intellectual idea among New World Negroes had become in effect the training school for the future leaders of the independence movements in Anglophone Africa, and West Africa in particular (Fage, 472). Within a few years, the political map of Africa changed drastically and independence became the order of the day. Thereafter, as independence was achieved by more African states, other interpretations of pan-Africanism emerged, including: the Union of African States (1960), the African States of the Casablanca Charter (1961), the African and Malagasy States (1962), and the African-Malagasy-Mauritius Common Organization (1964).

It was also with the same pan-African vision that the OAU was founded in 1963 with a secretariat in Addis Ababa to promote unity and cooperation among all African States and to bring an end to colonialism. As we are probably aware, the pan-African Historical Society in collaboration with the Department of History and International Studies of the University of Uyo organized a major conference in 2008 to commemorate fifty years of pan-Africanism in Africa. Most presentations at that event emphasized the towering role of Kwame Nkrumah in the growth of pan-African consciousness in Africa and there is a need for us to comment briefly on his immensely important role before we end this discourse.

Let it not be forgotten that Egypt, Morocco, Tunisia, Liberia and Ethiopia had been independent before the independence of Gold Coast (Ghana) and nothing had been heard from them about the Pan-African dream; Kwame Nkrumah changed all that: his speech at independence rather than revel in the glorification of Ghana's independence, staked out the bold claim that Ghana's independence would be meaningless without the total independence of other African states. As Bolaji Akinyemi argues:

> Without wasting time, he moved beyond a declaratory posture to give structure to his position. A Bureau of African Affairs was set up in the Presidency and was manned by non-Ghanaian Africans and Diaspora Africans from the United States and the West Indies. No African leader had done this before and none had done this after Nkrumah (5).

It has to be emphasized that Nkrumah's hatred for the maltreatment of any blackman was the same as that of a Ghanaian in any part of the world and he was determined to use the resources of Ghana to fight the African battle. This is demonstrated clearly in the following words of his:

> The fortunes of the African Revolution ... are linked with the world-wide struggle against imperialism. It does not matter where the battle erupts, be it in Africa, Asia or Latin America, the master-mind and master-hand at work are the same.

> The oppressed and exploited people are striving for their freedom against exploitation and suppression. Ghana must not, Ghana cannot, be neutral in the struggle of the oppressed against the oppressor (Chinweizu, 23).

Evidences are clear that Kwame Nkrumah sought to achieve the following objectives: to lock independent African states into a commitment to pursue the pan-African dream; to ensure that African states which were still to become independent would not become independent in a pan-African vacuum; recognizing the seductive nature of atomistic state power, he inaugurated the concept of a peoples' driven pan-Africanism through the instrumentality of the All-African Peoples' Conference where non-government political parties were in the majority (Akinyemi, 6). As Akinyemi argues, the resolutions coming out of series of All-African Peoples' Conferences have been consistently more radical than decisions coming out of the Conference of States. Indeed, the Peoples' Conferences were holding the feet of African President, to the fire of radical pan-Africanism. Nkrumah, was without doubt, motivated by Garvey's opinion that the Negro peoples of the world should build for themselves a great nation in Africa, a nation strong enough to lend protection to its members scattered all over the world. Let us end this rather sketchy discourse on pan-Africanism by stressing the need to be once again ruthlessly committed to the ideals of the concept. The need for this becomes imperative when we realize Uya's unmistakable assertion that "we should always remember that no one can do as much for us as we can do for ourselves and that there is no free lunch and handout in this world of concrete interests where blood and race are still dominant factors shaping interconnectivity and globalization" (*Slave Trade and Slavery,* 67).

In another presentation, Uya insists that we must confront our difficult present and threatened future, inspired by the faith of our fathers, the blood of our martyrs and the unwavering determination to convert the obstacles on our pathways to opportunities and stepping stones to success (*Our Future in our Past...,* 22). Peoples of African descent wherever they are, must, in the tradition of our forebear Pan-Africanists unite our vision and talents to survive in the increasingly hostile global village. There are significant lessons from pan-Africanism. Africans supported the African-Americans quest for civil rights while African-Americans canvassed for the independence of African States (Jeter, 8). It should always be remembered that Pan-Africanism has generally taken a larger than state-centric strategic approach to defining the parameters of the global African predicament and the solution to it, within a broader, collective vision of a Pan African idea. Indeed, the language of Pan-Africanism was, and should still be, directed against foreign and indigenously based oppression.

WORKS CITED

Akinyemi, Bolaji A. "Kwame Nkrumah and Pan-Africanism in Africa". Being a Paper delivered at the International Conference on Fifty Years of Pan-Africanism in Africa: 1958 – 2008, Retrospect and Prospect. University of Uyo. September 8-12, 2008.

Alkalimat, Abdul. "The Contribution of African-Americans to the Development of the United States of America" in R. Uwechue (Ed) *Africa Today.* London: African Books, 2000.

Anene, J. C. (Ed). *Essays in African History, 19th and 20th Centuries.* Ibadan: Onibonoje Publishers, 1977.

Ayandele, Emmanuel A. *et al. The Growth of African Civilization: The Making of Modern Africa in the 19th Century to the Present Day.* London: Longman, 1971.

Berghain, M. *Images of Africa in Black American Literature.* London: Macmillan, 1977.

Chime, C. *Integration and Politics among African States: Limitations and Horizons of Mid-Term Theorizing.* Uppsala: The Scandinavian Institute of African Studies, 1977.

Chinweizu. *The West and the Rest of Us.* New York: Vintage Books, 1975.

Esedebe, P. O. "The Emergence of Pan African Ideas" in Onigu Otite (Ed). *Themes in African Social and Political Thought.* Enugu: Fourth Dimension Publishers, 1978.

Esedebe, P. O. *Pan-Africanism: The Idea and Movement, 1976-1991.* Washington D. C.: Howard University Press, 1984.

Fage, J. D. *A History of Africa.* London: Hutchinson & Co. Publishers, 1978.

Jeter, Howard. F. *Reaching out to the African Diaspora: The Need for a Vision.* Lagos: JFR Publishers, 2003.

Legum, Colin, "The Nature of Pan-Africanism" in P. J. M. McEwan (Ed). *Twentieth-Century Africa.* London: Oxford University Press, 1978.

Mckay, Vernon. *Africa in World Politics.* New York: Harper & Row Publishers, 1963.

Northrup, David *Crosscurrents in the Black Atlantic 1770 – 1965: A Brief History with Documents.* Boston: Bedford/St. Martin's, 2008.

Thompson, W. B. *Africa and Unity: The Evolution of Pan-Africanism.* London: Longman, 1973.

Uya, Okon E. *Contemporary Issues in Slavery and the Black World.* Calabar: Clearlines Publications, 2005.

Uya, Okon E. *Slave Trade and Slavery Abolition: An Afrocentric Perspective.* Uyo: Diamond Ville Digital and Publishing, 2007.

Uya, Okon E. "Our Future, Our Past: The Legacies of the Pre-Colonial and Slavery Eras". Being a paper presented at the International Conference of Fifty Years of Pan-Africanism in Africa, 1958-2008". University of Uyo, September 8-12, 2008.

CHAPTER 5

AFRICAN NATIONALISM

By

NWACHUKWU M. ANYIM

Introduction

African nationalism emerged as part of the struggle by Africans to achieve self-determination or self-rule. It shares similar characteristics with the concept of nationalism, especially with respect to the pursuit of national interests and goals through the attainment of sovereignty for a group of people who may be said to constitute a "nation". Thus, the emergence of African nationalism can be situated within the context of a sense of patriotism, loyalty, or devotion to the national interests of indigenous African societies against colonial or external domination. Although we cannot discountenance the fact that, before the advent of colonialism in Africa, there was "tribal" or "sub-national" consciousness, it is pertinent to note that it is within the context of the struggle against colonial rule that African nationalism was clearly articulated. African nationalism has been viewed from different perspectives – either positively or negatively. In positive terms, it has led to the independence of African nation-states but, in negative terms, it has been viewed as the struggle by self-seeking African elite to replace the colonial powers with their own form of internal domination over their societies.

There are cogent arguments in support of these two perspectives. What is pertinent to note is that many "national" or ethnic groups are clamouring for self-determination in different African countries, years after such countries became liberated from colonial rule. This explains why there is a great deal of instability in various parts of the African continent. Part of the reason for this phenomenon is the fact that the colonial powers, for administrative and economic convenience, had merged different ethnic groups with different socio-cultural and political systems. There were clear signs that, after independence, there would be a problem of instability arising from the struggle for superiority among the different ethnic groups. In fact, because of the fear of domination among the ethnic groups, some of the African countries had to have their independence delayed.

The point being made is that ethnic nationalism replaced African nationalism at the independence of several African countries. I have argued somewhere else (Anyim, 2002) that unless genuine efforts are made to minimize the negative effects of ethnic nationalism it would be difficult for an African country, like Nigeria, to achieve sustainable development. The bottom line is that African nationalists are seen by some individuals as heroes and by others as villains. What cannot be denied is that African nationalists were able to unite in their struggle to achieve the common objective of attaining independence. The task that remains is how to articulate common national goals which would effectively neutralize the latent ethnic or tribal consciousness. Where there is effective and responsive leadership among African leaders, it will be possible to forge national identities and histories without necessarily sacrificing sub-national identities. This is the task that must be tackled in the present dispensation. Unfortunately, corruption and ineptitude are rife in African countries. It has been difficult to sustain democratic principles and practices on account of the fact that those in power usually attempt to perpetuate themselves in office. But, all hope is not lost because African rulers are beginning to learn their lessons in the face of opposition from their citizens.

We argue, therefore, that African nationalism contributed significantly to the liberation of African societies but that because of the heterogeneous nature of African countries the task of achieving social, economic and political freedom is far from being over. We shall highlight the fact that some of the failures associated with African nationalism apply to other regions of the world and also we shall show that nationalism, aside from the objective of achieving autonomy, is often not an articulated set of principles. Nationalism has a high level of emotional content. This has led scholars such as Karl Popper to repudiate its claims. He considered nationalism as absurd. According to Popper,

> ...the nationalist faith...is absurd. I am not alluding here to Hitler's racial myth. What I have in mind is, rather, an alleged natural right of man - *the alleged right of a nation to self-determination*...The principle amounts to the demand that each state should be a nation-state: that it should be confined within a natural border, and that this border should coincide with the location of an ethnic group; so that it should be the ethnic group, the 'nation' which should determine and protect the natural limits of the state (367 - 368).

Popper's position touches on one of the weaknesses of nationalism but he also recognized that, even in the face of obvious facts against it, nationalism has continued to receive wide acceptance as an article of moral faith. While we agree with Popper that nationalism is not the ultimate solution to problems within a given nation-state, we disagree with him that it is absurd. We believe that, within reasonable limits, it is not absurd for a given ethnic group to demand for self-determination or autonomy if its interests and welfare cannot be guaranteed in a larger nation-state. So, whether in Nigeria, Rwanda, Sudan, Somaliland, or Western Sahara, the clamour for self determination will continue until African nation-states are run based on justice in the distribution of national resources. The clamour by some ethnic groups for autonomy is therefore in consonance with the spirit of African nationalism.

Nationalism

Meaning and Sources of Nationalism: The concept of nationalism was derived from the concept of nation which is used to refer to a group of people who are bound by the belief that they possess a common history, culture and identity. Although the concept of nation is often used to refer to nation-states or countries, it is basically the belief by a group of people that they have a shared identity. Sodaro (145) highlighted this phenomenon by stating that "a nation is a large group whose members believe they belong together on the basis of a shared identity as a people". Within the context of Africa, a nation can be equated to an ethnic group or tribe. Indeed, Sodaro identified ethnicity as one of the sources of a people's sense of national identity or nationhood. The other sources are civic identity, shared patterns of social communication and an imagined political community. These sources of nationalism explain why nationalism conveys a sense of patriotism, loyalty and devotion to a nation because of the feeling of shared identity among a group of people bound by a common language, common history or biological ancestry, traditions, and so on. As a result of shared values, nationalism emerges as a patriotic effort to; achieve self-determination for the people involved. In a way, therefore, it can be stated that the conditions which favour the emergence of nationalism include common history, language, culture and some forms of definable geographical territory. We can now attempt to give some definitions of nationalism. For Sodaro,

> Nationalism in its broadest meaning is an idea, a consciously formulated concept that emphasizes the distinctiveness of one's "nation" and articulates certain "national" interests, purposes or goals for action (146).

From this definition, one can deduce that nationalism has two components - the principles outlining the shared identities of a national group and the action required to achieve self-determination for the group. This same view has been corroborated by another writer who stated that:

> The term "nationalism" is generally used to describe two phenomena: (1) the attitude that the members of a nation have when they care about their national identity, and (2) the actions that the members of a nation take when seeking to achieve (or sustain) self-determination (http://plato. standard. edu/ entries / nationalism/ Nationalism, 1).

These two important aspects of nationalism show that nationalism is an ideology which is used in achieving a political end - self-determination. Sodaro has pointed out that domestic nationalism involves the demand by a group of people who consider themselves as a nation to govern themselves without interference from other governments or political forces. In this case, nationalism entails the control of a defined territory as constituting the national boundaries of the group which demarcate it from the international boundaries of other nation-states. But there is another variant of domestic nationalism and this comes in the form of partial self-determination or autonomy. Partial self-rule or self-determination entails territorial independence within the larger nation-state. Since self-determination is an important aspect of nationalism, it is not surprising that it is steeped in emotion rather than fact. This has resulted in the formulation of myths to show that one race or nation is different or superior to another. Nazi Germany was a classic example of nationalism based on the myth of the superiority of the Aryan race over others.

In the African context, apartheid South Africa was another good example. These are some of the negative aspects of nationalism which have sometimes led to pogroms or ethnic cleansing. However, the demand for self-determination over a territory is often impracticable. This is because many national groups live in different territories controlled by different nation-states. For this reason, the feeling of nationhood may simply be imagined in such a territory. But it does not make the feeling of nationhood less intense.

History of Nationalism

Scholars have noted that the earliest forms of nationalism can be located in the history of some societies which regarded themselves or their cultures as being superior to others. This can be seen in the history of the Jews and Greeks in the ancient period. However, after the ancient period, a variety of factors aided the growth of nationalism ranging from the rise of federalism, mercantilism, the evolution of regional languages, and the rise of the middle class. Within the context of European history, nationalism became a potent force in the nineteenth century based on the theoretical backing by philosophers such as Hegel, Fichte, and others. This led to social changes in Germany, France, Italy and others. In the twentieth century, after the end of the First World War, the concept of nationalism incorporated the right of nation-states to self-determination. However, the nationalism of Hitler's Nazi Germany led to the Second World War. So far, it would be seen that the notion of nationalism is a uniquely European phenomenon but this is not accurate because the history of most nation-states in the world is replete with accounts of their struggles for self-determination or self-government. This means that the feeling of national identity and self-government is an integral part of the history of different human societies. African societies are not an exception. In the African context, especially after the Second World War, it assumed the form of a struggle for political liberation from colonial rule and domination.

At the moment, although most African societies are independent, there are still ethnic or national groups clamouring for self-determination in their affairs. This is the case in other regions of the world. We cannot overlook the nationalist struggles of the people of Southern Sudan, Tibet, Western Sahara, Kosovo, etc. The history of modern nationalism in Africa is linked to the struggle for liberation from the shackles of European imperialism and chauvinism. This explains why the history of colonial Africa is replete with cases of confrontation between European colonialists and natives. However, after independence, nationalism has continued to exist as a result of the clamour for some degree of autonomy by some ethnic groups. It is debatable if nationalist feelings will ever completely disappear because it is very resilient. In the contemporary period, it is an important part of international relations, especially in matters of trade or security. We cannot understand phenomena such as racism and xenophobia without understanding the dynamics of nationalism. Different nation-states have put up measures to check the menace of unbridled nationalism.

Africa Nationalism

Meaning and Sources of African Nationalism: We had noted that there are parallels between African nationalism and nationalism in other regions of the world, especially Europe. African nationalism cannot be separated from the pan-Africanist movement which was created to act as a rallying force for the unification and liberation of Africans. The history of African nationalism cannot be separated from the struggle to achieve independence. So, colonialism was an important factor in the emergence of modern African nationalism and this caused Africans to demand for the right to self-determination. According to one writer,

> African nationalism has its roots among the educated elites (mainly 'returned' Americans of African descent and freed slaves or their descendants in West Africa in the 19th century. Christian mission - educated, many challenged overseas mission control and founded independent churches...Africa's direct involvement in World War II, the weakening of the principal colonial powers, increasing anti-colonialism from America (the Atlantic Charter in 1941 encouraged self-government), and Soviet criticism of imperialism inspired African nationalists (http: //www. talktalk. co. uk reference /encyclopaediahutchinsonlm0029 55 8. html).

From this view, we can conclude that the sources and factors which caused the emergence of modern African nationalism were both external and internal in nature. This means that the African elite who constituted the vanguard of African nationalism were aided by events which took place outside the African continent. Basically, pan-Africanists proclaimed the common destiny of Africans and the need for pride in African cultures. The pan-Africanist movements promoted the idea of a unified Africa which is self-governing. In discussing the sources of African nationalism, we must take special note of the role that pan-Africanists played towards it's emergence as an instrument for the struggle for the emancipation of Africa from colonial rule. Jessica Powers have highlighted the link between African nationalism and pan-Aricanism. For Powers,

> The ideology of Pan-Africanism promoted racial pride and claimed Africa for the Africans; it spoke for all Africans rather than focusing on a particular ethnic group or nation. With no political power, it could not change the colonial system, but it did articulate the problems that Africans experienced under basis of nationalism (1).

We agree with the position of Powers that pan-Africanism was one of the important sources of African nationalism. Based on this link with pan-Africanism, we can assert that African nationalism formulated a theory of the distinctive nature of the African for the purpose of achieving political, economic, and cultural emancipation for the African continent. It emphasized that Africans share common identities and destiny which they should be proud of. Moreover, it stressed that Africans must fight for their own independence. This shows a parallel between other forms of nationalism and African nationalism because it integrates the two important components of nationalism - common identity and a course of action to achieve self-determination. However, only the ideal of self-determination has been fully achieved from the standpoint of independence from colonialism. The notion of shared common identity for which pan-Africanists called for the unification of Africa is far from being achieved. This is because most of the nation-states of Africa are heterogeneous, that is, they are composed of diverse national groups which were merged together by colonial rulers. In many instances, these national or ethnic groups have very little in common with each other-historically, culturally, etc. This explains why the pan-Africanist movement declined after the attainment of independence by African nation-states. In Nigeria, for example, "at different periods of her history, leaders of the major ethnic groups have expressed secessionist sentiments" (Anyim, 1999:32).

Scholars have attributed this difficulty in forging a common identity to the fact that the different ethnic groups in a heterogeneous society tend to owe more allegiance to their different ethnic groups than to the nation-state. Rabushka and Shepsle (39) have contended that such loyalty to the different ethnic groups undermines the nation-state because it tends to contend for ultimate political authority and to rival the state for legitimacy. The inevitable fall-out of this struggle is that there is instability in many African nation-states at the moment.

History of African Nationalism

The history of African nationalism tends to focus on the struggle for the decolonization of the continent from European powers. This focus is inescapable because of the partition of Africa into colonies by Britain, France, Portugal, Belgium, Italy, and Germany. These European powers controlled all parts of Africa with the exception of Liberia and Ethiopia. Some of the roots and sources of African nationalism which we identified in the preceding section are also connected with the struggle against colonial rule. But, even though these sources are important aspects of the history of African nationalism, we need to note that prior to colonization, the African continent was made up of different ethnic or national groups which were fiercely nationalistic. For example, there were kingdoms or empires such as Ghana, Mali, Songhai, Kanem-Bornu, Bini, and Oyo empires in the West African region. This was also the case in the eastern, southern, northern and central parts of Africa.

While there were trading activities between some of these empires or national groups, there were also constant conflicts and wars among them because of the belief that they were different nationalities. This was one of the factors that contributed to the slave trade. From historical records, there was contact between Europeans and Africans as early as 200 B.C through Greek sailors who sailed round the continent. But it was not until the 15th century that Portuguese sailors visited West Africa for the purposes of trade, religion and colonization. Initially, contact between Africans and Europeans was based on trade but as a result of the rivalry among the European powers because of natural resources there was the need to acquire territories. It is on record that Africans resisted the colonization of their territories. This resistance continued even during colonization but was heightened by a combination of internal and external factors after the Second World War. The point we are emphasizing is that there was strong nationalist consciousness among the different national groups before the advent of full colonization. The different national groups resisted domination of their territories from both internal and external forces. Such nationalistic consciousness has not totally disappeared in the nation-states that now make up Africa. This explains why the idea of unified Africa by pan-Africanists has not been achieved. The nation-states or countries of Africa cannot really be said to be nation-states in the sense of being composed of a monolithic nation, that is, a group of people bound by one culture, language, religion and biological ancestry.

What obtains, rather, is that a nation-state, such as Nigeria, is made up of different nationalities which were merged together by colonial powers to achieve their own political and economic ends without considering that the national groups did not really have much in common with each other. However, we note that colonization helped to douse ethnic rivalry among Africans in order to focus on the liberation of the continent from Europeans. It was this common desire for political freedom that created the platform for the emergence of modern African nationalism with a set of principles and goals.

It should be pointed out that the different patterns of administration adopted by the colonial powers influenced the growth of African nationalism. While France, Belgium and Portugal saw their colonies as parts or extensions of their home countries, Britain preferred to rule her colonies indirectly through native authorities. The French, Portuguese and Belgian governments pursued the option of assimilating their colonies into their own cultures - as citizens of their countries by granting them privileges that Africans in the British territories did not enjoy. It was natural, therefore, that the spirit of nationalism was stronger in British colonies. But Africans generally were united that there must be self-determination for the whole of the African continent.

Apart from the resistance of the national groups to colonization in the 19th century, the 20th century witnessed an articulated and purposeful attack on colonialism. Pan-Africanists played an important role in this regard with their rebuttal of the notion of inferiority of African races. Notable pan-Africanists included Edward Blyden, Booker T. Washington, Casely Hayford, W. E. B. Du Bois, Marcus Garvey, and George Padmore. The importance of Pan-Africanists in the emergence of African nationalism cannot be overlooked. Wallace G. Mills (10) has enumerated the significance of pan-Africanism to include the following:

i. It affirmed the worth of the black people by rejecting the inferiority ascribed to Africans.
ii. It helped to launch the struggle for the right of blacks in diaspora.
iii. It asserted the right of independence for Africans.
iv. It held out a lofty ideal for the future of independent Africa.

The above efforts by pan-Africanists helped to provide the intellectual foundation for African nationalism which was used by nationalists such as Nkrumah, Kenyatta, Nyerere, Senghor, Kaunda, Azikiwe, Awolowo, Mandela, and so on. Thus, it is correct to assert that pan-Africanism provided the fundamentals of African nationalism. Marcus Garvey (2) summed up this fact when he stated: "Black men the world over must practice one faith, that of confidence in themselves, with: one cause, one goal, one destiny". This kind of opinion is found also in Senghor's *negritude* and those of other prominent African nationalists. Thus, before the end of the Second World War in 1945, there were several political and cultural organizations which championed the cause of independence for Africans. However, the history of African nationalism took a dramatic turn in 1945. According to Timothy D. Sisk,

> World War II had significant and psychological effects on the continent and its people. As a consequence of the war, the colonial powers were weakened and the legitimacy of occupation began to erode; at the same time, the message of the struggle for civil rights in countries such as the United States spread abroad. U.S. Presidents such as Eisenhower pressed for decolonization to open Africa's markets to free trade (813).

Sisk also identified some other important factors such as the emergence of a middle class and the fact that it was discriminated against by the colonial administrators as some of the factors which boosted African nationalism. Some writers have been critical of African nationalism because of the activities of the middle class which perhaps engaged in the struggle in order to enjoy the same privileges accorded to Europeans. Indeed, after independence, many of the nationalists who took over the reins of power were no better than the Europeans that they replaced. Perhaps, this is the reason that one writer has sarcastically defined African nationalism as:

> A mass movement drawing on racial hostility to replace an advanced leading group of a different ethnic origin by a "new class" of privileged despots of the same ethnic origin as the masses in the name of democracy, human rights, and so forth (http://www.rhodesia .nlbackgrl176 .htm, 4).

This replacement of external domination and oppression by internal ones is a sad part of the history of African nationalism. Nkrumah had stated that the paramount objective of nationalism must be political freedom and it seems that there was not enough consideration on how to instill democratic principles in the emerging African states. This explains why attempts at democratization have not succeeded in many African states.

Meanwhile, another major turning point in the history of African nationalism occurred in the 1960's. This was the period that the majority of African states became independent. In 1960 alone, countries such as Nigeria, Benin, Burkina Faso, Chad, Central African Republic, Cote d'Ivoire, Chad, Zaire, Togo, Cameroon, Senegal, Mali, Mauritania, Gabon, etc became independent.

Ghana had earlier obtained its independence in 1957. The case of South Africa was unique in itself because of apartheid but the blacks achieved their political freedom in 1994 with Nelson Mandela as the first democratically elected black president. At the moment, Africa has been rid of European colonial rule but there are still some areas in Africa where some national groups are bent on seceding from their existing states, such as Southern Sudan, which has just succeeded in 2011. What seems to be the case at the moment is that national or ethnic groups within African states are struggling to control political power and where they fail to achieve this objective they demand for autonomy within the existing states.

African Nationalism: Prospects and Failures

There is no doubt that African nationalism achieved the primary objective which was the decolonization of Africa. A combination of internal and external factors helped in achieving this purpose. Africa is now a clearly defined territory made up of different nation-states which have sovereign rights in the comity of nations. As far as political liberation from European colonialism is concerned, a vital aspect of African nationalism would seem to have been achieved. However, in terms of "freedom rating" in the world, only a handful of African states are rated "free" while the rest are either "not free" or "partially free". The reason for this is that there is lack of good governance based on democratic principles in the majority of African states. Thus, in a way, European oppressors have been replaced by African oppressors. There is widespread electoral fraud and corruption which allow incumbents to retain power against the wishes of their citizens. Some have retained power for three decades! In order not to be accountable to the citizens, such rulers have enacted laws to deny their citizens of basic human rights. Political repression is, therefore, rife in many states.

The above scenario can be counted as some of the failures of African nationalism. Another important failure is that the pan-Africanist dream of uniting the whole of Africa has not been achieved. Indeed, we have had cases of xenophobia in different parts of Africa resulting in riots and deaths. These cases, it can be argued, are not peculiar to Africa. This is because nationalism is usually emotional. This tendency gives rise to confused objectives among nationalists. In some cases, there is no scientific evidence or proof to back up the theories or myths of the nationalists. It is not surprising, therefore, that nationalism has helped to promote racism. This is the reason that some liberal writers like Karl Popper have rejected it. If African nationalism has not lived up to its potentials as envisaged by its founders, part of the explanation is that nationalism itself contains some inherent weaknesses. But, African nationalism is not dead yet. There are regional groups within Africa which are fostering cooperation among states in the regions. Although, the African Union is mostly in name and not substance; it has helped to forge a common front on some issues in the larger world politics. It would be easier to defend African positions but for the weak economic conditions of the African states. Thus, in the face of economic domination by other regions of the world, there is need to emancipate the African continent from internal forces. The strengthening of weak democratic structures will help to add economic freedom to the "political" freedom that has been won. This means that some form of moderate nationalism is still relevant in the contemporary period but it must be based on liberal principles in order to curtail some of its excesses.

WORKS CITED

Anyim, N. M. "Ethnic Nationalism and the Sustenance of Democracy in Nigeria" in *Ibom Journal of History and International Studies*. No. 10, 2002.

Anyim, N. M. "Philosophy and Nigeria's Development: A Critical Analysis" in Agbafor Igwe (Ed). *Philosophy and National Development: A Periscope of the Next Millennium*. Uyo: MEF Publishers, 1999.

Popper, K. R. *Conjectures and Refutations*. London: Routledge and Kegan Paul, 1969.

Rabushka, A. and Shepsle, K. A. *Politics in Plural Societies: A Theory of Democratic Instability*. Columbus: Charles Menil Publishers, 1972.

Sisk, Timothy. "Nigerian and South Africa" in Michael J. Sodaro (Ed). *Comparative Politics: A Global Introduction*. Boston: McGraw - Hill Publishers, 2001.

Sodaro, M. J. *Comparative Politics: A Global Introduction*. Boston: McGraw - Hill Publishers, 2001.

INTERNET SOURCES

Jessica Powers, "Early Nationalism and Pan-Africanism" in http: //www. Suitel 0l. com /article .cfm/ african_history 162933, March 13, 2001.

Wallace G. Mills, "African Nationalism" in http://stymarys .ca/IVw.mills /course322/17African_nation.html

The Hon. Marcus Mosiah Garvey, "African Fundamentalism" in http: //www.africawithin .com/garveY/ garvey fundamentals. htm.

http://plato.Standford.edu/ entriesl nationalism I Nationalism.

http://www.talktalk.co.uk/reference/encyclopaedia/hutchinsonl 00 2958.html.

CHAPTER 6

POST-COLONIAL AFRICA: PROBLEMS AND PROSPECTS
By
ENYIMBA MADUKA

Introduction

Colonial Africa was a period that African states were under the rulership of some foreign countries for a number of years. It was Africa whose identity, culture and values were submerged into that of the colonial masters. As Eze rightly observed, "colonialism is therefore, the indescribable crisis disproportionately suffered and endured by the African peoples in their tragic encounter with the European world, from the beginning of the fifteenth century through the end of the nineteenth into the first half of the twentieth." Thus, for centuries Africa was suppressed, manipulated, exploited, deprived and dehumanized. This continued to be the case until the emergence of the African elites, who having been educated became aware of the deplorable condition of their people. Hence, the struggle for self-determination, identity, fundamental rights and indeed independence began. Despite the rough terrain of the road towards independence, freedom was eventually gained. This marks the emergence of post-colonial Africa. The phrase post-colonial Africa is used here to refer to the African states immediately after the colonial period. It connotes the present and contemporary African states in their effort to manage and control their domestic affairs with undue influences from the west. Indeed, the post-colonial Africa can be construed as the era of concerted attempt at nation-building through the reconstruction of the image, cultural identity and personhood of the African which were bastardized by the European.

However, evidence has shown that most of the problems which Africa grappled in their colonial days have continued to trail her till the present. The question is what is the nature of these problems?

And what are the possible solutions? In an attempt to answer these questions, this chapter shall use the post-colonial Nigerian state as a case study of post-colonial Africa. The point will be made that these problems are to be seen as challenges of nation building. And until it is construed as such with a determinate effort to overcome them, then the future will remain uncertain and therefore bleak. But if otherwise, then, it has great prospects for the nation. Thus, we employ problems and challenges interchangeably in this essay.

Post-Colonial Africa: Challenges or Problems
In the making of any given nation, there have always been hurdles in the form of challenges or problems. It has never been smooth and crisis-free. Even the nation's recognized today as developed nations, had a lot of problems and challenges to contend with before getting to where they are today. Yet in as much as they are still moving towards the actualization of their real self, they continue to experience some troubles from time to time. Hence, problems and challenges are necessary gadflies that sting the growing nation into a full-fledged nation. This is the case with the Nigerian state which is saddled with numerous problems since its independence in 1960 and indeed most African states after their independence. Some of these problems include bribery, nepotism, tribalism, corruption, naira-counterfeiting, occultism, smuggling, avarice, unbridled-sexual-promiscuity, favouritism, dishonesty, embezzlement of public funds, willful destruction of public property, political thuggery, electoral malpractice, armed robbery, inflated constracts, examination malpractice, injustice, oppression, etc (Uduigwomen, 61). To adequately examine these problems and challenges so as to proffer practical solution, we shall divide them into three major kinds, namely, economic, religious and socio-political challenges.

Economic Challenges and Problems

The economic problems facing the Nigerian state and indeed most African states lie in the fact that the major source of foreign exchange is from the oil sector to the overall neglect of other sectors. One can then begin to understand why it is in this sector of the economy that many economic fraud and financial ineptitude in such countries are mostly found. Mberu identifies three major economic problems of all societies of which Nigeria and of course

Africa is one (155). According to him, the first is to determine what goods and services are required and how much of each and where (in what regions of the country) and what manner they could best be produced. Second, it has to allocate the aggregate or total amounts of goods and services produced, that is, the gross domestic product, consumption by society as a whole in the form of government expenditures and future growth of the economy. Third, it has to decide how to distribute its total material benefits (national income) among the various members of the society, in the form of wages, interest payments, rents, profits whether public or private.

Evidently, Nigeria and indeed Africa is not exempted from these tasks and challenges which usually breed problems and conflicts if not properly managed. It is in the area of resource control, resource management and resource allocations that Nigeria has always had ethnic bias and sectionalism, which eventually results in bloody crisis and tribal conflicts. At this point, many sectors of the society cry against marginalization: commenting on the acidic effect of ethnic violence in the globe, Uka states that:

> These inter ethnic conflicts have caused dreadful havoc (all over Africa) even here in Nigeria; the activities of Oduduwa Peoples Congress in Yoruba land, the Arewa Congress of Northern Nigeria, the Bakassi Boys of Abia State, the Odi episode in Niger Delta Region, the clash between the Jukuns and Tiv, the ethno-religious riots in Kaduna, Kano, Jos, the disturbing clashes between border communities, between Cross River and Akwa Ibom States and between Cross River and Benue State etc all point to the seriousness of the issue (109).

Further observation must be made about the poor state of the economy which has led to a poverty-stricken population where the rich gets richer and the poor gets poorer. It is no longer news that most inflation experienced in some African countries like Nigeria is artificially created. In other words, it is man-made with a self-centreed underpinning. Most business moguls, economic merchants and other individuals and companies and most times government themselves, who have monopoly of a given essential economic commodity would selfishly decide to mortgage it to create scarcity which will eventually result in inflation and this continue to wreck more havoc on the economy. How to overcome these economic vagaries is one of the greatest challenges facing post-colonial (Nigeria) Africa.

Religious Challenges and Problems

According to Asira "religion is an instrument for the unification of the Supreme Being and man on the one hand and man and man on the other hand; However, in Nigeria, religious adherents tend to be at loggerheads with themselves" (95). Asira could not have been more correct, especially when it is recalled that this is a country whose citizens are very religious. Asira describes this as the "irreligious attitudes of religious adherents" (98). Most of the problems facing post-colonial Africa and indeed Nigeria in particular are religiously motivated. There have always been clashes between the two major religions in the country – Christianity and Islam. This crisis of religions interests between these two religions has led to several riots and destruction of lives and properties. This has impacted negatively on the country's attempts or efforts at realizing its democratic ideals. In the 20th and 21st centuries there have been a number of clashes resulting from fanaticism of certain religious adherents that had threatened and still threaten to disrupt the country's match towards national integration and development. Stephen made this point when he states that;

> ... conflicts between the stated religions occur when fanatical adherents of either religions in any society, community or state, engage in acts of fanaticism and bigotry in religious matters, by attempting to compel fellow citizen of the opposite religions to worship and abide by their parochial theological doctrines, with the aim of securing political, economic or cultural supremacy and dominance (63).

This is the root cause of numerous religious problems which are evident in Nigeria and most African countries since the beginning of self-rulership in Africa. For instance, it is an established fact that, since May 1999 about 40 violent clashes, most of which are inter-religious Muslim/Christian conflicts, have been recorded. One of such is the religious disturbance which erupted in Yehwa, in Shendam Local Council of Plateau State. Beginning on the 11th of May 2004, the conflict rapidly spread to Kano, Bamitu and other northern states, with the greatest casualties recorded in Plateau State, which almost led to the declaration of a state of emergency and the temporary removal of the democratically elected Christian governor – Joshua Dariye of (Stephen, 55).

Socio-Political Challenges and Problems

This appears to be the most prevalent and corrosive of all the crisis besieging African nations. Sometimes, politically motivated factors breed religious crisis at the centre of Nigerian predicament. Socio-political problems in Nigeria is found in the area of social injustices of all kinds, marginalization of the less privileged, poverty and unemployment, illiteracy and poor educational facilities, rigging of election, arson and murder, political assassination, insecurity of lives and properties, forceful removal from office, sit-tight or second term syndrome, examination malpractice and cultism in both secondary and tertiary institutions. In fact, the Nigerian socio-political scenario is steeped deep with terrible challenges which have proved over the years to be difficult to surmount. In this country like most African state where there is supposed to be security, exercise of freedom and fundamental human rights, assassination and deprivation of fundamental rights have become the order of the day. There can be no mention of any transition process from one political regime to another without a mention of assassination of political stalwarts, massive rigging of elections, money laundering and other financial ineptitude. It is sad to recall the cold-blooded murder of an attorney general of the federation – Chief Bola Ige, the involvement of one time governor of Bayelsa state, Chief Alamieyeseigha in money laundering and financial misappropriation. Indeed, the story surrounding his imprisonment in London and his subsequent escape is most pitiable and portrays the country in a very bad light.

Again, with the military punctuation of our democratic process and the subsequent cry of the masses and the civilian-political elites for them to return to the barracks for them to take over, one begins to wonder what difference it makes in the socio-political scenario as in other aspects of the society. It goes without saying that it appears to be even worse now than before. At this juncture, one cannot but agree with Chinua Achebe that "the trouble which Nigeria and therefore the challenges before Nigeria and Africa as a whole is that of leadership" (27). It is possible that the picture painted above of Nigeria and African society as a whole can create some cold feelings in the minds of Nigerians or a gloomy expression for the future of Nigeria or African nation states in the light of its leadership.

No wonder Wole Soyinka was reported in the newspaper as saying that the present political scenario of violence, assassination, removal from and replacement in office of officers of the state and the second term syndrome, is an ominous sign that Nigeria is heading towards another spate of military intervention and ultimately a disintegration of the democratic process and the nation at large. But in all these challenges, predicaments and problems facing the Nigerian nation state the questions remains, what does the future hold, what prospect for Nigerian leaders? Is there any hope for the future or are we doomed for disaster? In what follows, we shall examine these questions and conclude by suggesting what steps must be taken to ensure a better future of the nation states. The point will be made that, the gloomy state of the nation, not withstanding, there is still hope for the nation, what these challenges and problems present is an opportunity for reconstruction, re-directing, re-learning and unlearning certain attitudes, decision-making and re-engineering of not only the material resources but also the human resources.

Concluding Remarks

In our thinking, the purpose which the numerous challenges and problems x-rayed above seek to serve is to create a situation so intense that will inevitably open the door to re-organization and re-conscientization of the people especially the ruling class. It is our opinion that, such violent crisis as evident in Nigeria and some African nations are not meant to create disaster and rock the boat of the countries progress to disintegration. Instead it merely brings to the surface the hidden tension or conflict that is already alive so that it can be seen and dealt with. When one views the various challenges facing the Nigerian state from the above perspective, then it will be discovered that there is great prospects for the future, as the solution for a better future lies in the hands of both the rulers and the ruled. Thus, we must do a lot of learning and re-learning. We must imbibe the principles of morality and eschew ignorance, materialism and what Okolo calls squandermania mentality (Nwankwo, 35). For this is the bedrock of all problems and challenges in the country. There must be an ideological resolution which will create in the minds of the people the urgent need to be united to re-discover themselves and fight for an inclusive Nigeria. According to Uwalaka, an inclusive Nigeria would mean:

> A Nigeria in which every citizen or component group, enjoys all the rights and privileges of belongingness, a sense which imposes a corresponding obligation to members. It is a Nigeria in which there are no official policies or actions to marginalize or exclude certain individuals, groups or cultures and in which even unofficial or clandestine actions of private groups to do the same are officially combated (157).

Furthermore, for a better utilization of the opportunity created by the numerous problems in the country to better the Nigerian future, each individual must seriously and sincerely undergo self-examination, being truthful enough to acknowledge that the situation demands the corporate effort of every Nigerian. Finally, we uphold Socrates' disposition that it is necessary to create a conflict or tension in the mind, so that individuals would rise from the bondage of myths and half-truths to the unfettered realm of creative analysis and objective appraisal. So we must see these various challenges and problems in the state as antecedents that will enable Nigerians (both the leaders and the led) to rise from the dark depths of prejudice, oppression and ethnicity to the majestic heights of understanding, liberation, unity, brotherhood and development. Only then will we be able to avert this looming socio-economic, religious and political eclipse in our dear country.

WORKS CITED

Achebe, Chinua. *The Trouble with Nigeria*. Enugu: Fourth Dimension, 1989.

Asira, E. A. "The Paradox of Religiousity in Nigeria: A Threat to National Unity" in *Sophia: An African Journal of Philosophy. Vol. 6*, No. 1, 2003.

Eze, E. C. (Ed). *African Philosophy: Anthropology*. Oxford: Blackwell Publishers, 1998.

Mberu, B. U. *Social Structures and Institutions*: Abakaliki: Willy Rose and Appleseed, 1999.

Nwankwo, I. J. "Practical and Theoretical Problems in the Emergence of Responsible Governance in Africa" in *Sophia: An African Journal of Philosophy 7,* No. 2, 2003.

Stephen, J. O. Religion and Clash of Civilization: The Incidence and Consequences of Islamic/Christian Religious Conflicts on Democracy in Nigeria" in *Sophia: An African Journal of Philosophy*. Vol. 7, No. 2, 2003.

Uduigwomen, A. F. "Leadership and Nigeria's Socio-Political Malaise" in *Nigeria: Government and Politics*. (Ed). Ozumba G. O. Aba: AAU, 1999.

Uka, E. M. *Equipping the Saints for the Challenges of Our Time*. Aba: Executive Press, 2002.

Uwatata, J. *The Struggle for an Inclusive Nigeria*. Owerri: Snap Press, 2003.

CHAPTER 7

AFRICAN SOCIALISM

By
ETIM O. FRANK, Ph.D

Introduction

Ideas cannot be divorced from the society in which they flourished, and they are not completely dependent on social structure. Political ideas can legitimize the political structures, and consequently increase political stability...when certain ideas are widely accepted and agreed upon in the political system, we speak of a consensus (Ball, 1979: 31); thus, philosophy occurs wherever there are people with inquisitive minds agitated by the events in the environment. Therefore, it was so that Africans thought of the beauty of their past and overvalued it in what Professor Ali Mazrui termed 'primitive gloriana'. Many scholars also basked in the euphoria of earlier period in a manner of 'primitive romanticism'. Sevin Hirschbein (1978) termed these as 'appeals to a golden age of the past to serve as a model for the present', which was obtained in the state of communality and sought to develop further into a form of governance in the colonial and post colonial years. As scientific or Marxian socialism is subjected to considerable revisionism and versions African socialism would have been refined to a near perfect stage for application today. It is therefore not uncommon to find its variants such as, Tom Mboya's African socialism (1963), L. S. Senghor's Senegalese socialism, and Nwalimu J. K. Nyerere's *ujamaa* – the non-Marxist path to socialism, etc.

Scientific socialism grew out of two major antecedents; the agrarian reforms in Europe, which created the class of land owners, landless population, and the industrial revolution of the early 19th century, which produced the antagonistic classes of the proletariat – industrial wage earners and the bourgeoisie, the industrial owners who are locked in an aggressive relationship. Thus, these two opposing classes are brought together because of the industrial background hence connected to one another by 'social solidarity.' African socialism on the other hand grew out of the sanguinary blood ties, which existed between the people of African descent, who often came from the same patriarch, thereby constituting family ties. Mechanical rather than social solidarity informed African socialism. This was the basis to avoid exploitation as much as possible in the African socialist context. The intention of this piece is not to compare the two and condemn one as being unprogressive as many have done before now. This analysis is however to examine the contribution of Africans to political theory by evolving the philosophy of African socialism. It would in addition discuss the problems besetting further development of the concept in Africa. This subject-matter is dealt with in three parts; introducing the point of departure, dealing with the values and norms derived from African tradition and custom which informed the theory of African socialism, and the structure, power organization, the economy and the problems which confronted the concept and practice of African socialism.

African societies emerged like all others through the stages of growth. Like western and Greek societies, it was once at the pre-civilization stage, which Thomas Hobbes described as the 'state of nature'. It was the stage that was characterized by the absence of the 'Leviathan' (political authority). Men exercised their fundamental human rights without restriction. These rights conflicted with one another, which resulted in excessive conflict in the society. The persistence of conflict and the inconveniences it created, led Hobbes to describe life in such a primitive state as being 'short, nasty brutish and solitary' (Sabine, 1973: 425). Man being a reasonable, community building and a gregarious animal, sought order to rule his relationship with another. Thus, man entered into social contract with other men to institute order in their relationships, this created to Africans, and men elsewhere, communal society with social order, which formed the basis of the political theory.

A detailed and comparative study of facts made available by archeologists, pre-historians, historians, social geographers and anthropologists reveals that there have existed in history six broad kinds of social systems. These are; the communal, the slave-based, the serf-based, the mercantile, the capitalist, and the nascent socialist systems. Human society everywhere started with the communal type. The social order, which prevailed in the African communal society, which defined the rights, duties and privileges of everyone, was that of communal ownership of land, the major means of production. Land in the African communal society was owned by the community, or by extended families. Each family owned land and there was no landlessness. Every family worked for its own upkeep, and no individual worked permanently for another outside the family. Its members according to rights derived from age, sex and work used the product of the family. Communal work was common (Toyo, 2008: 3).

It is instructive to note at this point that African communal society was concerned with everybody within the inclusive community. The society was structured along patriarchal lineages. Each lineage head had a duty not to allow anyone within his fold go hungry. Pursuant to this objective, the only means of production being land was held in common for all. Whenever anyone came of age, a piece of land was made available to him, and his age grade would contribute labour to cultivate his land and during harvest. This sharing of the major means of survival was for lack of another term referred to as African socialism. It comprised production, ownership, distribution, and consumption. This is the issue highlighted in detail in the subsequent sections of this paper to indicate that Africans also contributed to the development of political philosophy.

The Philosophy of African Socialism

The philosophy of African socialism radiated from the communal background of African society. This is because every philosophy is masterminded by the objective physical conditions in which the bearer of the philosophy finds himself. It is important to outline the norms and values that prevailed in communal African societies, which were coalesced into the concept of African socialism.. In this system, the main item of property was land. Communal work was common. All other rights; political, economic or cultural, were related to these. Life as anthropologists report about such societies that existed in the 19th and 20th centuries was egalitarian. This means that the families had the same rights and no one within the family had superior rights to another that did not derive from age, sex, or nature and amount of work (Toyo, 2008: 4). This is where the following principles were derived which included;

i. Africans are all related by blood in every settlement hence the patriarchal nature of African societies, arranged in clans and lineages. As a result, it was an abomination to be instrumental to the hunger or poverty of one's relations. This explained the essence of communal ownership of the means of production, land.

ii. The idea of planning, direction, control and cooperation. It was a common phenomenon for the family-head to decide which of the farmlands would be cultivated with what type of crops and which would be left to fallow for the next cultivation season.

iii. The African communal society guaranteed political equality and democracy in whatever crude form. Issues were freely debated and resolved and everyone was equal in his contribution within his/her social class.

iv. Social justice was also upheld in African communal setting. According to Professor Dudley Seers; the question to ask about a country's development are three; what has been happening to poverty? What has been happening to unemployment? What has been happening to inequality? If all three of these have declined from high levels, then beyond doubt this has been a period of development for the country concerned. He reviewed this and added 'self-reliance' and ownership as well as output in the leading economic sectors (Gana, 1983: 91). This is because in the African setting everyone had access to the means of production and appropriated the product of his labour maximally, hence there was no exploitation.

v. There was communal labour where an age grade would all go to a member's farmland and contribute labour to tilt his land and at other time it was another's turn to also help tilt his land. This was distributive justice. Human dignity was thus upheld in African communal society.

These are some of the determinants derived from the African traditional practices, which informed the later philosophical postulation of African socialism. It is instructive to note that just as scientific socialism (Marxism) had several brands, so it was with the concept of African socialism. The common denominator of all these, were the norms and values prevalent in the African communal societies. Be mindful that the use of the term 'socialism and communism' is not original to Karl Marx nor Lenin or Hegel, but borrowed from Moses Hess, hence Africans could adopt it without meaning scientific socialism.

The conceptualization and articulation of African socialism was derived from the sociology of communalism, which made Africans to believe that everyone in the family, lineage, village or clan originated from the same putative ancestor (patriarch). Thus, everyone was connected to one another because of sanguinary blood ties, termed 'mechanical solidarity' by sociologists. This explicates extensive political behavior in Africa and subsequently informed African socialism based on the belief that 'we are all sons and daughters of the soil'...From this belief springs the logic and the practice of equality, and the acceptance of communal ownership of the vital means of life, the land (Mboya, 1963: 603). This philosophy gave primacy to material condition, particularly economic factors, in the explanation of social life, for man is *'homo-economicus'*, an economic man. It is true today as it was in the African communal society that economic need is man's most fundamental need; man must eat before he can do anything else – before he can worship, pursue culture or become an economist. When an individual achieves a level of economic necessities, particularly his daily food, for granted, the urgency of economic need loses the edge; in short, man must eat to live but he must work in order to eat (Ake, 1981: 1). This attitude of the mind of Africans remained the foundation of *ujamaa* and indeed underscored all brands of African socialism. In the words of Nwalimu J. K. Nyerere, socialism is an attitude of mind, which ensures that the people care for each other's welfare.

Democracy: The governance and the power structure in African socialism rested with the elders who represented the families, lineages, or clans. They held the power and the mean of production in trust for the people. They meet together to take decisions, contribute warriors from the clans, lineages in defense of the territory. The leaders of the various groups decide who becomes the overall head or king based on the seniority of their progenitor. This explains why the practices of the ruling house are rotated among ruling houses in most African states.

The Economy: The nature of the economy under African socialism is essentially distributive and in accordance with one's inputs. You appropriate what you sow and contribute proportionally to the commonwealth for the sustenance of those who suffer from an act of God such as famine, drought or fire disaster as jointly recommended by the family head, lineage or clan. For instance, when a hut had to be built, everyone was expected to go out cut the trees and erect the frame. The women would bring the cow-dung and the earth to make the floor, and drew water and make the plaster for the walls. Then the men would bring the grass for the thatching, and the work would be done together. The owner of the hut would cook food for everyone and the work would finish in a day. If someone refused to take part, then he would find that when his time came to build a hut, few people came to help him and he might be completely boycotted. This was the kind of sanction, which operated against the lazy man (Mboya, 1963: 604). Other sanctions range from ostracism to many others.

Scientific and African Socialism: Their Relationships

Too often, the philosophy of African socialism is not given a place in the discourse of political thoughts. This part of the paper presents the relationship between the two concepts in comparative terms. Scientific socialism is at the same time a theory and practice. Engel defines it as a method, not as a dogma; it is a series of steps that the mind takes to discover and demonstrate the truth', or preferably 'a series of reasoned steps to reach an objective in any field whatsoever. In other words, method as at once theory and practice, more precisely a theory conceived to be applied towards a definite objective. Engel was perfectly right to define socialism as a method (Senghor, 1964: 1). African socialism on the other hand is not an end in itself, but a 'means' to an 'end' of a good life. It is where the worker owns the means of production, and appropriates the benefit thereof maximally, thereby eliminating exploitation and alienation from the product of his labour. To this extend, both are/were 'means' to an 'end'.

One of the ends of Marxism is the destruction of capitalism, the major instrument of alienation and exploitation and the taking over the power of the state, which is sustained by the state apparatus (bureaucracy, justice, army, and police). African socialism by its nature abhors capitalism, and subverts this by its basis which rests on 'mechanical solidarity' by which every person is related by blood ties through the community or clan's patriarch. This created an attitude of mind towards one another, which repudiates exploitation through pursuit of profit. Karl Marx distinguished between socialism and communism. Socialism is not communism, it is the preparation for communism, a temporary stage on the road to communism both involve dual task - political and economic – but of a different type. Politically, socialism retains the apparatus of the state in order to transform it (Senghor, 1964:1). African socialism is a stage towards high socio-political formation; a stage which one cannot predict what it would have been if 'colonial – capitalism', did not distort it. This is because all human social organization is subject to changes. It was in the hands of workers of the land and leaders of the clans.

One of the goals and objective of Marxism will be the age of abundance where each will receive according to his needs, because the division of labour into manual and intellectual pursuits will vanish. Nwalimu J. K. Nyerere a theorist par excellence of African socialism averred that when a society is so organized that it cares about such individuals within that society, the individual would not worry about what will happen to them tomorrow if it does not hoard wealth today. Society itself should look after her widow and orphans. Both the rich and the poor individually were completely secured in African society (Wikipedia, 2006). Scientific socialism establishes democracy at the stage of the violent takeover of the state and at the level of eschatology. Power organization under African socialism was a collegiate system, where the leaders of the clans came together to take decisions and execute it democratically. In some traditional African societies such as the old Oyo Empire, it was known as the 'Oyomesi'. This was replicated all over Africa. Democracy was embedded in African socialism.

In a capitalist society, like great Britain, for instance, the owners of capital will similarly, predominantly determine the substance of law. In a socialist society, like Soviet Russia, the substance of law will be determined by the fact that the common ownership of the means of production subordinates the interest of a class to the interest of the society as a whole (Laski, 1966: vii). This is precisely what African socialism did in pre-colonial Africa. Lastly, the motive, and the force in Marxism consisted in the thesis, anti-thesis and synthesis. By this progressive process, socialism breaks down into its contradictions and glide towards communism. It is a possibility that communism could not generate its contradictions and give birth to what neither you nor me nor Karl Marx could predict. Similarly, because no human society is ever static, for forces of social intervention would have generated a new form of African socialism, which this author would, be playing god if he attempts the prediction of the nature of what it would have turn into. Finally, while Marxism rests on the existence of antagonistic classes in the society, African socialism was founded on the extended family system. Thus, they both need different framework for its analysis.

Ujamaa: The Practice

African socialism like Marxism was subjected to several interpretations and brands. It is only the ujamaa brand, which created social structures for its realization in Tanzania based on the principles enunciated in the Arusha Declaration of 1967. It is within its created structures and functioning that we herein examine the policies, programs, achievements and challenges in a bi-polar world with rising capitalist influence. It should be recalled that the global socio-economic system in which "ujamaa' operated consisted of scientific socialism in the Eastern bloc on the one hand and the liberal capitalist system in the Western hemisphere on the other, all of which were searching for converts. Sandwiched between these two extremes Ujamaa in practice observed it principles contained in the Arusha Declaration strictly. The principles as derived from Arusha Declaration included: self-reliance, absence of exploitation where all people are workers, these were wrapped in the mega principles of the 'people, land, good policies and good leadership' (Nyerere, 1968: 520).

The Tanzania leadership decided to do this by a system of village communities engaged in a group work. These villages were subsequently called ujamaa villages and the aim was to place the entire rural population in these villages. The 1978 villagization programme was explained in 'The Development Plan of 1969-74 as follows: 'the objective is to farm the village land collectively with modern techniques of production and share the proceeds according to the work contributed. People who are farming together can obtain the economic advantages of large-scale farming in the better utilization of machinery, purchase of supplies, marketing of crops, etc. It becomes easier to supply technical advice through agricultural extension officers who can teach a group more easily in one place, rather than traveling from one small shamble to another. It is also easier to provide social facilities such as water supplies, medical and educational services, to farmers who live in groups rather than in scattered holdings (Ake, 1981: 116).

The Tanzanian government had refused West German aid when it was tied to the non-recognition of East Germany, which Tanzania eventually recognized. It pursued non-aligned development. It opens its economy to gifts, loans and private investment as long as it was not tied to any condition that may interfere with Socialist Development in Tanzania (Hirschbein, 1978: 1). It is instructive to note that the principal strategy of ujamaa was to avoid profit, which arose out of the exploitation of one man by another. It was rather to be attained by all men working and producing; the surplus would then be exported to accommodate capital for development. Nevertheless, this was difficult to be attained.

The Challenges

Is it possible to develop socialism while subject to the imperative of international capitalism and its international credit institutions (WB and IMF)? It is possible to withstand the forces of both Western and the Eastern blocs, which were searching, for allies? These posed grave challenges to ujamaa. These problems arose because socialism in ujamaa is equated with Marxism. Nevertheless, it is at most a brand of it. The pitfall of comparison with Marxism must be avoided. The other is being the natural poverty of the state of Tanzania and its underdeveloped nature, which made it near impossible to generate and accumulate enough surpluses from the inputs of the peasants. While attention was focused on cash crop production to earn the desired foreign exchange, a gap was created in the production of food crops, leading to subsidies in the ujamaa villages. This was a function of management, technology and the vagaries of the weather because most of the east African countries had a bout of drought.

Success of Ujamaa

The invention of the concept of ujamaa, a brand of African socialism is in it a contribution to political theory and philosophy by an African, based on African value system. It was a means to an end as Marxism. Nevertheless, because of its substantial pressure experienced by the phenomenon in the post-colonial era, none of us is able to foretell what would have been its level of development now.

Considerable state farms were set up which served as models for the ujamaa village cooperation to learn techniques and other skill there from. Employment was thus created and the commanding height of the economy passed to the state. The logic was that of self-reliance for as Nyerere averred: if every individual is self-reliant, the the house cell will be self-reliant; if all the cells are self-reliant, the whole ward will be self-reliant, and if the wards are self-reliant, the district will be self-reliant, if the districts are self-reliant, then the region is self-reliant, and if the regions are self-reliant, then the whole nation is self-reliant and this our aim (1967).

It is worth submitting that because of the practice of ujamaa, the public sector has now become very dominant in the Tanzanian economy. To illustrate this, in 1973 public sector capital stock had risen to Sh. 2,077 million or 70.7 per cent of the national capital stock, while the public sector's share of wage employment had risen to 64 per cent of total wage employment. Thus, enormous expansion of the public sector has meant a radical change in the distribution of ownership in factor of localization (Ake, 1981: 118). It is the opinion of this paper that if aggressive ujamaa was insulated from capitalism for independent development, it would probably have attained the level, which other development theories had attended.

Conclusion

The practice of ujamaa or African socialism, brought to the fore the centrality of the principles tangential to development as self-reliance, the people, land, good public policies and good leadership. An evaluation of development in post-colonial African states indicated that these central elements are often missing hence vicious underdevelopment. Ujamaa if nothing else has set the agenda for independent development in post-colonial state. African socialism would perhaps have done much more than Marxism.

WORKS CITED

Ball, Alan R. *Modern Politics and Government*. London: Macmillan Press, 1973.

Gana, Jerry. 'Strategy for a Progressive Rural Development' in *Towards a Progressive Nigeria*. (Ed) Asikpo Essien-Ibok. Kano: Triumph Publishers, 1983.

Hirschbein, S. "Tanzania: The Non-Marxist Path to Socialism" in *Monthly Review: Journal of Philosophy*. Lewis and Clark College, Portland Oregon. No 32 (8) 1978.

Laski, Harold. J. *A Grammar of Politics*. London: George Allen & UnWin, 1966.

Mboya, Tom, *African Socialism - Freedom and After*. London: Andre Deutsch, 1963.

Nyerere, J. K. 'The Arusha Declaration: Socialism and Self Reliance' in *Freedom and Socialism*. Oxford: University Press of East Africa, 1967.

Sabine, G. H. and Thorson, T. L. *A History of Political Theory*. Illinois: Saunders: Dryden Press, 1973.

Senghor, Leopold. S. *On African Socialism*. London: The Pall Mall Press, 1964.

Toyo, Eskor. 'Capitalism and the Niger Delta Crisis' in *Lecture Delivered at the University of Uyo*. November 27, Graduate Students' Association, AKS. 2008.

Wikipedia.org: Julius_Nyerere 'Ujamaa – The Basis of African Socialism' in *ChickenBones: A Journal for Literary & Artistic African-American Themes*. 12/22/2006.

CHAPTER 8

TOWARDS AN IDEOLOGY FOR AFRICA: AN INTEGRATIVE HUMANIST APPROACH
By
PROF. G. O.OZUMBA
&
JONATHAN C. OKEKE

Introduction

For any ideology to be visibly driven through to achieve the desired effect in the body – politic, there is need to put in place laws, the fear of which will enforce compliance and obedience. The natural man cannot pursue excellence unguarded by law and moral principles and checks. An African ideology must distance "itself" from the postmodern chaotic ensemble of maxims which characterize the ideology of the so-called developing nations. We must always ask development in terms of what? Is it in terms of technology, capital, infrastructure, armaments and stockpile of destructive weapons? Africa should not develop along these lines. Our focus should be in terms of moral quality of human lives, peace with one another, congenial environment, integrative harmony of the ecosystem and provision of basic human needs like water, food health services, good roads, power supply, employment, provision of food through well planned agriculture, high productivity, zero tolerance for corruption, continual restitution of stolen wealth of the common wealth, punishment for erring public servants, service for immortalization and not for aggrandizement, public spiritedness and sacrificial service. The above should constitute the engine providing the impetus to drive the African ideology. When each African nation is able, to achieve internal harmony and cohesion through the above cardinal principles, the same principles elevated to a transnational level within Africa will achieve the same level of success and the same substance and form of development that is desirable for Africa. We are afraid that western development may be a developing chaos which may soon consume them. We can see the arms race, the scramble and partition of the world, the Palestinian-Israeli imbroglio, the Eurozone (Greece, Italy, Spain, Iceland, etc.) debt burden, the expedition to annihilate despotism in North Africa, the moral decadence in our world and so on.

Ideology for Africa: A Quest

Ideology, for us is a set of well articulated ideas that is shaped by the mistakes of the past, the rumblings of the present with a view to fashioning a better vision for the future. To this extent every good ideology must be futuristic (forward looking), visionary, utopian, idealistic and perfectionist. Perfectionist so that if we can not get at the perfect system, we may end up somewhere near it. As the common saying goes "when shooting shoot at the moon so that if you miss the moon you may get the stars".

Ideologies are not tinkered out of the debris of worn out practices but are formulated to provide a holistic mould into which the future life of a people can organize for a more fruitful earthly and external existence. Ideologies must contain values, goals, expectations, ideals and programmes of action which delineates the trajectories and road maps that show how to realize a convenient eventual existential outcome when we follow through.

Some scholars look at ideology from the socio-political and economic standpoints but we are of the view that any ideology that is to worth its name and provide the needed guide to action in firm expectation of the good life must be holistic. It has to touch on all aspects of human needs. Here, we are referring to the economic, political, social, religious, spiritual, cultural, scientific, technological, environmental and institutional aspects of human existence. Ideology provides a charter, a window through which we can see the future from the present. Ideologies' main end is to provide hope amidst hopelessness, faith amidst frustration and determination amidst daunting challenges.

The ideology we posit or postulate is determined by the side of reality we are looking at. It depends on our disposition and our "purchase quality of ideas". Those fed up with life (on the negative side) are bound to paint a nihilistic picture whereas those on the positive side are bound to paint a promising picture. Ideology is like a set of conditional commandments, if you obey its injunctions you reap the el-dorado of its promises. And if you disobey, you reap the gloom of its curses. Having an ideology therefore does not in itself portend success and a bright future. It is only the doers at the ideological blueprints that reap the fruit it bears.

It is imperative to note that, it is the philosophy that holds sway at any given point in time that determines the general course of events. For example, the Nietzschean mindset that was suffused with hate for the Jews, impregnated by his neurosis, captivated the minds of philosophers of the 19th and 20th centuries. It is this that led to the materialist philosophy of market economy and the consequent ideology of market forces. This is the ideology of survival of the fittest via multinationals. The developed nations have accepted this because they control the instruments of coercion and exploitation.

The question one may ask is, where does Africa feature in all these? It is a position of underdoggism and subordination. This is why it has become necessary to look in between the lines with a saner and more inclusive humanist mindset to articulate an ideology for Africa which surveys the options that are available to her mindful of the global nature of today's coexistence. It should be an ideology that while lifting Africa from its present socio-political and economic doldrums takes cognizance that we must foster a world community devoid of the acrimony, bad blood and angst that have trailed the pursuit of global free market under the auspices of the developed nations of the world. Africa must and should be able to slide herself through the motif of globalization and make a mark and live an authentic life of its own without necessarily playing the second fiddle or being an appendage to the developed nations. For example, all parts of the body are important by carrying out peculiar functions. Their importance and uniqueness lie in their peculiarity. Africa through a rationally scripted ideology should be able to strike a chord of uniqueness and sustain and entrench its uniqueness to its own advantage and for the general global good. This is what our integrative humanist ideology intends to achieve. Amidst multiculturalism, inter and intra culturalism, there should be a healthy symbiosis of beneficial give and take among nations on a level playing ground. An ideology therefore should be able to chart a course for this beneficial symbiotic relationship.

From the foregoing, we wish to state that Africa cannot continue with a wholly capitalist system. Ideology formulated solely within the framework of capitalist economy is subjugation and poverty reinforcing. We cannot get the best from the capitalist arrangement because the groaning of the ever increasing population of the marginalized will surely tear the system into shreds. This may be why we are having the clamour for Islamic banking, increasing indebtedness of nations among the European nations (Greece is at a very critical state of financial health), we have a proposal for communism of European debts, the fear of global financial depression, infectious bankruptcy, etc. There is therefore need to re-examine our entire global financial arrangement so that the contagion of Greece, Italy and others will not affect other nations.

The ideology we are proposing falls within the framework of our philosophy of integrative humanism. Any ideology that will propel and engineer genuine, positive change must have a human face and integrates the positive values in all ideologies (where possible and applicable) into a mesh of practicable blueprint. A laudable ideology must be such that is capable of taking care of the growing needs of citizens in all ramifications within reasonable limits.

Within the framework of integrative humanism, we are insisting on an ideology that articulates diligence, fear of God, selflessness, proactiveness and aspiration for earthly and eternal comfort for all men. Our world today is at the brink of destruction because of the increasing godlessness among world citizens. The family unit is fast breaking down; there is suicide bombing, kidnapping, wars, internal uprising war against terrorism, corruption and many moral maladies. The starting point of any worth while ideology must begin from a moral and spiritual rebirth.

Ideology should be a vehicle that could carry all willing and unwilling mass of mankind to the destination of satisfaction as much as possible. This transformational ideology must emphasize leadership by example, that is, servant leadership, people and leaders should live their lives in such a way as to leave worthy legacies behind them. This legacy centred ideology can be achieved through spiritual, social, cultural, ethical and political conscientization. The instrument for achieving this is through education for all, the churches, mosques, news media and civil society organizations. Proper education for instance, will phase out the Boko Haram syndrome (Western education is sin). No properly educated person will engage in suicide bombing. There is the need to reappraise and reorder our moral, cultural and spiritual values. A culture that praises people with ill-gotten wealth cannot lead to any meaningful progress.

Ideology therefore should be a rational construct suited for education and not indoctrination. According to Hanan Alexander "Ideologies are either Moral (ethical) or amoral (non-ethical). Moral ideologies should embrace the conceptual condition of human agency, free will, moral intelligence and fallibility (which makes ideology dynamic and constructivist). This should be against the amoral ideologies transmitted by indoctrination through the feigned infallibility of mere mortals in the fashion of papal fiat (excathedra pontification). Morally based ideologies should not be forced on people, but should be driven through by teaching and explanation until we achieve conviction. The rationality of such ideology should be evaluated by individuals and convinced only after the evaluation of the beliefs and practices which such ideologies enjoin (Alexander, 1).

A Resume of Different Ideologies – African and Western

Neo-Welfarism (Nmamdi Azikiwe): During colonial times, African elites believed that western exploitation was the cause of Africa's underdevelopment. But with independence from the late 1950s, socio-political thinkers shifted grounds. They set out for an inward search for the causes and possible solution to Africa's socio-political and economic backwardness. The result was race for a new ideology which would be genial to the ways of Africans. Suffice it to mention that the drive for a peculiar ideology was in part influenced by the ideological warfare between the Soviet Union and USA from the 1950s. In line with this, Julius Nyerere came up with Ujamaa, Leopold Senghor with Negritude, Kwame Nkrumah

Consciencism, Obafemi Awolowo with Democratic Socialism with and Nnamdi Azikiwe with Neo-welfarism of which were brands of socialism or the admixture of socialism and democracy like Awolowo's postulation. Let us first consider zik's neo-welfarism.

As a political philosopher, Zik always favours the middle coruse. He believes that the leading world ideologies of capitalism, socialism and welfarism and even the African native ideology have both good and bad elements. It is the later elements which render them inadequate and unsatisfactory (Omoregbe, 43). He therefore pushes for a harmonization of the good elements. This yielded what he calls 'new-welfarism'. In his book, *Ideology for Nigeria: Capitalism, Socialism or Welfarism?* (1979), he defines neo-welfarism as a socio-political and economic system which embraces belief in private enterprise, reinforced by state participation in the private sector and state collaboration in management technology for completely and efficiently administering on a profitable basis statutory corporations and parastatals, commercial enterprises including government-controled and government-sponsored companies (127). This obviously gives us a good summary of neo-welfarism. But permit us to mention a few other stellar points. Azikiwe sees his method as eclectic, pragmatic and harmonizing of vital ingredients of leading ideologies with a good dose of local content. This is because he believes that Nigeria has her own traditional ideology and what was needed was augmentation and modernization. According to Nwokereke (109), Azikiwe claimed that our traditional political system was socialist in structure but capitalist in content, and maintained that since this idea of combining elements of capitalism and socialism was also practiced by our ancestors, and it was practicable, that all we need do is to update it to suit our contemporary complex society.

Also, the neo-welfarist government Azikiwe says shall aim at fair and equitable distribution of the country's goods among the citizens and avoid building a society where some citizens are extremely rich and others extremely poor. As an economic system, neo-welfarism aims at building a society of abundance as opposed to an affluent society, organized on the basis of the economics of scarcity. According to Igwe (214), an abundant society would be characterized by abundant good, abundant shelter, abundant clothing, abundant necessities of life and abundant amenities within reasonable cost and within the reach of many. And as a political system, the aims and objectives of neo-welfarism would be to restore democracy by building a new political polity where there will be political freedom, economic security and social equality. As a result, a neo-welfarist government would be made up of four arms, namely, the electorate, the executive, the legislature and the judiciary. For want of space we shall limit our exposition of neo-welfarism to these few key points.

Ujamaa (Julius Nyerere): Julius Nyerere of Tanzania was a staunch part of African nationalism and an unwavered believer in African traditional ways. According to Nwokereke (62), African socialism or Ujamaa as he calls it to make it distinct from other brands of socialism is more than a political system. It is a philosophy, a world-view as well as gateway to Africa's true selfhood. In his work "African socialism: Ujamaa in Practise" Nyerere (113), holds that the foundation and the objective, of African socialism is the extended family, the true African socialist does not look on one class of men as his brethren and on another as his natural enemies... he rather regards all men as his brethren-as members of his ever extended family "Ujamaa", or "familyhood" and this describes our socialism. It is opposed to capitalism which seeks to build its happy society on the basis of the exploitation of man and it is equally opposed to doctrinaire socialism, which seeks to build its happy society on a philosophy of inevitable conflict between man and man.

Colonialism and its attendant problems were inimical to Africa's development. Africans therefore, need an ideology that is genial to their native ways and culture if they are to advance like other world societies. The African society under Ujamaa would aim at self-reliance and self-liberation. According to Nyerere (1970), liberation is inseparable from development; in fact he sees development as liberation and this is to be achieved in an egalitarian and communalistic society based on familyhood. Omoregbe summarizes that a nation under Ujamaa would be basically family units extended to embrace the whole society. The capitalistic spirit of acquisition, individualism, the exploitation of man by man, class struggle and conflicts will all be excluded from society (34). Ujamaa socialism therefore holds that all men are fundamentally equal because for Nyerere without the acceptance of equality of all men, there can be no socialism (Nwokereke, 68). As an ideology, therefore, Ujamaa socialism can be defined as a socio-political and economic system which involves a change in personal attitudes and a reconciliation of individuals, but gets beyond these to effect structural change consistent with the socialist outlook, creating a pattern of justice in which equality and freedom of all will be assured.

Negritude (Leopold Senghor): Senghor projects the old Negro-African communalism as the basis of African brand of socialism. He rejected the major trends of capitalism but did not accept a socialist state where the economy is totally nationalized. This is because African communalism gives room for minimal personal ownership of property. According to him however, what Africa needed most was a cultural independence and freedom of choice (Nwokereke, 49).

As the first president of the independent Senegal, Senghor's negritude was aimed at cultural emancipation of his people. Omoregbe (34) writes that negritude is a philosophy of re-discovery and cultural reawakening; it is also a philosophy of cultural emancipation intended to give the African people a sense of pride and dignity in their identity as Africans, by making them appreciate the values of their culture as distinct from the culture and identity of the colonial French. Thus, the African brand of socialism would for Senghor, be based on the cultural orientation of Africans. This is the main discourse of his paper "What is Negritude?" (1975); in it he describes the French policy of assimilation as slavish. It would lead to the erosion of African cultures and values and for this he rejected it. Africans he maintains, have a peculiar outlook to life which characterizes their identity. Such peculiar African ways are the basis of African socialism where everyone is somebody and no one is anybody. Means of production, distribution and exchange would be equitably shared and political spirit would not be rift with classification. To him capitalism is foreign to Africa and as such the Marxist theories of class struggle is irrelevant to African socialism. Senghor is a philosopher and a renowned poet.

Kwame Nkrumah (Consciencism): Kwame Nkrumah was a foremost African Nationalist under whose leadership Ghana won her independence and was the president of Ghana between 1957 and 1966 when he was toppled through a coup detat code named operation chicken roasted. His ideology is called consciencism or "philosophical consciencism". Consciencism is a political and an economic system based on materialist conception of the world where tension constitutes an inner dialectics that engender political and economic development. In his book, *Consciencism* he states, "It is out of tension that being is born. Becoming is tension and being is the child of that tension of opposed forces and tendencies" (103). Consciencism derives from the word conscientious meaning deep seated awareness of ... in this case, the plight of African people. This is why consciencism is a brand of socialism, but that, which is developed to fit the nature and needs of Africans. In other words, it is an African brand of socialism. Nkrumah contends that the African society is different from the western society in many ways. It is not capitalistic but communal. According to Okolo:

Traditional African society is not capitalistic, but egalitarian and communalistic. Nkrumah stressed that the traditional face of Africa includes an attitude towards man, which can only be described, in its manifestations and being socialist. This arises from the fact that man is regarded in Africa as primarily a spiritual being, a being endowed originally with a certain inward dignity, integrity and value. This idea of the original value of man imposes duties of socialist kind upon us. Here lies the theoretical basis of African communalism. This theoretical basis expressed itself on the social level in terms of institutions such as clan, underlining the initial equality of all and the responsibility of many for one. On this social situation, it was impossible for classes of the Marxian kind to arise (28).

Hence, it is Nkrumah's belief that the traditional African society has all it takes to build a modern viable socialist economy. For Nwokereke (46), Nkrumah maintains that originally Africans lived communalistic lives where everything was owned by the community and everything worked for the good of the community. It is therefore, foreseeable that capitalism was a western accretion that invaded Africa through colonialism. Nkrumah's consciencism thus becomes a revolution to topple the foreign capitalism from its position in Africa. According to Omoregbe:

> Traditional African society, Nkrumah says, is not capitalist, but egalitarian and communalistic. Capitalism is irreconcilable with the egalitarianism and communalism of traditional African society. African nations should reject the inequality, individualism, capitalism and imperialism brought into Africa by the European imperialists. Nkrumah admonishes African nations to go back to the egalitarianism and communalism of traditional African society (32).

For Nkrumah therefore, socialism is a modern form of communalism which Africans are already used to. For this fact, it is more suited to the African peoples. Consciencism becomes its localization in Africa where the welfare of the people is central. Though, the Marxist economic stages of feudalism and class struggle do not exist in African context, the revolutionary struggle is still relevant, this time, to root out capitalism and its agencies. Such like in Marxism, would still be a revolution of the people oppressed by capitalism and consciencism would be its ideal substitute.

Obafemi Awolowo (Democratic Socialism): A foremost African nationalist, Omoregbe describes him as an eminent thinker with deep prophetic insight (52). His ideology is called democratic socialism suggesting an admixture of democracy as a political system and socialism as an economic system. In his book *People's Republic,* Awolowo posits that the main aim of a state is to ensure that its citizens "enjoy the fruits of their labour, and to live a full and happy life, including the enjoyment of the fundamental human rights" (119). It is the pursuit of these goals of happy life and guaranteed fundamental rights that made men to adopt two distinct economic systems namely capitalism and socialism.

Awolowo rejects capitalism as being exploitative, selfish and individualistic. For him, "for every single entrepreneur who succeeds or survives, there are probably more than a thousand or ten thousands that have gone completely under, never to rise again" (166). He embraces socialism as a better system. However, his socialism which he calls democratic socialism differs from that of Marx. It is a stage between capitalism and communism and it has as its principle "from each according to his ability and to each according to his deeds or needs as the case may be (192)". In summation Awolowo states:

> We declare that the aims of socialism are social justice and equity, and state of affairs in which the resources provided by nature belong to all the citizens equally and the products of the union of land and labour are appropriated to labour of all graduation and skills through the media of good wages, respectable standards of living, abolition of unemployment, free provision of social amenities such as education, health, etc (192).

Democratic socialism therefore aims at balancing the good of democracy as a political system with that of socialism as an economic system.

Capitalism: Capitalism has remained a dominant economic ideology since its emergence from the feudalist systems of 16th and 17th centuries AD. In one word, it is an evolution of feudalism. *The Macmillan Dictionary of Modern Economics* defines it as a:

> Political, social and economic system in which property, including capital assets, is owned and controlled for the most part by private persons. Capitalism contrasts with an earlier economic system, feudalism, in that it is characterized by the purchase of labour for money wages as opposed to the direct labour obtained through custom, duty or command in feudalism... under capitalism the price mechanism is used as a signaling system which allocates resources between uses. The extent to which the price mechanism is used, the degree of competitiveness in markets and the level of government intervention distinguished exact forms of capitalism (54).

A prominent feature of capitalism is less governmental control and higher private say. From the definition above, we can learn that capitalism as an economic ideology succeeded feudalism based upon recognition of the rights of private parties to choose how to employ their labour and capital in markets as indicated by market prices instead of tradition. It recognizes the price mechanism as its key coordinating device instead of command and control. On the whole, capitalist systems are distinguishable from one another based upon the extent and nature of governmental interventions and the competitiveness of their markets.

Further still, a capitalist economy is a free market economy. Workers are free to work for wages, capital is free to earn a return, and both labor and capital are free to enter and exit both from various lines of business. As a system, capitalism relies upon the pricing mechanism to balance supply and demand in markets; it relies on the profit motive to allocate opportunities and resources among competing suppliers; and it relies upon a political authority to establish the rules and regulations so that they include all appropriate societal costs and benefits. Government and its agents are held accountable to provide physical security for persons and property as well as the laws and regulations. Capitalist development is built from investment in new technologies that permit increased productivity, where a variety of initiatives are selected through a Darwinian process that favours productive uses of those resources, and from the periodic modernization of the legal and regulatory framework as indicated by changing market conditions and societal priorities. Bruce Scott (4), writes that capitalist development requires that government play two roles: one administrative, in providing and maintaining the institutions that underpin capitalism, and the other entrepreneurial, in mobilizing power to modernize these institutions as needed. On the whole, capitalism contrasts with earlier economic systems characterized by forced labour, self-sufficiency, barter, and/or reciprocal relationships based upon family, tribe, or locally known relationships. It also contrasts with more recent systems where governments have acted directly through ownership and/or central planning to control of the use of resources, finally as an ideology, it harps on human desire for liberty, freedom and individualism to gain acceptance around the world.

Socialism (Communism): Socialism may be defined as a theory and a movement aiming at the collective organization of the community in the interests of the mass of the people through the common ownership and collective control of the means of production and exchange (Appadorai, 115). Thus it is both an economic and a socio-political system which stipulates that great industries and land should be publicly or collectively owned, and that they should be managed in accordance with a national economic plan specifically for common good and not for private benefit.

Socialism rose in opposition to capitalism, a system which exploits the mass of the people, enthrones a few individuals to control the economic life wire of the nation. Karl Marx, the German philosopher was the founder of socialism which he together with his collaborator Fredrich Engels wrote the principal works that formed the basis of the theory.

In their *Communist Manifesto* (1848) and *The Critique of the German Ideology* (1846), they came from a historical survey to propound the major theses of scientific socialism. Marx calls his socialism scientific because he believes that history is crucial to economic development. For him, the civil society is the true source and the theatre of all history. The conception that history confines itself to the high-sounding dramas of princes and states is for him absurd. The real history is the material relationship which takes place within the civil society. The studies of such history give one a predictive power.

Discussing civil society and the conception of history in his *The Critique of the German Ideology,* Marx sees history as nothing but the succession of the separate generations, each of which exploits the materials, the capital funds the productive forces handed down to it by all presiding generations, and thus, on the one hand, continues the traditional activity in completely changed circumstances and, on the other, modifies the old circumstances with a completely changed activity ... the earlier history is nothing more than an abstraction formed from later history, from the active influence which earlier history exercises on later history.

Based on this, socialism predictively would emerge from capitalism just as the later emerged from feudalism. A number of factors would characterize this evolution or revolution as different schools of socialism would see it, they include; the doctrine of historical materialism, class struggle or warfare, theory of surplus value, Dictatorship of proletariat, concept of classless society, etc (Mukhi, 170). On the whole, the socialist agree on the focus of their ideology by disagreeing on how the ideal society or the communist stage can be realized. The revolutionary school chooses violent revolution while the evolutionary schools believe in gradual constitutional means. It should be noted therefore that at the highest point of its development, socialism would give birth to communism – a classless society without a government, just the masses!

Critique of Mainline Ideologies

Let us first point out that Azikiwe's treatment of ideology and philosophy as synonymous is erroneous. While ideology is a philosophy, philosophy is not ideology. Ideology is often a mirage claiming authentic existence within the fulcrum of a people's needs but philosophy is a baggage of problem solving tools for any people if not for all men.

Also Neo-welfarism, a political ideology of Nnamdi Azikiwe has been criticized as an adulterated socialism with the dangerous tendencies of capitalism (Omoregbe, 49). Here, we are more concerned with the modern insights from different welfarist world economies. The Americans, British, Irish, Spanish, Portuguese and the Greek capitalist economies have all been adulterated with socialist principles from 1970s down. They could in sum be described as Neo-welfarist economies. 30 years after this great transformation, these economies are crumbling with rapid force. It does seem therefore, that Neo-welfarism which seeks to remain socialist in structure but capitalist in content contains the seed of its own destruction namely; incubating a lazy and rebellious citizenry. Neo-welfarism renders the citizen of a nation lazy by regular handouts on one hand and at the other hand, makes them too powerful by recognizing their rights to demand whatever they want and also the power and the right to revolt. We can see that within 30 years, the citizens of these countries mentioned above had eaten away the wealth of their nations while producing less.

America currently owes thirteen trillion dollars to foreign nations and local lenders. The Spanish and the Portuguese owe more than 1 trillion a piece, the Irish owe close to 2 trillion, the British had to cut welfarist spending to remain afloat, while the Greeks have not only ran out of money, but owes more than they can ever repay. A BBC interview granted to a Korean labourer in Greece early in 2011 quoted the Korean as describing the Greeks as "lazy, fun lovers and rebellious people" (BBC world news, Feb. 2011). The current world economic crisis therefore started from the economies that can be described as Neo-welfarist. On this score, we reject Neo-welfarism of Azikiwe as producing a happy citizenry in the interim but an angry and chaotic people for all time to come.

In this way also, we can find one or two lapses in other political ideologies we have considered. Julius Nyerere's Ujamaa socialism is first criticized by its failure in Tanzania. An economic system that downplays the basic emotions of the individual man cannot thrive. Eliminating individualism might give happiness to the society but not to the individuals that make up the family units and the society at large. As an economic system, Ujamaa might work for sometime but the disgruntled individual would soon find a way to sabotage it. This was evident at the collapse of Ujamaa in Tanzania. We therefore criticize Julius Nyerere's Ujamaa for being too pro-society and anti-individual.

Negritude of Leopold Sedar Senghor is a remarkable ideology but like others, it also falls prey to the socialist influence of the time; or, betterstill, the extreme socialist influence of the time which is antagonistic to individualism. Omoregbe (33) states that Senghor also maintains that individualism and capitalism are foreign to African traditional society and the African way of life which is communalist. This is a way of saying that Africa should not be open to change. Capitalism by far is the driving force behind successful world economies, to glorify African communalism above it, which by all sensible judgments is the cause of Africa's backwardness is simply a show of lack of vision. The focal point of African theorists like Senghor should have been what ideology might push Africa forward not which one did our ancestors practice? Since it is all clear that the ones the native Africans practiced retarded the growth of the continent and led to other vices like slave trade and colonialism. So we criticize Senghor's negritude for opposing individualism which is a vital emotion of the individual man

These criticisms also apply to Nkrumah's consciencism, another brand of African socialism. According to Omoregbe, Nkrumah believes that capitalism is irreconcilable with the egalitarianism and communalism of traditional African society (32). Although, his call for African nations to reject the colonialist imperialism is a high point for consciencism as an ideology, its overt concentration on the past African ways is regressive. Consciencism would have to choose between a docile, peaceful but backward society and a vibrant and progressive one which capitalist tendencies engender. We criticize Nkrumah's consciencism for inadvertently choosing the former.

Awolowo's democratic socialism is one of a kind. It lays less emphasis on the African native ideological systems. It concentrates on creating something that would suit Africa from the western systems. For this, it is unique among its African contemporary ideologies. However, creating an admixture of a political system democracy, and economic system socialism would yield a Neo-welfarist system. In this regard, all the criticisms we leveled against Azikiwe's Neo-welfarism also apply to Awolowo's democratic-socialism. Capitalism, socialism and/or communism have been criticized for obvious reasons. Capitalism is exploitation, socialism is anti-individual and the extreme form of communism where the government phases away is utopian. Beyond these, what else?

Perhaps the most current criticisms which are relevant to the dynamics of the moment would concern the apparent failures of capitalism and socialism in the contemporary global economics. With the ideological war between the two, desperation set in and a mindless shift began to occur; a shift from which ideology is better positioned to account for world development to which ideology is more aesthetically appealing. For this, the capitalist economies led by USA began to incorporate some socialist elements so that capitalism would offer everything of itself and some key elements of socialism as bonuses – prominent is the wefarist package for the people. The same goes for socialist economies that now amended their codes such that reasonable private ownership of properties was admitted. The result is that both capitalism and socialism have become highly adulterated, a situation that offered temporary victories for the two gladiatory ideologies but which three decades on have accounted for the collapse of global economy in general.

Capitalism has been unable to sustain world economic development possibly because of the adopted welfarist packages which have created a revolutionary work force that wants more for less labour. American big industries collapsed with hundreds of thousands job losses because the workforce insists on earning more than the industries net as income. This trends which is also prevalent in European capitalist economies have seen the manufacturers producing goods at high cost and thereby dwindling sales. The welfarist tendencies of capitalist economies have transferred command and control power to the work force with the dictatorship of the proletariat who understands little of economic rules and dynamics. Hence with the selfishness of capitalist atmosphere combined with the proletarian revolutionary power, capitalism with its welfarist tendencies came crashing down. The Irish and Greek economics collapsed; American, British, Spanish, Portuguese and the Euro-economies are now under severe threat.

On the other hand, it is the socialist economies that are thriving. The capitalist elements incorporated into the socialist economic ideology brought it to a vantage footing. Command and control were extended to private corporations. Welfare was drastically reduced; industrial workforce in China was exploited. Like India, one of the fewest pure capitalist economies left in the world, China pays the labor force far too less for too much work. The result is increased productivity of cheap goods. With this, they invaded the capitalist economies with cheap goods. This led to the collapse we are currently witnessing among capitalist whose industries have been put out on business economics. Thus, the current recalcitrant economic crisis in the west which began in 2009 is nothing but the collapse of the ideology of capitalism. It has only one true solution, the purgation of the welfarist elements! That is what IMF and World Bank recommend to Ireland, to Greece, Spain, Portugal, USA and Britain to mention a few under the label, "austerity measures" – under it, the labor force would earn less, pay more and work more.

This is simply a return to pure capitalism. But the capitalist proletariats of Ireland, Greece, and recently USA are revolting – you can't kill off the socialist elements, they seem to say.

In this way, socialism can be criticized for bringing chaos to the global economy by destroying the heart of capitalism. What happened in 1989 therefore, was not only the collapse of socialism as we assumed but also the swallowing up of socialism by capitalism. But it seems socialism is poisonous. It gradually ate away the heart of capitalism and brought the world economy to its present sorry state. Pure socialism therefore can be criticized as a lazy ideology. Resources are shared according to individual need why work more. Individuals are expected to work according to their abilities, why show my true ability? In this way American and European banks collapsed because individuals who are insatiable keep bowing to get the most exotic things of life. It was their right according to the welfarist principles to be given what they need. For this, Americans and Europeans Squandered huge sums on frivolities while their Chinese counterparts were busy producing huge sums for their country.

An idle American lives in a cussy home, drives an exotic car and the banks pay his bill without single collateral. The result is that the banks eventually ran out of cash and wanted their money back only to realize their debtors wanted more.

Classically, one can also criticize socialism or scientific socialism as Marx called it as being unscientific. Karl Popper in his *Conjectures and Refutations* has shown that scientific socialism is unscientific because its theories and hypotheses are not falsifiable. When developed capitalist economies did not lead to proletarian revolution, Marxists formed an ad hoc explanation instead of admitting that their theories were wrong.

Again, the materialistic interpretation of history is not all there is, other factors play vital roles in history. The idea of class struggle as a necessity for the socialist stage is too pessimistic and has not materialized anywhere. The Marxist prediction of a revolution only at the highest development of capitalism has not happened anywhere, rather the revolutions which occurred in the east Europe took place at an early stage of capitalism. On the whole, the two ideologies have not been without some key flaws.

Thoughts on the Nigerian System

Is it federal or unitary ideology? From a close study of what we practice, we shall dub it "Unito-federal" ideology, that is, unito-federalism and in the spirit of integrative humanism there is nothing wrong with this. All we need to do is to harness the essential and positive elements in both systems of government and synthesize in a neat and rational crucible of welfarism. What is important is to adopt and adapt principles that will enable us to forge a formidable, progressive, and prosperous and welfarist nation in which all her peoples and constituent states and ethnic groups will have a sense of belonging and benefit equitably and fairly from the resources with which our nation is endowed.

Welfarism must be anchored on readiness and willingness to work hard. It is only the shortfall that government augments through welfare schemes. After all, there is no free lunch anywhere. Federal character in all wrungs of the administrative ladder federal, state and Local Government is an injection into the 1979 constitution which came as a result of the conversion of our system from federalism to unito-federalism, as a way of taking care of the injustice and the domination of one or more tribes over others. According to Peter Ekeh "the federal character is the principal innovation of the 1979 constitution intended to combat the threshold problem of competing primordial loyalties in the country. He goes on to say that federal character was formulated to command its own laws of equity, different from definitions of individual merit. Its aim is to achieve national unity by minimizing the disadvantages of ethnic groups that stand to lose in plain contest for political power and for benefits that derive from the public realm.

The highlights of the federal character which gave rise to the zoning policy also was well intended but with the unsavoury implication that when it is the turn of a zone to produce the president, it is incumbent on that zone to showcase its best candidate. What happens where the zone is made up of "blind people"? Should the rest of the federating units make do with a "one-eyed-man" who happens to be the best the zone could offer? Do we allow a one-eyed-man to rule a nation that has millions that are qualified who happen not to come from the presenting zone? To sit idly by and watch the one-eye-nonentity rubbish statecraft in the name of Zoning and federal character will not be rational. This is the most contentious issue in the art and engineering of the system of Zoning and Federal Character.

There is therefore the need to strike a rational balance between individual merit and the consideration of Zoning. We have to ensure that Zoning does not annihilate merit, quality service and competence. The mill of Zoning must grind not only on equity but on the platform of reasonable measure of merit and competence.

This controversy played itself out in the last elections where the concept of Zoning almost robbed Dr. Goodluck Jonathan the chance of contesting for the presidency. A combination of fate, incumbency, political adroitness, suavity and the patronage of power brokers made it possible for him to survive the "Tsunamic groundswell of opposition" that fought his ambition. What we have gained from that battle of political somersaults is that the Zoning formular should constitutionally be modified to read either of the following "that the position of president should remain open to all qualified Nigerians irrespective of tribe or party affiliation" and that as soon as the president emerges, he/she becomes duty bound in sharing political offices in conformity to the norms of federal character and zoning.

Or, we insist that the position of the president be rotated among the six geopolitical zones with each zone serving only a five year term, but with the proviso that each contesting political party must chose their presidential flag bearers from the zone whose turn it is to produce the president. This arrangement is necessary because of the lopsided nature of national constitution with the dominance of the Hausa/Fulani over the other tribes and the multiversity of minority ethnic groups, without a rational equitable power sharing, power is bound to reside with one ethnic group to the chagrin of other component groups of the federation – power rotation on the basis of the six geopolitical zones will be the best thing that can happen to our nation. It will engender a sense of mutual belonging, equity, fair play, and rational consideration of one another. This will reduce ethnic tension, fear of marginalization and domination. However, we must insist that this arrangement should not be abused or used as a platform to throw-up zonal mediocre.

To have an ideology that will inspire patriotism, we need to draw the contents of our ideology both from the mirror of the minority and major ethnic nationalities that make up Nigeria. This is the whole essence of convoking of sovereign conference of ethnic nationalities. As soon as people are assured that personal, ethnic and aggregate interests have been taken care of, they are bound to identify with the progressive ventures of national development and stability. The essence is to promote national loyalty in a multi ethnic society like Nigeria (Afigbo, 1).

The Nigerian experiment is undergoing a purification exercise. We see the continuous breakdown if stereotypes and status quo. In the last election, we witnessed the electorate voting on grounds of perceived political expectations from candidates and not necessarily based on party affiliation. Apart from Moshood Abiola's ill-fated victory, Goodluck Jonathan's, victory at this year's presidential election is another occasion, where the majority of Nigerians spoke with one voice with little consideration for ethnicity, party affiliation or religion. It appeared as if in one fell swoop we have overcome the ills of ethnicity, religion and partisanship that have always characterized our national politics. It was a window opened into the glorious opportunities that await us the day we jettison the politics of ethnicity, religion and partisanship, what should guide our choices should be the quality of personalities vying for elective offices and the tendency/bent to fulfill their promises to Nigerians. The days of the unholy trinity of North, West and East should be over.

The idea of Federal character will soon be sublimated as soon as we begin to act from a patriotic consciousness of belonging to one nation. The sooner we dispense with ethnic consciousness and see ourselves as one people forged together by providence, the better for us all. The ideology we forge strives to achieve this mindset and consciousness. As Achebe would say; let the Eagle perch, let the vulture perch and let the kite perch also for what is good for the goose is also good for the gander. As Godswill Akpabio a minority Annang man made it as Governor in Akwa Ibom State, and a Goodluck Jonathan from Minority Bayelsa made it to become the president of the country so should all Nigerians be given the opportunity of attaining the highest level of their ambition as long as they have the qualification – moral, academic, spiritual, political, social and otherwise to do so with no ethnic barricades.

Integrative Humanist Ideology for Africa

Our concern is that in spite of the many ideologies open to the children of men the quality of human existence continues to plummet. The popular saying that "all that glitters is not gold" is apt and applicable in our general human situation. The Holy writ describes it as painted sepulcher accommodating dead men's bones. The recent crash of the Euro-dollar and financial collapse of many European nations like Greece, Iceland, Italy, Portugal, Spain, etc., is a pointer to the fact that all is not well with our world; America and Britain are recently in deep financial stress. Unemployment is daily on the increase, job is highly insecure, and frustration is on the upsurge. Early in the Eighties communism, socialism collapsed in the then Soviet Union and now is the turn of capitalism to hit the dust. It is only countries like China, France, and Germany who seem to be practicing a mixed grill economy of capitalism and socialism appear to be remaining afloat. The question that immediately comes to mind is, where is the problem from? Is it with ideology or with human operators of the different ideologies? We have liberalism, capitalism, socialism, communism, welfarism, syndicalism, African socialism, etc. All these have not appeared to work to provide us with the much sought el-dorado.

Our analysis shows that any ideology that panders more to welfarist provisions will give room to idleness and laziness which burden the system instead of helping the system. Following Max Weber's exposition of the spirit of capitalism in his Protestant Ethic, it is clear that wealth is built through hard work, thrift and prudentiality. Any economy that is hinged on excessive handouts in form of welfare packages and laziness inducing interventions will soon hit the rocks. Capitalism had to introduce excessive welfare packages in order to cushion the effects of the hardship occasioned by the exploitative nature of capitalism. We cannot eat our cake and have it. A system which breeds unfairness should redress the same through equity and shared responsibility and reward.

Our advocacy is an ideology that ensures that hard work and the involvement of all in this virtue should be the driving pillar of our ideology. As Achebe would say, there is nothing wrong with the Nigerian climate, soil, or even her diverse peoples but for Professor Asouzu, the cause of the insensitivity on the part of our leaders is a consequence of and direct product of the long standing pains and suffering of these leaders who having suffered excruciating poverty now see the leadership position as opportunity to stockpile as much wealth as possible to avoid going through the dark road of poverty. Poverty hardens and makes one insensitive to others suffering. But this should not be the case. Poverty should be a tonic to make us to be empathic, sympathetic, sensitive and pitiful for the plight of others still in the dungeon of poverty.

The problem therefore is neither purely ideological nor leadership but rather spiritual. This is why we are recommending an integrative humanist ideology which insists on spiritual rebirth and moral renewal. It is only a person who is morally sound and spiritually alive that can provide sacrificial leadership. Without inner regeneration, sense of accountability before an omniscient God and a vision that, it is only through a clean and righteous earthly existence that we can be sure of peaceful and blissful eternal existence we cannot achieve the much touted progress which we envisage through vision 20-20-20. Any philosophy or ideology that makes men feel that it is only in this life that our existence is relevant cannot produce a society of moderation. This is why integrative humanism does not countenance all forms of technology. Some technologies are a bane on our moral psyche and spiritual aliveness. Leisure is good as a way of unwinding after an honest exertion of energy at meaningful labour. What we should strive to achieve in Africa is moral rectitude and to see our sojourn here as preparatory to eternal existence.

In African communalism, land was the sacred link between man and God, and man depends on land and God for his existence.

Desecration of land through corruption meant attracting the wrath of gods, divinities, ancestors and the Almighty God. Today, monetization of the system has up-rooted us from the land and from God our creator. We must go back to the sanctity of the land for production of our Agricultural needs and to God for our spiritual needs.

Conclusion

The business of philosophers at any given point in time is to examine situations, issues, realities from a dispassionate and objective point of view while taking, into consideration the votary of incidences and factors that interplay in the unfolding events. The philosopher's position has to be dynamic to take care of the changing times. The very critical and episodic events of last three decades have given impetus for the formulation of an integrative humanistic ideology for Africa and nay the global world. The collapse of systems, nations, ideologies and empires is largely due to the increasing depravity of man, continuing alienation of God and the excessive quest for material acquisition. All the major religions, namely Christianity, Islam, Hinduism, Buddhism and even African Traditional Religion stress the need for moderation in all we do. Integrative humanism shifts blame from leadership to the poor moral and spiritual quality of humans who aspire to lead others. The ideology we recommend is eclectic, that is, sifting and welding all the positive elements in capitalism, socialism, welfarism, African socialism, etc., with an insistence that we must seek first the kingdom of God and His righteousness and then with hard work all other things will be added unto us. If we fail to do this, whatever system we build will sooner than later crumble as mere pack of cards.

WORKS CITED

Achebe, Chinua. *The Trouble with Nigeria.* Enugu: Fourth Dimension Publishers, 1983.

Afigbo, A. E. "Federal Character: Its meaning and History" in *Federal Character and federalism in Nigeria.* Eds P. P

Ekeh and E. E. Osaghae Ibadan: Heinemann Educational Books, 1989.

Alexander, Hanan A. "Education in Ideology" in *Journal of Moral Education*. Vol. 34, No. 1 March 2005.

Appadorai, A. *The Substance of Politics*. Madras: Oxford University Press. 1878.

Awolowo, Obafemi. *People's Republic*. Ibadan: Oxford University Press, 1968.

Azikiwe, Nanmdi. *Ideology for Nigeria: Capitalism, Socialism or Welfarism?* Lagos: Macmillan Nigeria Publishers, 1979.

BBC News. "Greek Economic Crisis". Feb. 2011. www.bbcnews.org.

Cassels, Alan. *Ideology and International Relations in the Modern World*. London: Routledge Publishers, 1995.

Dictionary of Economics. NY: Macmillan Published

Ekeh, Peter P. "The structure and meaning of Federal Character in the Nigerian Political System" in P. P. Ekeh and E. E. Osaghae (Eds) *Federal Character and Federalism in Nigeria*. Ibadan: Heinemann Educational Books, 1989.

Hardin, Russell. "Ideological Polarization" in Barry Clarke and Joe Foweraker (Eds) *Encyclopedia of Demoncratic Thought* London: Routledge Publishers, 2004.

Hawkes, David. *Ideology*. London: Routledge Publishers, 2003.

Igwe, Agbafor. *Zik: The Philosopher of Our Time*. Enugu: Fourth Dimension Publishers. 1992.

Lloyd Dennis. *The idea of Law*. London: Penguin Books, 1999.

Marx, Karl & Fredrick Engels. *A Critique of the German Ideology.* Trans. Tim Delaney and Bob Schwartz. London: Progress Publishers, 1968.

Mukhi, H. R. *Political Thought.* Delhi: SDB Publishers, 2008.

Nwokereke, Eze. *Trends and Perspectives in African Socio-political Philosophy.* Abakaliki: Copycraft, 2005.

Nkrumah, Kwame. *Consciencism.* Accra: Panaf, 1974

Nyerere, Julius. *Freedom and Unity.* Dare' Salaam: OUP, 1966.

Nyerere, Julius. *Essays on Socialism.* Dare' Salaam: OUP, 1968.

Okolo C. B. *African Social and Political Philosophy.* Nsuka: Falladu Publishers, 1993.

Omoregbe, Joseph. *Knowing Philosophy.* Lagos: Joja, 1990.

Popper, Karl. *Conjectures and Refutations.* London: Routledge and Kegan Paul, 1969.

Pyenson, Lewis. "The Ideology of Western Rationality. History of Science and the European civilizing mission" in *Science and Education.* Vol.2, 1993.

Scott, Bruce. "The Political Economy of Capitalism". Draft Copy, 2006.

Senghor, Leopold. "What is Negritude"? in G. C. M. Mustoso (Ed). *Readings in African Political Thought.* London: Heinemann, 1975.

CHAPTER 9

AFRICAN CULTURAL VALUES
By
EMMANUEL E. ETTA, Ph.D

Introduction

The world is becoming a global village, but there seem to be a colossal damage going on unnoticed. This damage has to do with the collapse of cultures that were cherished in the past by their original owners, and African cultures are no exception. However, in the midst of these damaging circumstances, there is an urgent need to protect one's cultural identity, as this is fundamental towards sustaining his worldview and life as an individual, hence, a work of this nature. This work is aimed at exposing and fishing out cultures and values that are original and peculiar to Africa, as it will help to differentiate African cultures and values from those of our western brothers. In this paper, I have noted African cultures to include: art, craft, folklore, religion, languages and cuisine while its values are expressed in areas like sense of community, sacredness and of religion, respect for authority and elders, language and proverbs to mention a few. Extensive discussion on each will be a priority, with particular attention to their significance in the daily life of the African.

The Africans

Africa was the birthplace of the human species between 8 million and 5 million years ago. Today, the vast majority of its inhabitants are an indigenous origin. People across the continent are remarkably diverse by just about any measure. They speak a vast number of different languages, practice hundreds of distinct religions, live in a variety of dwellings, and engage in a wide range of economic activities. Over the centuries, people from other parts of the world have migrated to Africa and settled there. Historically, Arabs have been the most numerous immigrants. Starting from the 7th century A.D., they crossed into North Africa from the Middle East, bringing the religion of Islam with them. A latter movement of Arabs into East and Central Africa occurred in the 19th century. Europeans first settled in Africa in the mid 17th century near the Cape of Good Hope, at the Southern end of the continent. More Europeans immigrated during the subsequent colonial period, particularly to present day South Africa, Zimbabwe, and Algeria. South Asians also arrived during colonial times. Their descendants, often referred to as Indians, are found largely in Uganda, Kenya, Tanzania and South Africa.

The main split according to the *Wikipedia Free Encyclopedia*, is between North Africa and sub-Saharan Africa, which is in turn divided into a great number of ethnic and tribal cultures. While the ethno-linguistic divisions are Afro-Asiatic (North Africa, Chad, Horn of Africa), Niger-Congo (mostly Bantu) in most of sub-Saharan Africa, Nilo-Saharan in parts of the Sahara and the Sahel and parts of Eastern Africa, and Khoisan (indigenous minorities of Southern Africa) and parts of Oceania and India. A definition of culture would suffice now, having exposed the various components of the culture of Africa. It is envisaged that it will give us a clear picture of what the continent is made up of.

Simply defined, culture means the knowledge and behaviour of a people over time; it is the common way of life of people (Azenabor, 117). Historically, the word "culture" is derived from the Latin word "colere", which means to cultivate. In other words, it is an attitude of cultivating one's self in an effort to attain the ideal of wisdom through which humans become themselves (Ukpoloko, 24). According to Ebijuwa's definition, which seems to agree with the first definition, culture for him is the total way of life of people or community. The way, he adds, includes the arts, music, mode of dressing, beliefs and practices (24). This last definition, most appropriately captures the content of African culture, which is central in our subsequent discussions. The vast continent of Africa is so rich and diverse in its culture, which not only changes from one country to another but within an individual country many different cultures can be found. The culture of Africa encompasses and includes all cultures which were ever in the continent of Africa. As a home to innumerable tribes, ethnic and social groups, some representing very large populations consisting of millions of people, Africa has diverse beliefs. Much of these Africa's culture centres on the family and the ethnic group. Art, music, folklore, traditional religion, language, or oral literature serves to reinforce religious and social patterns.

African Culture

The concept of African culture as earlier mentioned embraces all cultures found within African continent from time immemorial. Though a simple concept, it can also be understood or used interchangeably with African worldview as the case may be. This is because both concepts are complementary in outlook, when it concerns the logic, ethics, aesthetics, knowledge, ontology and socio-political events contemplated upon by the African mindset. Thus, when one defines culture of a people as the total way of life, this manifests as well in their work and reaction, worship and courtship. It is seen in their ways of investigating nature and utilizing its possibilities, as well as in the way they view themselves and interpret their place in nature. That is why, to gain an adequate idea of the nature of a people, one has to take account of the manner in which they house and clothe themselves, their mode of conducting war and arranging peace, their systems of statecraft, of education, of rewards and punishment and the way they regulate personal relations generally as well as understand ideas underlying their institutions and practices (Wiredu, 10). A people's culture in view of the definition given by Kwash Wiredu can also be likened to their philosophy. It can therefore be said that African culture, African worldview and African philosophy are complementary in the endeavour of revealing the ideas, mindset as well as giving meaning to the practical manifestations (practices) within the African environment.

Essentially, the African is conscious of his culture. Basic features of African culture can no more be said to be hidden. Iwe avers that African culture is spiritual in the sense that it is the culture that is intensely religious and ethnically oriented to the point of superstition or fanaticism at times (69). Here again, justice stands as the ethnical foundation of Africa's religious life and spirituality. It has a social perspective, in which case it is characterized by self-reliance, collective egoism, domestic-life-centreed, mass illiteracy and lack of modern social institutions and amenities. Economically, its characteristic features are primitive agricultural ways and methods of life, super-abundance of raw materials and mineral resources, disguised unemployment, incipient industrialization, and greed for money among the elites. Politically, Iwe adds that African culture exhibits intense tribal and sectional feeling and organizational instability, inordinate desire for power and command, bureaucratic malpractices, abuse of office and other forms of corruption. He however, admits that, the true spirit of African culture is that it values and cherishes purpose and integrity in leadership, as well as service in leadership. While also acknowledging the fact that Africa is noted for oral and objective tradition with no practice of literary recording and documentation. Other aspects of African culture are as follows:

African Arts and Crafts: These terms are interrelated, but with slight difference. Art is a means of self-expression, guided by Western education in designing, sculpting, drawing, using elements or motifs as materials, while craft is a traditional means of self-expression without western education. It is more of a trade than a profession. These art and craft in most cases explain issues about a people's past, present and future, and also reflects the types of material resources available in each locality (Ver Steeg, 531). Africa has rich traditional arts and crafts. African arts and crafts are mostly expressed in various forms of wood carvings, brass and leather art works. African arts and crafts also include sculpture, paintings, pottery, ceremonial and religious headgear and dress. According to the *Wikipedia Free Encyclopedia*, African culture has always placed emphasis on personal appearance, in which jewelry has remained an important personal accessory. This is because many pieces of such jewelry are made of cowry shells and closely related materials. Also masks are produced with elaborate designs and are important parts of African culture. These masks are used in several ceremonies to represent ancestors and spirits, mythological characters and deities (1).

Traditional arts and crafts of Africa most times showcase some themes that are significant to African culture. Such themes where African culture recur includes; for example, a couple, a woman with a child, a male with a weapon or animal, and an outsider or a stranger-couples. It is argued may sometimes represent ancestors, community founder, married couple or twins. The couple theme rarely exhibit intimacy of men and women. The mother with the child or children reveals intense desire of the African women to have children. The theme is also representative of mother and the people as her children. The man with the weapon or animal theme symbolizes honour and power (Stanley, 96). This simply implies that African cultural arts and crafts contain within themselves multiple messages and speak simultaneously of history, of technology, of aesthetics, of philosophy and of value, whether material or existential (Serageldin and Taboroff, 281).

Languages: The continent of Africa speaks hundreds of languages. All these languages and dialects do not have same importance; some are spoken by only few hundreds of persons, others are spoken by millions. *The Wikipedia Free Encyclopedia* specifies that among the most prominent language spoken are Arabic, Swahilli and Hausa. But the truth is that very few countries of Africa use any single language and for this reason several official languages coexist, African and European; while some African may also speak different languages such as Malagasy, English, French, Spanish, Bambara, Sotho, and many more. The languages of African present a unity of character as well as diversity, as is manifest in all the dimensions of Africa. Four prominent language families of Africa are: (i) Afro-Asiatic; (ii) Nilo-Saharan; (iii) Niger-Kordofanian and Khoisan. *Wikipedia* avers that, by most estimates, Africa contains well over a thousand languages, and that nearly all African countries have adopted official languages that originated outside the continent and spread through colonialism or human migration. For example, in numerous countries English and French are used for communication in the public sphere such as government, commerce, education and the media. This is probably because language is basically the medium through which ideas are expressed by means of speech sound combined into words (Sweet, 642). Language is the basis of man's uniqueness and the essence of his culture (*The World Book Dictionary*, 1178). And above all, language enables accumulated knowledge to be transmitted forward, allowing us to profit from other's experiences as though they were our own. It conceals and justifies, compelling us to suspend our doubts about its claim to validity. It also stands behind all of the massive legitimation necessary to hold civilization together, this is because, it is at the root of civilization (Zerzan, 1).

What is also significant about African language is brought to the fore in the words of Iroegbu, who says that the linguistic expression of a people is definitional of their essential being and acting; For it is the soul of culture, the heart of the environment and the spirit that innovates and directs a people's life (134). Ijiomah, while agreeing with the above, argues similarly that language has an in-built cognitive function and the assertion that language is power, implying that through its effects our human world is known and subdued (71). It follows also as he maintains that under normal circumstances (i.e. moral situation), language unifies the total human self by directing man to the ontology of his circumstances. To further buttress the salient importance which African language occupies in its different domain, Dorothy Motaze is impressively optimistic, that though the languages found among a people, cultural and international cooperation for development through such language is inevitable. Arguing further, she opines that for a people or group of people traditionally embedded in their culture and native ways of speaking, such change, she maintains would only be allowed as an ultimate necessity for development (Abasiekong and Modo, 173). And that what should be considered as an objective and intelligent task for the owners of a language is not just to feel strongly or be chauvinistic about the language they speak, but as well to relate feelings and sentiments to the physical and practical aspects of their development, through arts, education, and technology in the nation, possibly where such languages are spoken as native and original to the people (174).

Folklore and Traditional Religion: African folklore and folktales like all human cultures represent a variety of social facets of African culture. And like almost all civilizations and cultures, where flood myths have been circulating, this is also peculiar to different parts of Africa. For example, according to a pygmy myth, chameleon hearing a strange noise in a tree cut open its trunk and water came out in a great flood that spread all over the land (*Wikipedia,* 2). It opines that, the first human couple emerged with the water. Similarly he had, and that the God Ouende rewarded him with riches, and advised him to leave the area, therafter the Ouende sent six months of rains to destroy his selfish neighbours (2).

Folklore is a combination of the oral traditions, the beliefs, the dances, and the songs preserved by a people through custom over centuries, while religion on the other hand, whether African or western is a spiritual pilgrimage characterized by, the guest for and recognition of some supra-human power (God), the acknowledgement of man's limitations and self-sufficiency, and the adoption as well as formulation of doctrinal code and practical-moral in life, in explanation and answer to the fundamental issues and problems of human existence (Iwe, 48). What is strikingly significant about the relationship between African folklore and its traditional religion is the fact that both forms of African culture are perpetually involved in guiding human beings as they try to actualize themselves in their various societies. It is in the light of such unitary and complementary purpose that Mbunwa Samba posits, that folklore and fairy tales are the largest and most common genre of our African oral past, and that there play important part in the regularization of lives of people. This according to him, manifest in areas like self-control and is achieved by the morals they teach, and through such method, order is restored to a society, as well as serve as a means for the education of children (Okpoko, 8). This salient role played by folklore within the African cultural setting is similar to the aim of its traditional religion. The African traditional religion as an essential dimension of its culture is no doubt a dimension of human nature which stands to inject fundamental and ultimate meaning and explanation into human existence and life.

Cuisine: Africa is a large continent and the food and drinks of Africa reflect local influences as also glimpses of colonial food traditions. These include use of food products like peppers, peanuts and maize introduced by the colonizers. The African cuisine is a combination of traditional fruits and vegetables, milk and meat products. Locally, diet is often milk, curds and whey, as well as fish. Traditional African cuisine according to the *Wikipedia Free Encyclopedia* is characterized by the use of starch as food, accompanied by stew containing meat or vegetables, or both. Cassava and yams are said to be the main root vegetables (3). Africans, also use steamed greens with hot spices. Here again, dishes of steamed or boiled vegetables, pea, beans and cereals, starchy cassava, yams and sweet potatoes are widely consumed. Other fruits and vegetables which are used as food within African locality include watermelon, banana and plantain as some of the more familiar fruits.

African Values: The first question one will envisage in a concept of this nature has to do with wanting to know the meaning of the word "value". This is necessary because it would enhance a quick and easy understanding of such a concept. It is therefore expedient to define value. The word "value" has been defined severally by different scholars depending on their context of discussion, but according to Clarence L. Ver Steg, value is anything that is important to someone. It could be an idea, a belief, a custom or a thing (6). Values give meaning to life. They establish priorities. They set moral boundaries and define rules of behaviour (*Awake*).

Any response to a question like, what is it that you want most, shows, no matter what it is, some ideas of your set of values. Each day, each one of us faces situations that force us to make decisions. Every choice we make therefore is based on what we feel is desirable. In other words, they are based on our beliefs and values, and the values one holds affects one's conduct, what one thinks of. The belief of other people and other cultures are also influenced by the value they hold. Just as every person has a set of values, so every culture has a set of values. They help determine a group of people's whole way of life. Values affect how people treat others. Values influences how people earn and spend their money, how they share ideas, and why they adopt one set of rules instead of another. Hence, the values people hold are usually part of the custom and behaviour of their cultural group. Every culture has its set of values, its way of governing itself. How people are governed also reflects their culture. Questions like, can individuals go where they please? Can they move elsewhere? Do they decide on their own leaders? Demand answers which tell one about the culture and values of that society. What religious beliefs people follow tell one something about a culture and its values. This is because in-as-much-as knowledge of value cannot be separated from valuation that is from life in the world of values. It is as well impossible to posit a value as an object of knowledge without making a valuation that is, without making a creative spiritual act (Berdyaev, 13). It follows therefore as Azenabor opines that "the values aspect of culture is the way the people view reality and this reality in an African culture is metaphysical" (117). What it simply implies is that African cultural values have spiritual and physical undertones and relevance. However, it is pertinent to note that in the case of Africa just like elsewhere, the value aspect of culture is well able to place sanctions and embargos on material culture; Meaning that spiritual values within the African context have overriding significance and authority over material culture. This of course happens in a way that does not hinder or jeopardize the complementary interaction between the spiritual and material aspects of the African culture.

Some Aspects of African Values

Sense of Hospitality: The African sense of hospitality is among African values that are still quite alive. The African easily incorporate strangers and give them lands to settle hoping that they would go one day, and the land would revert to the owner. Thus for the Africans, one cannot opt out of his original community completely. So they did not imagine that others could. Again, the hungry stranger could without penalty, enter the garden in a village and take, say a bunch of banana to satisfy his needs; While the slow, inept and incapable were accepted as valid element in community life (Shorter, 5). Africans have symbolic ways of expressing welcome. These are in forms of presentation of kolanuts, traditional gin, coconuts, etc in various communities. These are given to a visitor to show that he is welcome and safe. Among the Igbos, the basis of hospitality is the generally accepted principle that a guest should not harm his host and that when he departs, he should not develop a hunch back on the way home. Similarly, it amount to incredible bad manners for one to eat anything however small, without sharing it with anyone else present, or at least expressing the intention to do so.

Sense of the Sacred and the Religious: Religion in the traditional African societies was and is still characterized by secrecy. For example, in African religion, the drum plays a very important role; this is because Africans are very fond of music. Music is used most times to transmit knowledge and values. Although the drum is the primary musical instrument often used to send and receive messages, Olupona declares that "in African religion the drum is considered sacred. The drummer must be skilled as an oral communicator, and skilled at the art of drumming precise rhythms, connected with religious ceremony and ritual as well as entertainment (2). This is because African people depend upon oral tradition to teach their listeners important traditional values and morals pertaining to how to live. Oral tradition delivers explanations to the mysteries of the universe and the meaning of life on earth. For these reasons, African religion considers oral tradition and its values, as guiding principle in which to make sense of the world according to Mbiti (Wilson, 1).

Mbiti argues further that in traditional African societies there were no atheists, because religion in the indigenous African culture was not an independent institution. Rather it is an integral and inseparable part of the entire culture. Religion here was practical, in the sense that one's entire action is reflective in one's religious concepts and practices as is seen in the ordering of society, because social morality is dependent on religion (141). To corroborate the above position, Idowu avers that among the Yorubas, morality is certainly the fruit of religion. They do not make any attempt to separate the two; and it is impossible for them to do so without disastrous consequences (146). This implies that in traditional African culture, moral, religious and philosophical attitudes were accepted as complementary in life, given that all were interrelated in reality. Probably, the result of inseparability of religion from morality was that; the ancient African was far from being an abode of laissez-faire morality. There were strict moral principles and determined code of conduct. Custom laid down the code of law which established the nature or right doings and custom established penalties and taboos against malefactors. Moral sanctions were mainly religious sanctions. And these metaphysical sanctions were truly effective. In other words, the sense of respect, and the idea of the sacred filled the African as he approached religious elements and matters.

Respect for Authority and Elders: African traditional societies are characterized by a deep sense of respect for constituted authorities and for their elders. This African value is rooted in its very foundation. It is a cultural and intangible value inherited from generations of African ancestral tradition. If one says that respect for elders within the African setting come within the era of colonialism and Christianity, it would be erroneous, because before the advent of colonialism, respect for elders was an already entrenched moral code which formed part of our customs and tradition. In the words of Willaim Conton "Africans generally have deep and ingrained respect for old age, and even when we can find nothing to admire in an old man, we will not easily forget that his grey hairs have earned him the right to courtesy and politeness" (1).

The elders are actually respected not based on sentiments, not even due to adherence to the biblical injunction, but because of the significance attached to their presence within any society. There are numerous reasons why elders are accorded respect in African societies; these includes the fact that they play both earthly and spiritual roles in traditional society, the experience they have garnered over the years. Also they are seen as custodians of wisdom, and believed to be morally upright persons in whom the people repose a lot of confidence. They are believed to be teachers and directors of the young. This is because they play leading roles in the moulding of the character of the young ones (Ebijuwa, 35). No wonder it is said that when an old man dies in Africa it is like setting a whole library on fire and burning it down (Ojoade, 16). In other words, the memories which were custodied in the African man were likened to the book libraries of today. In a nutshell, the words of one's elders are cherished, and one who listens to an elder is like one who consults an oracle. A typical example of the practical moral effect of the elders' words is contained in this poem of Matei Markwei: "In our little village when elders are around, boys must not look at girls and girls must not look at boys because the elders say, that is not good" (2). The respect given to the elders has its practical effect in the maintenance of custom and tradition. The young are always looking forward to being elders and they are often told that if a child respects an elder, he would be respected by the young when he becomes an elder.

Language and Proverbs

According to Vincent Muli Wa Kituku, the human voice is the key element in oral tradition. He avers that Africans have been primarily vocal people; and that for such reasons, language is regarded as a powerful force. Despite the multi-lingual nature of the African culture, he notes many ethnic languages still coexist in Africa, and enables African stories and folklore to be communicated across different regions (Wilson, 3).

Africans so value language because it gives them insight into their cultural worldview. It carries a lot of the people's culture and history. Here, Jenkins posits that learning a language can be an exciting adventure, because one is learning about a people, a part of history and culture, as another way of organizing the world we all share. Language is thus integral to worldview (4). He argues that learning a language, offers one the opportunity to learn an exciting, frustrating and equally valid way of thinking. For when we think in the way of our first language, we indirectly learn how to think in that culture. Put differently, language expressed in speech is an important vehicle of thought and culture. For the African therefore, if an individual is not able to communicate with the native language, the individual ideologically, puts himself out of community. Speaking a language does not in the African sense, depend on the peripheral knowledge of the language. It depends on the ability to express oneself adequately in the proverbs and idioms of the language community. An African saying has it that, the child who carries an elder's bag has a very good chance of being a wise man in his life. This is because they usually make use of proverbs to drive home their point (Ebijuwa, 36), as he follows his father to meetings and places and listens to the wise words the elders speak. The result is that he knows at an early age those idioms and proverbs with which we fool and battle the stranger, and also the custom of the land. These proverbs, riddles and idioms of a community, give one a thorough knowledge of that community. This is because they are drawn from and refer to the environment, social order and behaviour common in that community. They determine the norms of action in that community and above all, they are didactic in nature.

Sense of Community: Communalism in Africa is a political arrangement which emphasizes community feelings and togetherness. Its origin is the political belief that traditional feelings of the pre-industrial society can be harnessed and made the basis of development. In other words, communalism is based on the belief that in the traditional setting there was some symbiotic relationships among men (Etta, 29). It is therefore not surprising that the African idea of security and its value depend on personal identification with and within the community. Communalism is thus a system that is both supra-sensisble and material. Both are found in a society that is believed by the Africans to be originally "god-made" because it transcends the people who live in it now, and its "man-made" because it cannot be culturally understood independent of those who live in it now. The implication here is that the authentic African is known and identified in, by and through his community.

The community is the custodian of the individual; hence, he must go where the community goes. The individual must go to the community centre. It is the communal village square, which is a social, political, judicial and religious centre. It is the communal meeting place for political discussions, communal tribunals, sports and games. In trying to support the above, Sogolo asks a simple question, "How is the African conceived as an individual and what is his place in the community? In response, he posits that "there seems to be a consensus among such scholars as Nyerere, Nkrumah, Senghor and a host of others that man in Africa is not just a social being but a being that is inseparable from his community. Similarly, Mbiti as quoted by Sogolo, argues that "only in terms of other people does the individual become conscious of his own being, his own duties, his privileges and responsibilities towards himself and towards other people" (191). Again, the African mentality is that while individuals as persons come and go, the community as an entity remains. It is on this basis that African emphasizes community life and communalism as a living principle of which the basic ideology is community-identity. Its aim is to produce and present an individual as a community-bearer. In other words, culture is a community property and must therefore be community protected.

In the words of Steve Biko: "We regard our living together not as an unfortunate mishap warranting endless competition among us, but as a deliberate act of God to make us community of brothers and sisters jointly involved in the quest for a composite answer to the varied problems of life. Hence, in all we do, we always place man first and hence all our action is usually joint or community oriented action rather than the individualism" (12). Essentially, the African man is therefore not egoistic, but altruistic, he loves his neighbour, and above all, adheres and obeys the golden rule of do unto others, what you would want them to do unto you. The community is the foundation of all activities; the source of all wisdom and the individual life is sustained and destroyed through the community. According to i Wiredu, African traditional values can be found, or are imbedded in several beliefs and practices of the African; these values are most times hidden in such beliefs and practices among Africans like:

i. The idea of the existence of one great God as integral member of society as distinct from the western and Christian idea of God staying aloof in heaven in the community of the spirits, looking down on the evil one in hell, and yet seeking to govern a mixture of the sinners and the righteous on earth.
ii. The belief in the perpetual existence of life, in which there is a cycle of pregnancy, life, death and a period of waiting in a universal pool of spiritual existence with a subsequent state of reincarnation, by which it is possible to change one's lot for better or for worse.
iii. The belief in the sanctity of man as opposed to woman in society.
iv. The belief in the idea that man is born free from sin and the idea that he remains so until he becomes involved in some polluting circumstances in life, as opposed to the Jewish and Christian idea of man born with original sin which he is said to have inherited from his ancestors, Adam and Eve.
v. The idea of beauty of thought, speech, action and appearance as a basic and necessary prerequisite for appointment to the high office of state.
vi. The ability to produce a child as a necessary factor for the continuance of marriage.

vii. The importance of marriage as a criterion of social status.
viii. The principle of age as a vital criterion of wisdom.
ix. The tendency to stress, in all forms of art, the quality of significance as a criterion of beauty and virtue as opposed to the eternal emphasis on the slogan "art for art's sake, which is tending to render human life in modern Europe so grossly pointless and not different from that of the beast of the field.
x. Spontaneity of self-expression (the lack of) which is the greatest weakness of modern western diplomacy; and
xi. The peculiar conception that it is improper and obscene to say thanks soon after one has been offered food by a neighbour (7, 8).

What is implied in the above beliefs and practices is simply that apart from being expressed intangibly, that is independent of its tangible culture, African values are often times exhibited in the numerous material cultures of Africa. At such times these values are seen as the hidden essences of certain material cultural displays.

Conclusion

From the foregoing, this work has been able to show that Africa is a vast continent, rich and diverse in its cultures and values. These African cultures embrace and include all cultures which were ever in the continent of Africa. These cultures change from one country to another, as well as from one ethnic group to another. As time goes on, some of these cultures as in other continents, countries, and ethnic groups are modified to reflect contemporary situations. It is wrong therefore to admit the opinion of European colonial powers, that Africa is "the dark continent" when they began their explorations. Their perception about Africa as a vast and dangerous place filled with savage people is also completely erroneous and faulty (Haley, 1). This is because Africa is home to innumerable tribes, ethnic and social groups, with large populations consisting of millions of people with diverse beliefs. These beliefs and practices constitute both its material cultures and values.

In this paper therefore, African culture are found in some African practices like: art and crafts, folklore and traditional religion, languages and cuisine. While African cultural values are exhibited in its beliefs and practices such as; sense of community, sense of sacred and of religious respect for authority and elders and sense of language and proverbs to mention but a few. What is significant about the African cultures and values mentioned above is that, they are not cherished and handed down from generation to generation just for nothing, rather these African cultures and values are transferred to younger generation because African cultures and values serve very specific purpose, provide meaning, purpose, pride, enjoyment or emotion in the daily lives of African people (Coetzee and Roux, 43). Coetzee and Roux add that African culture is positive and productive in itself. To corroborate this view, William Abraham avers that, our traditional culture or past has what we need for a great leap into the future and all we need to do is to tap, modify, retain or reflect. In other words, African culture can be refined and used as a basis for present or future development in Africa (Azenabor, 121).

Azenabor notes that it is the material aspect of culture that is today subject to relentless change, but however, avers that, the value aspect of culture is well able to place sanctions and embargoes on material culture and institutional culture. This value aspect of culture for him is the way the people view reality, and this reality in an African culture is metaphysical (117). This is perhaps due to the fact that metaphysics is a dynamic base upon which every aspect of human endeavour is situated (Alphern, 99). Thus, if reality is truly the foundation upon which African values are based, it is indubitably rational to uphold Momoh's insistence that the value of traditional African cultures should be the measure of all things (121). It follows therefore as Imaah avers that spiritual significance shows that something exists that has power but not material, and that we assume to be the more powerful immaterial and invisible metaphysical significance, subsequently subdues the subsidiary visible material aspect (5). Conclusively, suffice it to say that African culture and values are essential in the life of African people. These are complementary in the sense that each is subsumed in the other, and the superiority of one over the other should not be echoed, since they are products of each other, rather they should be cherished as a single culture of Africa.

WORKS CITED

Abasiekong, E. M. and I. V. O. Modo. *High Points in Development.* Uyo: Dorand Publishers, 1994.

Alphern. C. *The March of Philosophy.* New York: Macmillan, 1934.

Awake. "What has happened to Values?" New York: Watchtower and Tract Society, 2003.

Azenabor, G. *Understanding the Problems in African Philosophy.* Lagos: First Academic Publishers, 2002.

Berdyaev, N. *The Destiny of Man.* New York: Harper and Row, 1960.

Coetzee, H and Roux, A. P. T. *The African Philosophy Reader.* London: Routledge, 1998.

Ebijuwa, T. *Philosophy and Social Change: Discourse on Values in Africa.* Ibadan: Hope Publications, 2007.

Etta, E. E. *The Concept of African Humanism as a Unifying Force in Itigidi Worldview* (Unpublished), 1999.

Idowu, B. *God in Yoruba Belief.* London: SCM, 1962.

Ijiomah, C. "Methods and Systematic Reflections: Reference to Ultimate Reality in an African Language" in J. F. Perry (Ed). *Ultimate Reality and Meaning.* Canada: University of Toronto Press, 2004.

Imaah, N. O. "Influence of Religion on Society and Architecture" in Sophia: An African Journal of Philosophy. Vol. 10, 2007.

Iroegbu, P. *Enwisdomization and African Philosophy.* Owerri: International Universities, 1994.

Iwe, N. S. S. *Christianity, Culture and Colonialism in Africa.* Port Harcourt: Department of Religious Studies, 1979.

Jenkins, Orville Boyd. "Dealing with Cultural Differences: Contrasting the African and European Worldviews". http://strtegyleader.org/langlern/pdf/dealdifboklt.pdf.

Mbiti, J. S. *African Religions and Philosophy.* Nairobi: East African Educational Publishers, 1969.

Okpoko, I. *Culture and Development: An African Perspective.* Jos: University of Jos Press, 2004.

Ozumba, G. O. *A Colloquium on African Philosophy.* Calabar: Jochrisam Publishers, 2004.

Seragelin, I and Taboroff, J. *Culture and Development in Africa.* Washington D. C: Library of Congress Cataloguing-in-Publication Data, 1992.

Shorter, W. F. *African Christian Spirituality.* New York: The Macmillan, 1978.

Sogolo, G. *Foundation of African Philosophy: A Definitive Analysis of Conceptual Issues in African Thought.* Ibadan: University Press, 1993.

Stanley, T. L. *The Arts of Africa.* London: British Museum Publishers, 1979.

Ukpokolo, I. E. *Philosophy Interrogates Cultures: A Discourse in Philosophical Anthropology.* Ibadan: Hope Publications, 2004.

Ver Steeg, C. L. *World Cultures.* New York: Scott Foresman, 1993.

Wikipedia. The Free Encyclopedia: Culture of Africa. http://en.wikipedia.org/wiki/culture of Africa.

Wilson, S. *Africa Oral Tradition.* http:// www. Black and christian .com/articles/academy/swi/son-09-03.shtml

Wiredu, K. *Philosophy and an African Culture.* London: Cambridge University Press, 1980.

World Book Dictionary. Vol. 2. Chicago: Scott-Fetzer, 1996.

CHAPTER 10

ETHNICITY AND AFRICAN POLITICAL PHILOSOPHY
By
EPHRAIM A. IKEGBU, Ph.D

Introduction

Customarily, federalism is clearly seen as a welcome institutional framework properly engaging disruptive degrees of intra-societal ethnic pluralism. In any case, federalism is a form of political arrangement with a constitutional division of powers between and among tiers of government in order to ensure that jurisdiction and decision making authority of the tiers of government is protected. Suffice to say that federalism is a political arrangement that ably recognizes ethnic groups to carefully exercise significant authority within a recognized and defined territorial boundaries and not losing sense of the need to provide hegemony for national political institutions. Today, Africa's political history has been evidently characterized by sign post of ethnicity determining the direction to which the political, economic, social, cultural and religious pendulum would swing. The over bearing demonstration of ethnicity and the glaring display of ethnic psychology and assumptions greatly affected the growth and development in Africa in all the spheres of existence. On a personal, unprejudiced ground, there is nothing wrong for an individual to discover his root and goes further to acquaint himself with the cultural/traditional enablement of the ethnic enclave he naturally belongs to. However, where it becomes rather an issue, is when a particular ethnic configuration and/or fragment feels that it can operate without contemplating and in complete isolation of the other ethnic groups/fragments that constitute a state. To buttress the above, the trinity of Socrates, Plato and Aristotle had placed the foundation of the formation of the 'polis' on co-operation. Aristotle argues further;

> Any man who by nature or simply by ill luck has no state is either too bad or too good, either subhuman or superhuman... He is a non cooperator like an isolated piece in a game of draughts (59-60).

The above Aristotelian expression in the *Politics* injects the psychology of cooperation and dismissal of supremacy by any group towards the other. Aristotle is not alone in the struggle to recognizing the potency of others in a given society, for a contemporary philosopher, Asouzu has been in the vanguard of promoting universal interest and recognition of autonomous units. In his book, *The Methods and Principles of Complementary Reflection in and Beyond African Philosophy,* he argues on the impossibility of an individual existing without the other. Asouzu sees the reflection of the existence of 'A' in the life of 'B' and with this, 'A' cannot be on its own but requires 'B' in a complementary perspective. The existing relationship of 'A' and 'B' is a relationship ad continuum. It is not a relationship of ad hoc character and status which terminates at the expiration of their individual pursuit. But this relationship continues to exist in as much as humanity continues to be in time and space. The logic above defeats though, arguable, every supposedly existing argument favouring the engineering and re-engineering of the fluidity of ethnicity. This paper therefore, is an attempt to fashion out a formidable platform upon which ethnicity can harmoniously be viewed as a unifying driving force for the realization of peace and unity within and among different fragments of the society. Considering the palpable tension and conflicts that the present society is faced occasionally and its possible consequences, a study in political philosophy of this magnitude is required to sensitize the various fragments of the need to embrace the new philosophy of "live and let live" which is in tandem with globalization, communitarianism, and welfarism.

Ethnicity and Its Origin

All over the world, the phenomenon, ethnicity, reverberates and to a large extent determines activities with the promotion of ethnic interest and advancement of policies that have direct positive bearing and impact on their peculiar parochial needs. Sharing the above expression, Rotimi Suberu defines ethnicity as:

> a social collectivity whose members not only share such objective characteristics as language, core-territory, ancestral myths, culture, religion and political organization, but also have some subjective consciousness or perception of common descent or identity (4).

From what is stated above, ethnicity evolves as a result of members of a particular geographical location with common characteristics and belief prepared to pursue a common goal. Maduabuchi Dukor corroborates the above view when he argues that:

> Ethnicity as a progeny of unpatriotism sets the state's economy backward since the individuals have no regard for centralized economic planning … ethnicity or ethnic nationalism also, contributes negatively to political development and democratic processes of the nascent nation state; the ethnic group in the majority controls the economic and political affairs of the state while the minorities remain underdogs struggling, gasping and yearning for participation in a democratic process (131).

It is a truism that ethnicity is an anathema that has eaten deep into the fabric of any given socio-political formation. It is a dangerous phenomenon because of its ability to hamper development and consistently destabilize the entire political, economic, social and religious structures of the society. For instance, an ethnic group that is privileged to capture political power in the African continent (as in the case of Nigeria) uses same to build a formidable political and economic platform principally for the growth of its peculiar enclave with little or no attention to other parts of the nation state. This being the case, would arouse the consciousness of other ethnic nationalities to the glaring cases of discrimination, marginalization, deprivation, neglect and other perceived negative treatments. An ethnic group that responds to the challenges of domination and arbitrary use of state powers against it, is only responding to the logic of the environment. It has to be clearly explained and understood that obvious deformities in sharing and allocation of resources and devolution of power give rise to the issue of ethnicity. At any given time, power and resources of a given state are not evenly distributed or not shared as to balance the needs and aspiration of each fragment; this brews a psychology that could greatly affect the peace and unity of the state. To this, Maduabuchi Dukor contends,

> The political consciousness of the people is an ethnic motivated-political-consciousness which does not augur well for the political and economic emancipation of the collectivity, the nation. In all, the socio-political scene of a nation state is characterized by ethnic rivalry and chauvinism. The necessary cause of ethnic nationalism could be traced to the realm of psychological ideas like racism, ethnocentrism, prejudice and superiority complex (131).

Dukor's contention cannot be very much different from the definition offered by Okwudiba Nnoli. Ethnicity and/or ethnic group must not showcase commonality in language and culture. There is the accommodation of the existence of linguistic boundaries. However, Okwundiba Nnoli defines ethnicity as:

> a social phenomenon associated with interactions among members of different ethnic groups. Ethnic groups are social formations distinguished by the communal character of their boundaries. The relevant communal factor may be language, culture, or both (5).

With this, ethnicity becomes an interaction between and among people with a common disposition, belief, and aspiration towards the governance and administration of a given state which they are largely members. In Africa (Nigeria), parochial sensibilities, pursuit of sectional goals and allocation of resources with the intent to favour a particular fragment of the state has become a reoccurring decimal. In the event of this ugly situation the country is plagued with incessant conflicts ranging from religion, politics and social economic differences. Ethnicity creates inevitable dichotomy in the psyche of humans, making them realize at one spot and respond almost immediately that the next person who ordinarily ought to be his neighbour is of different descent and as such, should be treated with contempt. This ethnic cum sentimental psychological feeling is a signpost for the polarization of the society into ethnic divisions and clans. Ojukwu corroborates the above when he perceives an imminent polarization of the country, Nigeria into several divisions. According to him:

> Already, I can see many areas of possible polarization, north versus south; Muslims versus Christians; majority versus minority; capitalist versus socialist. None of these augur well for the future of Nigeria (153).

Another issue that is so striking in the attitudes of the people and/or leaders with the application of the tools of leadership is the issue of identity. The demand for one's state of origin has indirectly demonstrated the tendency to discriminate against the fellow. A pluri-ethnic state is encouraged and continues to function in such capacity when and if citizens of the state are required to clearly identify themselves. This opinion was further corroborated by Ojukwu who in his effort at ensuring the unity of Nigeria recommended thus:

> We must actively remove or minimize the language barriers within our society by encouraging a lingua franca; we must prevent religious strife by insisting on the secular nature of our state. We must diffuse ethnicity by laying more emphasis on citizenship and place of residence rather than state of origin or tribe (40-41).

It is a truism that independence of language within a given polity accelerates the growth of ethnicity and its consequences. Wittgenstein while praising the beauty of language in our everyday discourse and advancement of knowledge, however, stresses the need for the language to be carefully analyzed so as to avoid ambiguity and also, capture the interest of the audience. Language embarks on vacation the moment its audience could not understand the epistemology of the language in use. Language therefore, is a formidable asset evidently used by ethnic majority and minority groups in the pursuit of their parochial and self-motivated goals. In the opinion of Ojukwu, the elimination or minimization of language barrier would afford the next neigbour the epistemic warrant to carefully deduce what is stated and whether such spoken language is against his/her interest bearing in mind his/her geographical location. In Nigeria, most conflicts today are caused by religious differences being propelled by the two contending religions - Christianity and Islam in their efforts to dominate one another.

The Emergence of Ethnicity in the Nigerian Polity

Before the colonialists found their root in Nigeria, the Nigerian people had existed and lived in a cooperative manner. The entity, Nigeria, was perceived to be the creative coinage of the British administrative colony. Nevertheless, different ethnic nationalities were already in existence before the colonial contraption. Nevertheless, it can not be dismissed outrightly that the emergence of ethnic politics in Nigeria has colonial blessing. On account of history, the colonialists in their efforts to ensure success and complete control of the nation state divided Nigeria into regions so as to ensure administrative convenience and efficiency in service. Regionalism which allows for the independence of the regions was introduced by Arthur Richard's constitutional history. Apart from administrative convenience as a major factor for the division of the country, the structure of the division ideally demonstrated a somewhat natural dichotomy between "region A" and "region B". The colonial act metaphorically, meant that there was absence of commonality of language, culture, religion and other core traits or values between and among the regions. The Richard's constitutional history was not alone in fostering the colonial intention of festering ethnic character in Nigeria as John McPherson added to this through his policy of federalism.

The inherent logic in federalism is that regions were allowed to manage and control resources found on their land, and pay royalty to the central government. This act of federalism implies that states (regions) enjoy political, social, economic and cultural autonomy. This was the logic that governed the political economy of Nigeria in her pre-independence and independence era. Okwudiba Nnoli in one of his famous books writes that the colonial urban setting was the cradle of ethnicity in Nigeria. For him, "it was there that what we refer to today as ethnic groups first acquired a common consciousness" (35). He was unequivocal when he states that

tribalism or ethnicity in Nigeria is a creature of the colonial and post-colonial order. He buttressed this further when he argues that:
> It was only after colonialism that the term Yoruba-land began to be used to refer to the domains of all rulers who claim descent from the mythical Oduduwa, instead of the kingdom of Oyo to which it was previously limited (35).

The effect of the argument presented by Nnoli is that ethnicity in Nigeria was a foreign commodity shipped to Africa by the colonialists. The implication of Nnoli's position if accepted and judged in its face value means that, prior to the scrambling and partitioning of Africa by the whites, Africans had demonstrated high level co-operation in the affairs within and among themselves. The second limb of the deduction is that at no time had there been any form of sectional and/or regional gathering within and among peculiar members with sameness of religion, language, culture and social interest to articulate issues bothering on their welfare. However, it is interesting to note the contrary view of Ihonvbere as cited by Asouzu which goes to debunk the earlier position that ethnicity in Nigeria and Africa had foreign link. Ihonvbere argues that "prior to the advent of colonial domination, ethnic groups in Africa fought violently between and within themselves" (67). It is very possible to contend that foreign link of ethnicity to Nigeria may be on political basis going by the policy of regionalism and federalism adopted by colonial heads of state at one time or the other. This would not succeed for all understanding of the emergence of ethnicity in the political and social vocabulary of Nigeria. This is because, prior to colonial invasion, sectionality of groups in Nigeria had at one time or the other convened to carefully deliberate and articulate issues relating to the leadership and governance of the state, and welfare of the citizens of the regions. The possibility of the absence of central political fora may be evident; nevertheless, this may not negate the convocation of such meetings at town unions, village square, age grade assembly halls, council of elders, the Obi in council, Igwe in council, and other possible ethnically-inclined gatherings.

The feigning of ethnicity does not primarily involve one group against the other of different descent. It also exists and evidently revolves within and around an existing ethnic group. This brings to the fore, the issue of majority and minority. Ethnic minority is that group of people enveloped and/or sandwiched in a major ethnic group but is culturally and linguistically distinct from the major ethnic group. The minority group has no opinion of its own as its expresses its existence boldly in the context of the majority. This being the case, cries of marginalization, domination, oppression and others are frequently complained about by people of the minority group. In Nigeria today, it is so evident that the development of political parties and other striking political events followed regional, tribal or ethnic posture. Before the 1946, Richards' constitution, political parties of the NCNC, NNDP were nationalistic in both ideological and geographical rating which showcased evidence of co-operation and togetherness. In view of the above, Obialor and Nganya contend that:

> It was not until 1959 that NCNC was reduced to a regional and ethnic party as a counter weight to the already regionalized and ethnically-based political parties. The Action Group started as a Yoruba party (14).

Ethnicity, objectively perceived, comes with high degree of negative implication. This is why a new orientation and enlightenment have become so necessary to impact on the psyche and/or sensibilities of citizens in Africa. There is nothing wrong with the promotion and propagation of ideological, linguistic, religious and cultural leaning by an individual or group of individuals with commonality of the above; it is then a problem where and if the promotion of these parochial traits as enunciated above by a group of individuals take preeminence over the generality of the populace. The danger in allowing the promotion of ideological, cultural, religious and linguistic leaning to flourish is that national issues that ought to have been discussed with nationalistic interest would be approached with ethnically-oriented posture. Take the case of national political or constitutional conferences held at different times, because of the existence of different descent and fragments, each fragment did all it could to present argument that would favour it regardless of the obvious consequences on other regions. A conferee from a particular ethnic group is only out to defend its own region. This being the case, primordial politics and parochial sensibilities clearly influenced the reasoning faculties of the African people. With ethnic mindset, decisions reached at any convoked conferences could not reflect the ever-sought unity that members had come to achieve. This ugly phenomenon was observed by Ojukwu who berated the attitude of Nigerian nationalists with the exception of Nnamdi Azikiwe in the pursuit of ethnic agenda. He argues that:

> With bitterness, we began to learn that Zik, whom the British colonial administration could never incarcerate, had willingly constituted himself a prisoner of what appeared to us as northern interests…the foregoing coupled with the fact that the Igbos appear today to be marginalized and lacking in any appreciable influence within the power structure of Nigeria, invariably has made the leadership of Igbos by Zik a subject of a vast amount of discussion. In my own candid opinion, Zik did not set out to lead the Igbos and has not in fact led the Igbos. He has been first and foremost a Nigerian who aspired to a Nigerian leadership. When the British withdrew in 1960, Nigeria was left in the hands of three great men. Of the three, Zik could be said to have been the dreamer whilst the others were hard-headed realists. Zik believed, worked for and made sacrifices for a Nigeria that had not yet come into existence - the ideal increasingly unattainable, they found themselves deflated and deprived vis a vis the realists, who from the beginning, ensured for their groups a share of whatever was going (158).

Even at the point of acknowledging Zik as a promoter of inter ethnic harmony and togetherness evidently deduced from the expression of Ojukwu, this was however contradicted by a statement credited to Azikiwe demonstrating that he favoured the dominance of one ethnic group over the other. According to Azikiwe as cited by Nnoli,

> It would appear that the God of Africa has specially created the Ibo nation to lead the children of Africa from the bondage of the ages…The martial prowess of the Ibo nation at all stages of human history has enabled them not only to conquer others but also, to

adapt themselves to the role of a preserver...The Igbo nation can not shirk its responsibility (230).

Little wonder that such an offending statement capable of throwing the entire continent into perpetual war and confusion is originating from an elder statesman whose roles at all times, should be geared only on building bridges of harmony and friendship. However, this singular statement credited to Azikiwe was a litmus paper upon which his credibility as a pan-Nigerian leader was watered down. Azikiwe was a true reflection of a patriot who believed and fought for the unity and integration of the African continent. He was to a large extent a detribalized African son, who fought with his contemporaries against colonialism of the African continent. The various organizations which were used to champion the cause of independence of the African continent were either founded and/or chaired by him. While doing this, Nnamdi Azikiwe demonstrated the spirit of oneness between and among other African brethren. At the local level (Nigeria), he demonstrated also, that he was no less a Nigerian. Although the party he founded had ethnic character, the ideology was very nationalistic. He eminently departed from the philosophies of other nationalists of his time.

In an atmosphere of ethnicity or the ethnicization of the nation would imply sponsoring policies that would favour a particular region with no contemplation of the needs and aspirations of others. Where this is the case, other known regions would do everything within their reach to resist this phenomenal situation. And by so doing, friction and violence of monumental degree will consequently erupt. A tour of the 1954 Lagos Conference meant for the review of the advice of the fiscal commissioner in charge of revenue allocation heightened the spectre of ethnic feelings and sensibilities. At the conference, each conferee, representing a region directed his/her logical pendulum on the axis that could benefit his/her own region maximally with no consideration of the fate of other regions that make up Nigeria. Granted that this was the case, Nigeria and her African allies were engrossed with the evils of ethnicity. With the above position, the colonialists may as well be absolved from any blame arising from the fragmentation of the society.

However, there seems to be a natural tendency towards ethnicity. Ethnicity is a psychology naturally discovered between and among people who are communalistic in language, culture, colour, tribe and similarity of political ideology. For an ethnic group to record success in its aspirations there must be a common belief in themselves and what their intentions are strictly speaking, "polygamy of culture" may not be a quality or feature of ethnicity. This is possible with language, but commonality of culture is one of the essential ingredients respecting ethnicity. There is a psycho-socio angle to the explanation of ethnicity in Nigeria and Africa respectively. Buttressing the above position Agi argues that unregulated competition over something in short supply always gives rise to ethnic and selfish feelings for the preservation of oneself and one's kinsmen. According to him:

> The arbitrariness of God's arrangements seems at first sight to be the source and cause of division and unhappiness among men... the scarceness of earthly goods available in an economy that God seems to have made is one more factor which contributes to the break up of humanity (9).

It is Agi's view that "divine parsimony seems an incitement to materialistic competition" (9). This paper agrees with Agi that preservation of one's interest and that of one's kinsmen is only natural and expedient. This is arising from the fact that humans are self-seeking beings. They are rapacious, aggressive, egoistic and insatiable. In order to conform to the law of nature of self preservation, their personal interest and that of others are likely to conflict which would bring about tension and violence in the state, especially, in a situation where what is being competed for is both minimal and scarce. We do know and it is the view of this paper that ethnicity and its overbearing influence do not accommodate the philosophy of "consensus value". This is so because, what constitutes value system is what a particular ethnic group accepts and not what is adopted by the entire nation. Ethnicity is not rooted only in Africa. All over the world, ethnic chauvinism, ethno-religious and ethno-political issues are very common and dominate the affairs of governance. This is drawn from the fact that there are people from different clan, villages, communities, states etc, who organize themselves to reflect on how the affairs of the nation are being carried out, by whom and from where? They also, assemble to determine the sharing formula and what proportion of the social goods of the nation gets to them.

The questions become more valid and legitimate when those posing the questions come from the zone (region) that produces the natural resources upon which the state economy is determined and strengthened. Perhaps, the above lucidly could explain the reason for the quest for resource control and true federalism by the Niger Delta region of Nigeria which has been plagued with series of crises, until recently whenolive branch was offered to it by the federal government through the amnesty programme for the repentant militants.

Prior to the amnesty policy of Yar'Adua's administration, socio-political and economic activities were under serious threat and tension, due to the activities of ethnic militia of different clout clamouring for absolute control of resources and self determination. In order to actualize this dream, several groups representing both individual and communal interests were formed. At any rate, inequitable distribution of social goods and structural deformities awaken the consciousness of people from the regions that feel marginalized and equally put them to action. The above explains the ideological trappings of the foremost African nationalists. Ethnicity and ethnic feelings negatively control the psyche of people and also, make them to respond irrationally sometimes. However, irrespective of the degree of discrimination and/or marginalization, the unity of purpose should be uppermost on peoples' mind. The actions and inactions of people should be geared towards building a harmonious, purposeful, virile and result-oriented society. The society should be more concerned on how best to promote the unity of the state, to be proactive in building a strong economic base. What should govern the psychology of people in this 21st century is cooperation and unity. Ethnicity brings down the structures of the society. It promotes individualism and sectionalism. It is a snare to a strong political and economic front. This is obviously the bane of African civilization.

The Consequences of Ethnicity

Some scholars of African political and social sciences accept the fact that ethnicity constitutes one of the most dangerous threats to the actualization of stable government in Africa. Conversely, ethnicity in Africa is not an accident of history, but a product of consistent strife and competition by stakeholders. Those who align to the evils of ethnicity only struggle to actualize the goods and happiness of their peculiar region with complete disregard of the feeling of other regions in the state. What is paramount within the framework of those that churn out ethnic sensibility is how best to protect their parochial aims without considering the plight of the totality of the nation. Adjusting his mind to the possible consequences of ethnicity, and disconnecting the colonialists from any blame, Bala Usman avers that:

> If there is a problem of ethnicity in Nigeria today, it is certainly not because these ethnic groups existed before the colonial conquest. The contemporary tribes and ethnic groups' action today never existed in any real historical past of the peoples of this country (46).

By way of clear and lucid explanatory understanding of the argument of Usman, ethnic and parochial feelings became fully expressive at the colonial era in Nigeria. This view in any case, contradicts the argument advanced by Okwudiba Nnoli. Emphasizing further, Usman argues that the overbearing and prevailing logic among the apostles of ethnicity is the pursuit and promotion of ethnic agenda and interest within and among the segments of the society. This he expresses thus:

> This process of enrichment of the leadership and the impoverishment of the citizenry continues in Nigeria because those engaged in the production of goods and services do not individually and collectively play a dominant role in political system. The political system is dominated by those who parasitically acquire wealth from their control of commercial and financial transactions often through their capability to block and put obstacles on the path of any transactions which favour

production. This is why they became richer while the rest of the country becomes poorer and poorer (33).

It is evident though arguable that the tactical alienation of those whose land produces the national resources from the scheme of affairs in Nigeria and Africa can cause monumental tension and violence. This is why Barongo having observed the prevailing lacuna in the political and economic structures of the society prefers a socialist political arrangement as a proper political engineering for peace and stability within and among the fragments of the country. Barongo believes that:

> The emergent capitalist mode of production, distribution and consumption in Nigeria tends to breed and intensify ethnic and elite conflicts of a kind that militates against the building and functioning of an integrated society and a democratically stable political system and that, if national integration and political stability are to be achieved and maintained, there is an imperative need for the country to escape from capitalism and adopt an economic system of a socialist type which has inherent mechanisms of minimizing conflicts and enhancing consensus and social cohesion (65-80).

What is said above by Barongo is the centrality of this paper. The African political society should thrive and compete favourably with political environments of other continents. The political and economic existence in Africa should not be theatrically known for war, conflicts, 'sit tight' syndrome, and poverty of administration, corruption, religious and ethno religious conflicts. The above stated developments do not encourage stability and even growth of the system. This paper further argues that if the political structure of the African continent is built upon solid foundations of socialism, not as an ideology, but a pragmatic system of political process, with the empirical imprints of addressing problems already enunciated, it would be seen as extending its hand of fellowship and co-operation towards familyhood. To buttress the necessity of the campaign for African unity,

Asouzu had argued against the possibility of individual person and/or state existing without the other. Asouzu sees the reflection of the existence of *Amadi* in the life of *Udeh* and with this reasoning, *Amadi* cannot be on its own but needs *Udeh* and as such *Amadi* cannot claim superiority over *Udeh*, but both operate in a complementary perspective. In this understanding the existing relationship of *Amadi* and *Udeh* is a relationship *ad continuum*. It is far beyond ad hoc relationship which terminates at the expiration of their individual pursuit. The implication of ethnicity is the difficulty in ensuring that people of different descents languages, cultures and religions fraternize and harmoniously pursue set objectives and goals without sectionalizing the objectives. But this is far from what exists in the minds of African populace. What occupies their reasoning faculty is how best to promote their own parochial interests against the general and/or public interest. This tribal logic of ensuring the good and benefit of a segment of the society in the spirit of *ndia bu ndi nke anyi* (these are our own people), is indeed a parochial reasoning virus and/or leprosy that has convulgated every part of the African bloodstream. This is not far from what Asouzu calls "the nearer the better and the safer" (2004: 65). This is a fallacious way of viewing reality and attending to issues of utmost concern.

Aspiring to do good for only those of the same clan and tribe with us and ignoring every other segment that does not share sameness of logic with us only demonstrates that ethnicity can not be concretely viewed as the evils of colonial contraption as been touted by some analysts. Colonialism in Africa could be responsible for infusing the spirit of individualism which could be another way of fostering personal interest. Ethnicity is different from individualism. Individualism is principally an economic motive, while ethnicity is natural and goes beyond economic protection of a segment to the struggle of protecting the segment in all facet of existence. Naturally, people have the desire to protect and seek for the interest and protection of the place or locality where they come from; tracing their identity and origin from a particular geographical entity and acting assiduously to protect this area from infraction by others. It is in the above premise that Asouzu argues;

The tendency to ethnic cleavage has a dimension that is natural to human nature but which can easily be misappropriated and manipulated. In other words, ethnicity is not a negative factor per se but one that has an inherently ambivalent dimension (*Redefining ... Philosophy*, 67).

Asouzu believes there is nothing wrong in one identifying oneself to have been a member of a particular descent. But the natural tendency in human beings would manifest in a negative dimension as these human beings press to defend and protect their locality. From the above, it only implies that the individualistic expression of people's existence manifests in their thoughts, associations and/or relationships entered with others and also, in the attempt to protect these parochial interests. This could be the fulcrum of ethnicity. In line with the above, Asouzu argues:

> Ethnic matters are some of those decisive moments where the mind seeks to convince itself that a person or group of individuals are better off and are safe in the midst of those that share certain common, unique or exclusive qualities. These are our kith and kin, our own tribal people, people of our race, of our nation, etc. Thus, in most contentious situations of life, we tend to act in keeping with this maxim. Worst still, tend to assume that there are certain natural rights attached to its dictates in the form of an ordinance of the natural law (*Redefining ... Philosophy*,63-78).

From the point of view of Asouzu as seen above, ethnicity revolves around a collectivity of people with sameness of aspiration, with the mindset of pursuing a parochial goal. This cannot be graphically far from ideology, but in ideology as stated earlier, different ideologues with different ideological trappings may exist within a defined ethnic environment. But to what extent can humanity proceed in its quest to achieve lasting peace and co-operation within the polity? There is a very common adage which says: "United we stand, divided we fall". This adage goes to expressing the utility and significance of commonality of purpose. The unity of members of a given society attracts benefits that are unquantifiable. This is not far from the philosophy of Anaxagoras in the ancient period of philosophy, which was also somewhat recapitulated in the philosophy of Leibnitz who extolled the wisdom of the "monads", their unity as being capable of producing results and when they operate differently, it became difficult to make any useful achievement. This pattern of thinking as demonstrated by these philosophers in the ancient and modern periods cannot be far from the inherent truth in the contemporary philosophical exposition by Asouzu.

In the *Ibuanyidanda*, Asouzu is of the opinion that the unity of ants (*ndanda*) provides the strength upon which every challenge and/or *ibu aru* can be tackled. Irrespective of the degree of the challenge or load upon the *ndanda*, in as much as it does not operate individually, the ants would be able and capable of overcoming what difficulty that comes their way in a full complementary manner. This is the world and wisdom of *ndanda* as x-rayed. The philosophical and symbolic depiction of *ibu anyi ndanda* is the magical and/or miraculous power of *ndanda* in carrying their heavy burden. This phenomenon only reminds humanity the indescribable and inexhaustible strength in unity. It goes to demonstrate that a state achieves all it intends to achieve if and only if it operates not as an individual unit, but as a corporate entity. This paper aligns itself significantly to the necessity of avoiding things that could bring dichotomy between and among others in the African continent. Obasanjo bares his mind on the need to eschew ethnic politics and pursue only nationalistic drives. This he argues from his observation in the Nigeria-Biafra civil war which gave rise to ethnic-based politics thus.

> The election of that year was fought on regional loyalty, with a strong tribal bias. But the government that emerged was a coalition of two regionally based parties leaving the third party, also regionally based, within the cold; with no patriotic feeling, sectionalism and tribalism being extolled ... North for the Northerners, West for the Westerners and East for the Easterners. Nobody seemed to care sufficiently for Nigeria as a nation (Nzeogwu, 79).

Due to the individualistic orientation of the African political mindset, it is the reason for people to pursue the safety and security of their own ethnic group or region. The danger in this kind of arrangement is that individually-driven states cannot compete favourably with other states of the world with high spirit of co-operation and understanding. Ethnic politicking tends to give the impression that I alone exist (solipsism), which is obviously a wrong philosophy and injurious to the society. Ethnicity punctures a nation's desire to advance economically, socially, politically and culturally. The presence of ethnicity in a given society is seen as anathema which is constantly perceived to be a clog in the wheel of progress and harmonious existence of all segments of the society. Nothing moves in an atmosphere of uncertainty and instability. This is the byproduct of ethnicity. Any state that finds itself in the theatre of it is greatly bewildered and cannot correctly locate its bearing. The African continent as a people should change their attitudes and come up with an acceptable and proper orientation that could bring about peace in the entirety. The nations of the world are gradually and consistently giving up practices that put them behind among others in the comity of nations, African continent should therefore gear up and put behind them primordial thoughts and other ethno-psychological sensibilities that had eroded their values. By this 21st century, Africa ought to be a great continent if only it clearly understood the importance of unity. So unity of purpose is what is required to navigate a strong economic base which would further give room to a strong political structure comparable to those of the Asian, European and American continents.

Conclusion

It is unpolemic that the degree of violence and conflict corrupting from the advocacy and practice of ethnicity has reached its zenith that urgent and pragmatic measures should be immediately enforced. Sadly, lives and valuable properties ranging from millions to billions of Naira are being lost each time there is one form of ethnic crisis or the other. In Jos, a city in Nigeria, hundreds of human lives and properties w0rth millions of Naira had been lost in ethno-religious crisis that started late last year and is still occurring in spite of concerted efforts by both the federal and state governments to avert further crises in the area. The peace committee that was set up which is headed by Solomon Lar has been criticized as incapable of producing dependable result. Reason being that it was elite-centreed. According to Mallam Shehu Sani:

> The committee headed by pioneer Chairman of Peoples Democratic Party (PDP), Chief Solomon Lar, an elitist and non-representative, it would not achieve the purpose for which it was set up...The committee is nothing new. It is not special; it has always been like that when you have a crisis of this kind. It has always been the elite who are invited for peace talks... I don't believe that it is going to achieve anything because there are fundamental issues that led to the emergence of the crisis. Some could be addressed at the short time and some could be addressed at the long run, but the underlining causes are poverty, underdevelopment and the disconnection between the government and the people. Such issues must be addressed before you have an end to those perennial crises (*The Nation*, Monday, February 8, 2010: 36).

The point made above cannot be graphically ignored if peace is to be achieved in Jos and other parts of the African continent that have been a beehive of violence. Poverty, underdevelopment and complete isolation of the masses have created widespread discordant posture in the minds of the people towards the select few. There is urgent need to begin to think and behave not as a part in a whole, but an inherent whole in itself. What is meant here is that the trouble in almost all the continent of Africa today remains the ethnicization of their individual mind. There is always reference to one's state of origin in all that one does or intends to do. This phenomenon is oppressive, discriminatory and inciting. Every African is a citizen of Africa and should be seen in that perspective, with openness of opportunities disregarding culture, race, religion and forms of discrimination.

In Nigeria, the issue of quota system and federal character principle in my mind are forms of oppression and discrimination. These practices take place only in areas where suspicion, cheating and fraud are prevalent phenomena. But states that are operating inconformity to standard of operation only aspire to give the best and qualitative services to the nation as a whole and not a segment of the nation. This paper is of the opinion that the practice of the principles of quota system, federal character and other forms are inciting and morally wrong. This practice is capable of denying a more qualified citizen of the continent the right to advance in the sector based on the irrelevant and fallacious logic of "your quota is filled". By applying the above principle, mediocres are rather selected to fill the vacant places where quota is still open. This act would evidently reduce productivity and quality of service.

The same act of unreasonableness of logic plays in the political arena where people talk about and chart the course of "it is our turn". This political syndrome and /or virus have negatively impaired on the quality and stability of socio-economic and political lives of African continent, and has greatly reduced it on the score board of reality. Taking clue from the leadership credential enunciated by Plato and his apostles, a good leader of the people should be one that is competent and knowledgeable enough irrespective of his/her descent or origin. This is to say that behavioural reform and improvement or review of our constitutional instrument should help to tackle these attendants prejudiced behaviour or practices. There is need to review educational curricula. In our primary, post primary and tertiary institutions; ethnic studies and conflict resolution principles should be compulsorily made to be undertaken by all school children. Because of the pragmatic and imperative nature of the contributions of all the segment of Africa, I had argued elsewhere that National Commission on Ethnicity should be established at both state and regional levels to address the problem of ethnic politics. The utility of this assembly would be to discuss matters that affect each region and find a lasting solution.

This paper would not negate the Rawlsian therapy of socially engaging every member of the society especially the disadvantaged region. The recognition and engagement of the people from this area would erase the thought of marginalization; this would rather be seen as a healing balm. This chapter also proposes that a strong enlightenment campaign be carried out to educate the people at both the urban and rural areas on the dangers of ethnicity. The rural areas should be recognized and policies initiated to attract developments to the area which would give rise to the engagements of the youths in skills and other profitable practices, by so doing rural-urban migration would reduce.

This chapter therefore aligns itself significantly to the new logic of "live and let live". This is so because; any socio-political formation that is structured to be harmoniously together would succeed irrespective of the mountainous pressure of ethnicity. The new logic which anchors on the strength of co-operation upon capturing the truth as enshrined in Asouzu's complementary ontology and Aristotle's insufficiency of the needs of man as the risen detera for forming a state will minister to the minds of Africans of the need to reorganize themselves for optimal growth.The new logic if properly understood would banish every sentimental feeling of ethnicity and this will evidently relaunch Africans to the path of political and economic supremacy.

WORKS CITED

Adigwe, Francis. *Essentials of Government for West Africa.* Ibadan: University of Ibadan Press, 1979.

Agi, S. P. I. *Political History and Religious Violence in Nigeria.* Calabar: Ushie Publishers, 1998.

Asouzu, I. I. "Redefining Ethnicity with the Complementary System of Thought" in Thirstem Botz-Bornstein and Jungen Hengelbrock (Eds). *Re-Ethnicizing the Mind: Studies in International Philosophy.* Zurich: Lit Verlag,GMBA, 2006.

Asouzu, I. I. *Ibuaru: The Heavy Burden of Philosophy* Zurich: Lit. Verlag GMBH, 2007.

Asouzu, I. I. *Ibuanyidanda: New Complementary Ontology.* Zurich: Lit Verlag, GMBH, 2007.

Asouzu, I. I. *Ikwa Ogwe: Essential Readings in Complementary Reflection.* Calabar: Seaprint Publishers, 2007.

Asouzu, I. I. *The Methods and Principles of Complementary Reflection in and Beyond African Philosophy.* Calabar: University of Calabar Press, 2004.

Barongo, Y. R. "Ethnic Pluralism and Democratic Stability: The Basis of Conflict and Consensus in *Democratic Experiment in Nigeria: Interpretation Essays*. Benin City: Omega Publishers, 1987.

Dare, L and Oyewole, O. *A Government Textbook for West Africa.* Ibadan: Onibonje Books, 1983.

Ikegbu, Ephraim A. "Complementary Reflection and Hierarchy of Social Order" in *Sophia: African Journal of Philosophy*, Vol.8, N0.2, 2006.

Ikegbu, Ephraim A. "Philosophy and National Development". *A Systematic Approach to Philosophy and Logic* in Ekanem, S. A. and Ogar, J. N. (Eds). Calabar: Unical Press, 2008.

"Lar Committee 'll fail says Activist". *The Nation*, Monday, February 8, 2010.

Obasanjo, Olusegun. *Nzeogwu.* Ibadan: Spectrum Books, 1987.

Obialor, C. F. and Nganya, F. C. *Organization and Fundamentals of Government and Constitutional Development of West African States.* Owerri: Cape Publishers, 2006.

Odimegwu, Ojukwu E. *Because I am involved.* Ibadan: Spectrum Books, 1989.

Okwudiba, Nnoli. *Ethnic Politics in Nigeria.* Enugu; Fourth Dimension Publishers, 1992.

Rawls, John. *A Theory of Social Justice.* Oxford: Oxford University Press, 1971

Rawls, John. *Political Liberalism.* New York: Columbia University Press, 1993.

Usman, Y. Bala. *The Manipulation of Religion in Nigeria 1977-1987.* Kaduna: Vanguard Publishers, 1987.

Usman, Y. Bala. *Katsina State in the Nigerian Federation: The Basic Realities.* Monograph, 1992.

CHAPTER 11

RELIGIOUS FACTOR IN AFRICAN POLITICS
By
INIOBONG UMOTONG, Ph.D.

Introduction

Every political decision has a social implication and the social fabrics are held together not merely by social contract or laws but by values dictated by religion. Taking political decisions entails considering the social implication of such decisions on the citizens and their faith. Social fabrics are built on morality therefore the assertion by Emil Brunner that "the good consists in always doing what God wills at any particular moment" (James Rachel, 48) is a confirmation of the great impact and grip religion has always exerted on politics, be it in the ancient or contemporary period. Political development in the entire African continent is laden and spiced up with peculiar religious influences that inter-play in such a nation. Considering the cultural vastness and divergences embedded in African continent, this work will be narrowed down to the experiences prevalent in Nigeria though peculiar cases in other African nations will be mentioned. Nigeria is taken as the case study here because she can be seen as a micro Africa viewed from the fact that it is a multi-ethnic and multi-cultural entity brought together by colonial political engineering. Therefore what happens in the micro entity called Nigeria can be extended to embody the macro entity called Africa.

Nigeria by colonial contraption has three dominant nations – the Hausa/Fulani, the Yoruba and the Igbo nations. In each of these nations there are many other dialectical varieties with cultural affinity. In these ethnic nations, the indigenous religious affiliation and belief varies, it is a common knowledge that in traditional society religion shapes and dictate the political direction for the people. The romance between religion and politics is viewed by Charles Quist-Adade (a professor of sociology at Kwantlen Polytechnic University in Surrey) as "a dangerous mix the world over". In other words, religion and politics are the two sides of the same coin with a dangerous grip on human society. Here one may be tempted to ask, what is politics? What is religion? What makes religion so powerful to the extent of controlling or dictating the trend of political progress? In describing politics, Umotong (3) asserts that it is the activities associated with government. The theory and practice related to power and authority to manage human and material resources belonging to a given group of people. Politics can also be seen as a power relationship between the people, groups or organizations in a particular area of life as far as it involve power and influence, or conflicts and its resolution. Wright also defines politics as "the art of influencing, manipulating or controlling (groups) so as to advance the purpose of some against the opposition of others (Collinson, 53). Politics is the "science or business of government" (Robinson and Davidson, 1075).

On the other hand, religion according to Procter (933) is "the belief in one or more Gods especially the belief that God made the world and control it and give men life after death". Religion can also be said to be a peculiar system of belief and the worship behaviour connected with it. It is an institutionalized or personal system of beliefs and practices relating to the divine. It is a set of strongly held beliefs, values, and attitude that someone lives by. On the other hand, a more elaborate and all-inclusive definition describes religion as an object, practice, cause, or activity that somebody is completely devoted to or obsessed by. This explains why some are so obsessed to the point of killing in the name of religion. Religion viewed from this perspective offers an explanation why Karl Marx described it as the opium of the poor. It is so influential in deciding the political trend in any given society. Religion being an appeal to the mind for certain social values in respect to the Supreme Being has a grip on the reasoning and overt behaviour of every individual so colonized by the dictate of such religion. It is upon such values that the political engineering of such a people are tutored. Where the gods are made to listen to mortals only upon expensive sacrifices, the political leaders hearken to the yearning of the people upon bribery and other inducement polished in the name of "lobbying". Where the gods are appeased by much noise, in the form of prayers and songs, the leaders hearken only upon media pressure, international sanctions, local strikes and protests. These are the legacies and influences of religion on our political psyche. The influence of religion on the political trend in Africa needs not be over emphasized. The African (traditional) gods and deities are visible stones, woods, water and such other items, yet despite their perishable nature, they are revered and conferred with eternal status once they are elevated to the status of a god or deity – likewise in politics, once given any political power – King, Emir, Oba, Eze, Obong, Governor, President, etc – irrespective of the territorial size such elevated being begins to see himself as an eternal ruler of the people, constitutional or legal tenure notwithstanding. Where they are limited to a number of years they feel it should be limited only by life and not calendar years, even where it is allowed to be limited by life they feel it should be a dynasty where any surviving kindred irrespective of the wit level of such a person should be allowed to continue as long as he is of the lineage. These are some of the peculiar nature of religious influences in African politics.

On the whole, religious factor in African politics can be seen as that of interplay and influence. Each religious belief has its own fair share of influence on African politics, the traditional religious beliefs and practices are that of endurance and mutual coexistence with the total loyalty given to whoever rules. This is so because in the traditional religion it was believed that no one can ascend to any political responsibility except approved by the gods, therefore every act of the leader is believed to be guided by the dictate of the gods. But this is not so with the two most dominant foreign religions that holds sway in Africa. The Islamic religion has a great tendency of violently resolving political issues differently while on the other hand, Christianity is more or less indifferent in the circular politics; their hopes and treasures anchor in the life after this. From here, one can clearly see that the faith one professes has a great impact on the political event around such a person either as a ruler or follower.

Influence of Traditional African Religion on Politics

Since this work is narrowed down to a micro Africa – Nigeria – a country with over two hundred and fifty ethnic nationalities and three major languages. Since Nigeria has numerous religious beliefs, thus it can properly be a true representative or sample choice for the study of Africa as a whole. In the traditional Nigerian society the north is predominantly Hausa-Fulani while the east is Igbo and the west Yoruba. But despite their minor dialectical differences, these three major ethnic groups had their cultural values before the advent of foreign religious beliefs. In the east for example, shrines were built for the worship of deities and gods of respective areas of need such as the god of fertility, the god of thunder, the god harvest, the god of the sun, etc. The interconnectivity of religion and politics in Africa has never been in doubt. For instance, the ascension of most rulers or kings in traditional African societies has often times been divinely connected.

In this way, every elevation or coronation must be expressly approved by the gods of the land. In some cultures, the ruler should be able to trace his ancestry back to ages, that is, from the pre-historic time through oral history to the semi-gods in human form. A typical example is the Oduduwa dynasty of the Yoruba people of Nigeria and the Kabaka of the Kintu of Baganda people of Uganda. For every Ooni of Ife there must be an oral history connecting him with Oduduwa and once this link is established such an Ooni is believed to have the backing of the gods in the conduct of political affairs of the kingdom. In summary, the oracle must give approval of one's candidacy before he assumes any socio-political office.

Beside the ancestral approval on who should sit on the throne, it is also a common feature in African political landscape that some spiritual beings or entities are often invoked and provoked to get hold of certain situation for solution. It is on record that in 1896, Ambuya Nehanda – the spirit god of war in Zimbabwe – took hold of a peasant woman who led them to the popular "stone uprising" against the British. Though the woman was executed for leading the uprising, it was predicted that the spirit cannot be killed or subdued that it will resurrect in another form and this was proven right when in 1971, Ambuya Nehanda again entered another woman who was used by ZANU rebel forces for their struggle for independence. This is likened to the Bible story that when the spirit came upon Saul he also prophesied as a fulfillment of his acceptance by God to be the king of Israel. "And the spirit of God came mightily upon him, and he prophesied among them" (I Samuel 10:10).

In most cases, religion can produce political personalities as in the case of Ambuya Nehanda spirit in Zimbabwe or the spirit of the God of Israel in the case of Saul; it can also lead to the choice of a political leader as in the ancestral linage of Oduduwa in Nigeria or the appointment of a Sultan – the political and spiritual leader of the Hausa-Fulanis. African history books are full of tragic incidents of ambitious Europeans who ran into a collision course with African ancestral spirits. This shows that politics in Africa cannot be divorced of religious influences either in its traditional form or the contemporary approach.

Influence of Foreign Religions in African Politics

As pointed out earlier, politics and religion cannot be separated, each has a great influence on the other, and they are all addressing social issues bothering on social engineering for optimum realization of the human purpose on earth. Society cannot function except it is solidly anchored on sound moral foundation; this brings the issue encountered in African continent since the introduction of foreign religion and its attendant moral values to the fore. It exposes these foreign religions as the foremost causes of our political ineptitude. Before now, Kings and Queens who swore to the oath at the shrine lived an upright life in line with the oath of office they swore, this is no longer the case, our political leaders who are made to swear by the Bible or Koran have no morality in living up to the oath, since violation will not bring an instant condemnation or wrath by the Gods they swore to as it was in the (ancient) African traditional society, thus they are now at liberty to swear falsely.

The infiltration of African traditional values by Islam from the east through the Sahara to Nigeria and the injection of Christianity through the coast witnessed the pollution of our traditional political values and this has brought in its wake a new political order devoid of the old value and respect to sacred things and value for human lives. Christianity though acknowledges autocracy as exemplified in its numerous stories – the Davidic dynasty, the trinity of God, etc - seems to negate this concept at the same time as seen in its New Testament teachings as well as the practice of government bequeathed to Africans by the missionaries, this then leaves followers of these religions to practice whatever suits their fancy as they are at liberty to choose oligarchy or democracy since any can be supported with their faith as the basis. The Old Testament accepts dynasty but the New Testament negates it. The election of a new apostle to replace Judas, and the election of the first deacons by the evangelists are all pointers to the contemporary democratic tendencies – self seeking, table serving, food conscious opportunities for leaders - this is in aberration to the traditional African oligarchy where the gods decide who should be the king and such kingdom will continue in the kingship of the lineage till there is no male child left to continue.

With the introduction of Christianity, some of the traditional values are ignored, new kings are beginning to emerge not by choice of the gods or by hierarchical hereditary or moral uprightness and courage through military exploit, but by social status which in most cases are decided by financial influence (rightly or wrongly acquired) as such there is no name to protect in being unjust and unfair in their dealing with the people. This to a great extent does dampen the respect and functionality of such kingdoms and the operation/cooperation of citizens to the rulers. In other words, the religious practices of these new religions dictate the trend of events in our political culture and this trend is in advances with our rich and morally sound values. In our society today we are witnessing the "stealing" of human being as a means of livelihood. These stealing have no regard for age, gender or profession. Infants, adults, men, women of all walks of life and even human corpses are not spared. In whatever guise or form, kidnapping or trafficking is carried out in exchange for money. This shows the debased level of our religious and social values.

With the Bible instruction to the children of Israel on their way from slavery in Egypt to utterly destroy nations standing on their path to Canaan, "Ye shall utterly destroy all the places, wherein the nations which ye shall possess served their gods, upon the high ..." (Deuteronomy 12:2) the new era politician whose firm belief in the Bible sees their political opponents as religiously acceptable obstacle that must be crushed if "Canaan" (any political office they are eyeing) must be attained. These new teachings and the conflicts with the traditional way of leaving vengeance and political wars to the gods have successfully eroded our hitherto peaceful political succession culture. Islam is not faring any better in upturning African political structure and values. In the traditional African culture especially in the north and the west – Hausa/Fulani and Yoruba – the Emirs or Obas were appointed from the descendant of Usman dan Folio or Oduduwa it therefore means that if anyone is to emerge from other ancestry it must be through military conquest like Queen Amina's military exploit. But with the infiltration of Islam any one can emerge as a Sultan, Oba or Emir provided there is a connecting cord to the economic powers of the day. These religious influences have eroded our traditional political values and in its place planted a new culture which has leaved most African countries with more woes than kudos.

Recommendations and Conclusion

It is no longer news that before the advent of foreign missionaries to evangelize Africa with Christianity and Islam, most African communities had no experience of dare devil crimes such as armed robbery, kidnapping, rape, and shameless corrupt practices, not because the primitive Africans had no human tendencies to develop these anti social lifestyle but because the gods and their mood of operation gave instant judgement on people adjudged to be antisocial. Their judgements were not postponed till in the life after or to the denial of good life in havana or heaven. And again the rulers were ruling with the fear of the gods. In any event of misrule, the gods will visit the land with calamity that may even begin with the household of the king. The fear of being punished by the gods or the wrath of the gods rekindled upon the entire community was the order of the day as such governance was seen as a service not only to humanity but unto the gods.

The gods of these foreign religions do not understand our psyche, our body metabolism and the operations of the deities in each of our communities, because of inadequate knowledge of the operation of the people and the land in which they are made to operate, they lost the operational manual to function politically in Africa, our political rulers who are guided by this foreign manual lost touch with the values of the land and everything went comatose as we can see today. One then may wonder why Africans are still fraternizing with foreign religions that do not guarantee her social and political well being, the answer will be partly because it is more convenient to be selfish under the canopy of foreign religion, the price to pay in case of misdeed is less and at times may be covered up or subverted, whereas in the traditional society because of the eagle's eye of the gods a cover up of crime was difficult. When a nit wit is benefiting from a practice that affects the entire fabric of the social setting, he may be happy as a person not minding the general damage done to the society, this is because of his wit level which may furnish him of the happenings as being development, whereas when the entire community suffers he must certainly bear part of the sufferings, or is it not suffering when a ruler concentrate only in acquiring all the wealth he can while in public office to the detriment of the society only to be hunted later or even killed by that same excessive wealth? This is rampant in our society, through worthless children or fake business proposal which robs them most of the time of all the wealth they have acquired at the detriment of the society leading to health complications that eventually drains them of everything and even life.

It is high time we go back to our traditional values, operating more with spiritual laws than constitutional laws that can be subverted with cash and power. Having lived with these foreign religions for centuries and experienced their antagonistic tendencies because of their quest for territorial conquest with little or no moral values on social issues, then we should fashion out indigenous hybrid socio-political blue print. This hybrid social blue print is necessary because one cannot claim total acceptance of the traditional ways of life in this twenty first century and one cannot at the same time accept totally the rivalry and violent approaches to issues these foreign religions have bequeathed to us, therefore we need a blend of all the good qualities but starting with individual acceptance that there is a need for change of attitude if we must enjoy this social contract.

WORKS CITED

Collinson, Diane. *Fifty Major Philosophers: A Reference Guide.* New York: Croom Helm, 1992.

Enwerem, Iheanyi M. *A Dangerous Awakening: The Politicization of Religion in Nigeria.* Ibadan: IFRA, 1995.

Etuk, Udo. *Religion & Cultural Identity.* Ibadan: Hope Publications, 2002.

Folala, Toyin. *Violence in Nigeria: The Crisis of Religious Politics and Secular Ideologies*: New York: University of Rochester Press, 1998.

Kempkey, Kristian. "The Political Relevance of Religion in Africa: Case Study of Nigeria and Rwanda" in *Bologan Centre Journal of International Affairs.* Volume 12, Spring, 2009.

Laitin, David D. *Culture Politics and Religious Change among the Yoruba.* Chicargo: University of Chicago Press, 1986.

Nzeh, Casmiri Chinedu O. *From Clash to Dialogue of Religion: A Socio Ethical Analysis of the Christian – Islamic Tension in a Pluralistic Nigeria.* Berlin: Peter Lang Press, 2002.

Procter, Paul (Ed). *Longman Dictionary of Contemporary English.* New York: Longman, 1978.

Quist-Adade, Charles. Religious Intolerance in Africa: www//http:pewforum.org 2009.

Rachel, James. *The Element of Moral Philosophy.* New York: Mc Graw Hill, 2003.

Robinson, Mairi and George Davidson (Eds). *Chambers 21st-Century Dictionary.* Edinburgh: Chambers Harrap Publishers, 2004.

The Holy Bible: King James Version. Korea: Thomas Nelson, 1972.

Umotong, I. D. *Social & Political Philosophy: A Simplified Approach.* Uyo: Minder International Publishers, 2004.

CHAPTER 12

WOMEN PARTICIPATION IN AFRICAN POLITICS
By
SYLVESTER M. EKA, Ph.D.

Introduction

The exclusion of women from political processes in Africa can be traced back to the colonial time. As a result of colonization, the resurgence of women's movements demanding greater political participation started late in Africa. Women living in Northern Nigeria received suffrage as late as 1978. Nigeria even now has not created quotas for women in political party and national elections. In addition, Afia Zakia at the National Democratic Institute for International Affairs (NDI) lists the following as barriers impeding women's participation in Nigeria:

Money Politics: Many women do not have access to their own funds, and they depend on their partners or relatives for raising money.

Marginalization of Women in Political Parties: Women are marginalized, not promoted to leadership positions within their parties, not nominated by a party, etc. Political party leaders refuse to take female aspirants seriously and label the as cultural deviants.

Patriarchal Attitudes: Men sideline women among men in political parties.

Weak Women Movements: Absence of substantive women's movement and cohesiveness among women groups that claim supporting women's political participation.

Absence of Legal Force: Failure to enforce existing legal norms and international agreements. The domestication of CEDAW has failed in Nigeria and constitutional mandates have been ignored.

Lack of Government Support: Strong mandate and real power of the Ministry of Women Affairs. No meaningful support from public donors, etc. There was dismal failure of Nigerian women generally in politics, particularly during the first, second and ill-fated third republic. The reasons are that in the memory lane of the political history of Nigeria, women have not been successful in politics. Mrs. Funmilayo Ransome-Kuti, Mrs. Margaret Ekpo, amazons of our early steps, fought for and gained respect for women.

Political Participation: Conceptualization

Political participation includes the right to vote and actual voting behaviour, the candidacy, election, appointment of women at all levels of government and within party structures, women's participation in grassroot organizations such as neighbourhood groups, among others. Following government reported figures, the greatest change and perhaps the highest level of political participation for women appears to have occurred in the East European countries. The recruitment of women for office by parties in the communist bloc nations is particularly high at the local level of government. Major efforts have been made to educate women and bring them into the workforce. Government commitment to providing childcare and other social infrastructure has also helped to make the transition of women from home to work place easier (Oladapo, 1990:32). In Western European countries and the United States of America, governments generally have a national policy favouring equal opportunity for women. Laws supporting women's rights in voting, marriage, inheritance and employment have been enacted in the last 49 years.

Historical Perspective

Historical evidences are available to prove that the Nigerian women have for long been playing crucial role in political life of the country, and this has contributed in no small measure in shaping the political system of the nation. Margaret Ekpo began to participate in only male rallies with the support of her husband Albert into the beginning. She struggled to fit-in into the political mainstream, mostly dominated by male activists and politicians. She was among the few women in the early days of her political career. She observed the likes of Nnamdi Azikiwe, Awolowo, Mazi Mbonu Ojike, M. I. Okpara, Jaja Nwachukwu, and Malam Aminu Kano, etc, confront foreign-occupiers with fiery speeches relentlessly, putting their lives on the line; She aligned herself with Flora Azikiwe, wife of Nnamdi Azikiwe, Olufunmilayo Ransome-Kuti and others.

By early 1940s or mid 50s, she had made her mark. She was appointed to the House of Chiefs, alongside Olufunmilayo Ransome-Kuti of the Western and eastern Houses of Chiefs respectively. By 1964, she has been nominated to represent Nigeria at the Inter-Parliamentary Conference; represented Nigeria in World Women's International Domestic Federation Conference in 1963; served as Member of the Conference on constitutional matters in the 50s and 60s and served in many other capacities. She also assisted in forming many women organizations for example: Aba Market Woman Organization in Aba, Ngwa North; while the husband worked in the famous Aba General Hospital. Recalling her experience, she states: "I faced seven men in that election, including late Barrister Anyiam Osigwe. I won the election, thus becoming the first woman to be so elected in Aba. I held that post until 1967 when the war (Nigeria Civil War) broke out. I tabled many motions, argued, and got some of them passed into laws. My accomplishments paved the way for women who were interested in pursuing political careers, and motivated them to do so with greater confidence" (Ekponta, 2009:3).

Historical and monumental roles have been played by feminine giants such as Moremi of Ife, Queen Kambassa of Bonny, Mrs. Funmilayo Ransome-Kuti, Queen Amina of Zaria and Mrs.

Margaret Ekpo, among other amazons, whose impressive contributions, *inter alia*, directly or indirectly aided political advancement in Africa. African women are yet to be accorded their right of place in the political decision-making process. They appear to have struck tenaciously to their old role of political appendages and second fiddlers, rather than moving to the gladiatorial level of political participation characterized by standing for and holding elective public and party offices or positions. In 1957 during the pre-independence era of Nigeria, a couple of women political activists such as Mrs. Margaret Ekpo, Mrs. Janet Mokeliu and Ms. Young were members of the Eastern House of Assembly. Mrs. Funmilayo Ransome-Kuti, though not a fully-fledged politician, was a very strong force to reckon with in the politics of the Western Region. And Hajia Gambo Sawaba waged a fierce battle for the political and cultural emancipation of women in the north. One can say that women have always played variable political roles in Nigeria in spite of all the limitations and encumbrances. The first republic offered women very little politically.

There were two female senators then – Wuraola Esan and Beatrice Kwango, out of 36 members. These senators were nominated by their parties rather than being elected. Then came the politics of the second republic when Chief Franca Afegbua was elected the only woman senator out of 91, and in the ill-fated third republic, the country had three women Deputy Governors, Hajiya Ojikutu of Lagos State, Pamela Sadauku of Kaduna State and Mrs. Cecilia Ekpenyong of Cross River State. Only six women were elected into the House of Representatives out of its total membership of 589; similarly, in 1999 out of 1172 seats in State Houses of Assembly, women captured only 27 seats. The same gloomy picture also applied to the third tier government. Even in the 2005 Constitutional Conference, women again were relegated to the background. The composition of one woman out of the nineteen members' commission is unfair to womanhood and an act of marginalization and exploitation in the Constitutional Conference despite the enormous population of women which accounts for 58 percent of the total population of the nation.

New hope for women to participate in politics began to emerge with the transition to civil rule in 1979. The civilian administration of

Alhaji Shehu Shagari gave women some leverage in political participation. Not only were women involved actively once again in joining political parties, many women contested the elections. Some of the important outcome of the 1979 elections was the presentation of a woman, Mrs. Oyibo Odinamadu by the United Party of Nigeria (UPN) as the female Vice Presidential candidate (Pinkey, 2003). In the second republic, 1979-1983, there was 1 female senator out of 95, 11 females in House of Representatives out of 450 members, 3 women Ministers in Federal Cabinet. Few were in State House of Assembly but not one was a Local Government Chairman (Chairperson). The vibrancy, radicalism of womanhood and the progress so far soon eroded with the coming of the Buhari administration without any female cabinet member. Yet the military regimes which Nigerians experienced for more than two decades had not accorded women their due recognition in the scheme of things. In the military government, there were no women in the Provisional Ruling Council of State and no woman Governor or Administrator.

Nigeria is unlike Britain where a woman was once at the helm of affairs for eight years, Mrs Margaret Thatcher, the Iron-lady of Britain and Prime Minister. Other women who were once the head of governments in their respective nations, include former Prime Minister Golda Meir of Israel, Indira Ghandi of India, Benazir Bhutto was the Prime Minister of Pakistan, Mrs. Chamarro of Nicaragua's Daniel Ortega, Prime Minister of Turkey and former President Corazon Aquino of the Philippines. A look at these national leaders reveals that the Nigerian women are yet to make any appreciable inroad into the male-dominated political scene because of gross misconception of her role in politics, though the Nigerian woman is by far more handicapped. Some of these handicaps include child-caring, family problems, cultural and religious barriers, financial handicap, political insults, violence and other murky practices that pervade Nigerian politics. Indeed tradition and religion pose as greatest problem to women participation in politics in Nigeria. Today, women are participating more actively in political issues than ever before, due to political re-awakening and awareness. More often than not, they are besieged with challenges of which discrimination is rifer. Majority of the men more on chauvinistic disposition are preoccupied with the notion that decision making is exclusively for the men folk while women are to be instructed on what to do. Despite the difficulties faced by women in politics, they continue with their political ambition, contributing enormously to the political and national development in their own way. Women over the years could be said to have recorded some measure of appreciable political achievement in other political fields of endeavours, meeting their political objectives with limited support and resources at their disposal. The Babangida era marked a turning point in the history of women struggle in Nigeria; Maryam Babangida institutionalized the office of the First Lady in 1987. She became the first working First Lady and launched the "Better Life for Rural Women" programme. Abubakar's transition in respect of women's elective positions shows: 3 female out of 109 senators, 12 females out of 360 State Houses of Representative members, 12 females out of 990 State House of Assembly members, 143 females out of 8810 L. G. Councilors, 9 females out of 774 L. G. Chairmen. In the 1999 general elections, 27 million women registered out of 47 million registered voters, which is about seventy-five percent of the total voters but only 1.6% of them won the elections. Women membership of political parties stood at five percent in 1999, female party executive members were seven percent, and only eight percent women qualified as party delegates. Other notable women who were appointed into political positions are Mrs. Ngozi Okonjo-Iweala, Mrs. Obi Ezekwesili, and Prof. Dora Akunyili.

Women Representation and Participation

There are myriads of women in politics even presently that have done very well and are still performing excellently well. In Nigeria the representation of women in government though has improved than before, is still very low compared to what obtains in other nations of the world particularly in the developed nations. The representation of women in the past 2003 elections was poor. Only 3 women: Daisy Danjuma, Gbemisola Saraki-Fowora, Mrs. Iyabo Anishilowo, of the 109 members Senate, while 21: Abike Dabiri, Azuma Namadi Debeji, Aonodona Sharon Adzuana, Binta Garba-Koji, Fanta Baba Shehu and others were elected out of the 360 member lower House of Representatives. As it were, the number of serving female ministers is still few.

Presently, there is no significant improvement in the number of women holding elective and appointive political positions in the country vis-à-vis their men, despite increased enlightenment campaigns by various women organizations at various levels as well as commendable efforts by the federal government under the leadership of President Olusegun Obasanjo and some state Governors to appoint more women into some key political offices. Notwithstanding, it is appalling that at this stage of Nigeria's democratic development, Mrs. Virgy Etiaba of Anambra State became the first female Governor in Nigeria in 2006 though in controversial circumstances. Alapiki (2004) makes a presentation of "political facts" about Nigeria with respect to women representation in public offices and decision making organs at various levels of government as follows:

i. Women constitute 49.7% of the total Nigerian population (according to the controversial 1991 population census report).
ii. In the first republic, there were two female senators (Wuraola Esan and Beatrice Kwango) out of 36 senate members, none out of 312 members out of the Federal House of Representative, and none in the Federal Cabinet. The two female senators were nominated by their parties rather than being elected.
iii. There were only 5 women out of 250 members of the Constituent Assembly that debated the draft Constitution of 1979.
iv. Women were said to make up 60% of the electorates. However in 1979, there was not a single woman presidential candidate, no woman contested for governorship in all the 19 states of the federation.
v. Of the 4 women who contested for positions in the upper House of Senate in 1979, none won.
vi. In 1983, there was only one woman member in the 91 member senate in the person of Chief (Mrs.) Franca Afegbua.
vii. In 1990, out of 1, 297 local govenment positions nation-wide, women won only 206, i.e. 15% of seats available.

viii. In 1992 there was only one woman in the 91 member Senate, and only 12 women out of 638 (1.e. 1.8%) in the House of Representatives.

ix. In the aborted third republic, there were three women deputy governors out of 30 states of the federation. They were Hajiya Ojikutu of Lagos State, Pamela Sadauku of Kaduna State and Mrs. Cecilia Ekpenyong of Cross River State.

ix. Out of every 100 Nigerian in paid labour, there are 25 women.

Nigerian women in the contemporary period have realized the need to participate more actively in politics. This need to participate derives from the understanding that politics is about the competition for the control of the public policy-making process. This control is achieved by persons and groups of persons through a process of participation which gets them to leadership positions. This need has cultivated in women a high sense of responsibility toward the minimal participatory level of voting on election days. Omoruyi captures these changing trends thus:

> At the level of partisan political involvement which induces the lower forms of political participation such as voting, Nigerian women cannot be said to be powerless...from the December 1990 local government elections, female voter turn-out usually matched the male in a ratio of 50:50. In many cases, especially in the rural locations in fact it tends to exceed by a proportion of about 60:40 percent (1992: 14).

It suggests that the stage has been prepared for Nigerian women to emerge in the Nigerian political arena. Since independence, there has been a remarkable improvement in women's political activities. Women education has been considerably improved and their economic role has undergone a radical change as they are now much better placed then than before. Their organizations have increased in number and the Nigerian government has a very high opinion of what has been taken to increase women participation in decision making positions. Due to deliberate government policy, women have been appointed into strategic policy-making positions such as deputy governors, chairmanship of corporations, and chief executive

African Political Philosophy

of public institutions and head of ministerial departments (Okwuosa, 1994). The activities of a host of women organizations have added impetus to these developments. These associations include the National Council of Women's Society (NCWS), National Association of Women Journalists (NAWOJ), Women in Nigerian (WIN), and Better Life Programme for Rural Dwellers (BLP).

The Challenges of Nigerian Women Participation in Politics

Traditional and Socio-Cultural Challenges: A number of traditional and socio-political constraints impede the successful participation of Nigerian women in democracy and the various democratization processes initiated by different governments in the country. Such constraints include excessive dependence of women on their husbands for decisions, early marriages and the confinement of women in purdah, which is common among the Moslems. Early marriages impose severe matrimonial responsibilities on women and deny them the opportunity of developing themselves intellectually, psychologically, spiritually and politically for the challenges of life; confinement in purdah is a devaluation of the status of women and offers Moslem women little or no opportunity to participate in the democratic process.

Patrilinial Descent: Other related constraints are the patrilinial system of descent whereby the man is the head of the family; widowhood; inadequate women role-models; the traditional perception of division of labour between women and men which provides the rationalization that women's role is that of child-bearing and managing the kitchen and related domestic affairs, as well as male chauvinism, especially where some men do not see anything good in women. Considering this sentiment, Eskor Toyo has argued that: it is impossible for a chauvinist to be a genuine democrat" (Pinkney, 1993:72).

Education: Despite the resourcefulness of women in Nigeria, a significant proportion of them are illiterates. Accordingly, Oruwari (1996:22) observed that a research conducted in 1990 showed that "only about 10% of Nigerian women are literate". Illiteracy inhibits the effective participation of women in democracy. This is because poor or lack of education on the part of women poses implications for effective political awareness, consciousness, enlightenment, mobilization, activation and democracy. No country can hope to place itself on the path of a stable democratic foundation, progress, sustainable development and greatness without enhanced access to the benefits and opportunities provided by education and the integration of women into the mainstream of its education system.

The Military: The domination of governance by the military in Nigeria constituted a major obstacle to the establishment of an enduring democracy in the country. Out of 50 years of Nigeria's "quasi-political independence", the military had misruled and de-democratized Nigeria for 28 years, without providing the enabling environment, favourable and objective conditions for democracy to flourish in the country. The inclemence of political environment created by the military partly denied Nigerian women (and men) the opportunity to participate in making relevant inputs towards the success of the democratic project.

The Challenge of Divine Nature of Women: By virtue of their sex, women are generally regarded as a frail with weak emotional disposition. They could hardly withstand the forceful and sophisticated manipulative and maneuvering tendencies of men in the struggle for political power, which in all magnifications negate the principles of democratic selection.

Challenges of Poverty, Money Politics and Democratic Space: Kalagbor (2007), citing Arikpo (2005), notes that poverty is a historical process of eliminating people from decision making machinery is manifested in hunger, lack of money, shelter, poor education. In Nigerian context it becomes a euphemism for pervasion of democracy against women.

Women Participation in Politics of Akwa Ibom State

Though those traditional barriers of culture, marriage, and others are there against women in Nigeria and Africa, the turn of events for women participation in politics in Nigeria, favour Akwa Ibom State. In 1999, Iquo Inyang Minimah was elected into Federal House of Representatives and Mrs. Ufot Ekaette was a Senator in the National Assembly. The wife of Governor Duke and now Mrs. Akpabio is occupying position of First lady with portfolios. Since the Abacha's creation of the Ministry of Women Affairs, women usually are appointed Commissioners and Ministers. According to *This Day Newspaper* of June 14 1999, Mrs. Eme Essien and Mrs. Arit Ekpo were appointed Commissioners in Akwa Ibom State. Writing on the "Sheltering the women of Akwa Ibom", Iniobong Ekponta (2009) explains that, Ekaette Akpabio, wife of Governor Akpabio of Akwa Ibom State exhibited her political power in her Shelter Support Programme (SSP) and the Family Life Enhancement Initiative (FLEI), where many lives of indigent people have been touched. However, Akwa Ibom State remains one state that has not accorded women the level of recognition women receive in other States. At the Federal level too, the Akwa Ibom State is least recognized in Federal appointments to women. As reported in the Vanguard of January 12, 2010, Governor Theodore Orji of Abia State leads Ekwunife's campaign. Mrs. Uche Ekwunife is (PPA) Progressive Peoples Alliance, Anambra State Governorship Candidate. Also the Committee of Elders of Anambra State (PPA) tips Mrs. Ekwunife and says, that our deep conviction is that this woman of courage through consistent hard work and through grassroots mobilization has confounded opponents. Here is the only woman in a male dominated contest who has given due respect to all including unkind opponents. This is the kind of support we expect women to receive in Akwa Ibom State, just as women should be courageous and work hard.

Interestingly as Kalagbor (2007) noted, as a radical departure from the past, between 1999 and 2007, Nigeria under President Olusegun Obasanjo has witnessed an increase in the number of women holding both elective and appointive political offices. Regrettably, all the efforts are cosmetic and a mere palliative since a significant proportion of Nigerian women are yet to be active in the democratic and democratization processes in Nigeria even in Akwa Ibom State. Between 1999 and 2008 only 2 women have been appointed Commissioners in Akwa Ibom State. They were Mrs. Eme Essien and Mrs. Arit Etim Ekpo.

Recommendations

i. Men and particularly husbands in Akwa Ibom should support their wives as Dr. John Ekpo supported Margaret Ekpo.
ii. A coalition of women organizations and groups should come together to raise support aimed at providing the requisite financial and technical assistance to women elective positions.
iii. There should be legislations to create quotas for women political offices in respect to the Beijing Declaration of 1995.
iv. Women should acquire more education and build confidence to contest elections.

Conclusion

This work dealt with women participation in African politics using Nigeria as a case study. The work also revealed that several forces of tradition, religion, finance, etc, hinder women participation in Nigerian politics. The work also exposed that right from the colonial period, Nigerian women have been very vibrant and can perform creditably if given the opportunity to participate with their male counterparts. The Shagari administration gave women new hope to participate in politics and hold high public offices. The military administration of Gen. Babangida also recognized women and appointed them into public offices. From 1999, the Olusegun Obasanjo civilian administration gave women more hope. In Akwa Ibom State, women also participated in voting and also occupied elective positions. However, women participation is generally less than expected. The work posits that women should try to acquire more education and build up more confidence to compete with their male counterparts.

Presently in Nigeria, women occupy elective and appointive positions as follows: Deputy Governor of Lagos State – Princess Sarah Adebisi-Sossan; Deputy Governor of Osun State – Erelu Olusola Obada; Deputy Governor of Plateau State – Dr. Paulin Tallen; Acting Director General, Securities and Exchange Commission – Mrs. Daisy Ekineh; Senator Mrs. Folashade Bent;

Chief Mrs. Senator Joy Emordi, Chairman, Senate Committee on Education; Abike Dabiri-Erewa, Member, House of Representatives; Mrs. Hairat Aderinsola balogun – Attorney General and former Commissioner for Justice, Lagos State; Minister of State, Water Resources, Mrs. Felicia Njeze and then full-fledged Minister, Ministry of Aviation; Former Director General of Due Process Office – Mrs. Nennadi Usman; Prof. Ndi Okereke Onyieku – Director General, Nigerian Stock Exchange; Mrs. Arinze Maduekwe – Director, NAFDAC; Dr. Ngeri Benebo –Director General (NESREA); Mrs. Belema Osibodu – Head, Public Affairs, DPR; Dr. Ada Okwuosa – Commissioner for Administration and Finance, ECOWAS Commission, Abuja; Minister of State for Works – Mrs. Grace Ekpenhire; Ondo State Commissioner for Women Affairs, Mrs. Bukola Tenabe; Prof. Joy Ogwu – Chairman, Senate Committee on Education; Mrs. Farida Waziri – EFCC Chairman. Others are Prof Dora Akunyili, Minister for Information and Communication; Delta State Commissioner for Youths – Mrs. Ishola Williams; Plateau State Commissioner for Education – Prof. Angela Miri; Executive Assistant to Delta State Governor on Micro Credit – Dr. Anthonia Ashiedu; Edo State Benin Zonal Head of National Agency for the Prohibition of Traffic in Persons Matters - Mrs. Adefinke Abiodun; Special Adviser to Lagos State Governor on Religious Matters – Mrs. Adefunmilayo Akitoye-Braimoh; Mrs. Juliet Oti Asoba - Delta State Commissioner for Education; Kano State Commissioner for Women Affairs – Hajiya Maimuna Kabir Khalil, Obong Rita Akpan – former Minster for Women Affairs; Akwa Ibom State Commissioner for Women Affairs – Hon. Mrs. Eunice Thompson; Hon. Dr. Louisa Ukpe, former Akwa Ibom State Commissioner for Health; Mrs. Akon Eyakenyi, former Akwa Ibom State Commissioner for Commerce and Industry; Barr. Valerie Ebe, former Akwa Ibom State Commissioner for Tourism and Chief Senator (Mrs.) Helen Esuene, representing Eket Senatorial District of Akwa Ibom State.

WORKS CITED

Arikpo, M. *Poverty and the Democratic Process: The New Face of Mass Poverty in Nigeria.* Port Harcourt: Uniport Press, 1995.

Anya, Okeke. "Women and Politics in Nigeria's Fourth Republic" in *Codesria Bulletin*. No. 4, 2001.

Alapiki, H. *Politics and Governance in Nigeria*. Port Harcourt: Amethyst Publishers, 2004.

Ekponta, Iniobong. Sheltering the Women of Akwa Ibom in *News Extra*. December 14, 2009.

Kalagbor, S. B. "Women and the Democratic Project in Nigeria; Signposts to Political Empowerment" in *Journal of General Studies*. Vol.1, 2007.

Mofe-Damijo, Mee. "The Rising Profile of Nigerian Women" in *Classique Magazine*, Lagos, 1990.

Oganwu, P. I. "Nigerian Women in Politics: Traditional and Religious Constraints" in Yomi Oruwari (Ed). *Women Development and the Nigerian Environment*. Ibadan: Vanatage Publishers, 1996.

Oldepo, O. (Ed). "Women in Nigeria: The Political Amazones" in *Newswatch Magazine*, Lagos, 1990.

Okwuosa, A. C. "Women in the Democratization Process in Nigeria: Gains and Limitations" in Omoruyi, O., Schlosser, D. B., Samba, A. and Okwuosa, A. (Eds). *Democratization in Africa: Nigerian Perspectives*. Abuja: CDS Bulletin, 1994.

Omoruyi, O. "Empowerment of Women through the Electoral Process" in *Abuja: CDS Bulletin*, 1992.

Pinkney, Robert. *Democracy in the Third World*. Oxford: OUP, 1993.

Umunnah, Carlisle U. O. "Margaret Ekpo: An Agent of Change (1914 – 2004)' in *Biafra-Nigerian World Magazine*, September 27, 2006.

Uchendu, P. K. *The Role of Nigerian Women in Politics*. Enugu: Fourth Dimension Publishers, 1993.

CHAPTER 13

THE CHURCH AND AFRICAN POLITICAL DEVELOPMENT
By
GABRIEL E. IDANG, Ph.D.
&
UDEME U. AFIA

Introduction

Holistic development within the context of this paper is the complete transformation of a person or group of persons to what God intends that person or group of persons to be. Appropriate philosophical reflections on the nature and destiny of the universe in general and man in particular would certainly point to God as the creator, owner and sustainer of everything whether physical or spiritual, particular or universal, concrete or abstract in its entirety. This is because philosophy itself is a holistic discipline that is foundational and fundamental in man's quest for reality, knowledge and value in all existential matters without exception. The church has its primary and ultimate mission, the realization of holistic development for the individual in particular and the society in general. The aim of this paper as the title suggests, is an examination of the role of the church in African political development.

St. Augustine, a Platonist philosopher and the greatest father of the church based his doctrine on God's plan and purpose and he was the one who declared in his Confessions that God has made us for Himself, and our hearts become restless until they rest in God. St. Augustine, like the Psalmist, must have felt some kind of surging within, a desire to know the truth. He probably must have wanted more material things, greater health and more harmony and security, but his yearning seems to have arisen higher above materialism. And he must have tried to find satisfaction of desire in all sorts of ways, to learn the great truth which is the fact that there is one desire and one fulfillment which brighten to all eternity. This is, unarguably, the attainment of holistic development, that is, the complete transformation of a person or a group of persons to what God intends the person or group of persons to be. And the fundamental question is: what is God's intention for man in particular and the world as a whole? To this question, many answers can be given, from the theological viewpoint as well as from the philosophical perspective as we shall see. Matters concerning development have been stated quite often and stressed by all and sundry. Man, from infancy to adulthood passes through stages of development. Each stage of development is influenced and enhanced by one thing or the other. Parents, guardians, churches, schools, and the society at large play various roles in developmental process of the person. And the ultimate aim of all developmental processes is the realization of the *summum bonum*, which is the highest good. And man is said to achieve this once he attains holistic development. The church has the onerous role to play in the task of leading people to holistic development. This is because the church is the foremost vehicle which God uses in actualizing is intentions for man.

When one considers the widespread acceptance that the Christian religion enjoys in both the developed and the developing world, we realize that it cannot be ignored if holistic development is to be attained. With its system of moral instruction which are routinely given whenever Christians are gathered, and its emphasis on such virtues as meekness, tolerance, humility, self-denial, and such values as love, peace, faithfulness and so on, it appears that the church is indeed central to the holistic development impetus of the society.

Very rarely do we consider the church as a very potent social institution that is capable of righting the wrongs and transforming individuals in the society from the darkness of moral laxity to the true light of moral development. Perhaps, our conceptions of development are often partial. This is why whenever the word "development" is mentioned; some immediately turn their attention to the availability or unavailability of state-of-the-art infrastructure and the social amenities. There is the tendency to conceive of development as the availability of modern gadgets and latest technological innovations or as the strengthening of political institutions and democratic processes. While these and other conceptions constitute one aspect of development or another, they are but a partial conception of development when looked at individually. This is why holistic development is a constellation of many aspects of development since development is itself a many-sided process. Holistic development as we shall see later is a total development that adequately takes care of man's material as well as his spiritual needs. Since man has a spiritual dimension, it can be inferred that any attempt at his development that fails to capture this dimension cannot be complete. It is in the light of this, that we want to examine the role of the church in holistic development. Let us see what the church is.

What is the Church?

Christian religious devotees often see the church as a "called out people", people of diverse backgrounds, professions, and callings who have heeded to the call of salvation and have given their lives to Christ". It is a gathering of Christians who are supposed to be Christ-like in thought, feelings and actions. Umoh (19) sees the church (Greek *ekklesia*) "as a religious organization that claims to include most or all members of the society as well as a unique legitimacy and has a positive relationship to the society". He further notes that the church is conservative in the sense that it does not challenge the leaders and policies of the government in power, but the Christian church, in fact, has the prophetic mission which includes challenging leaders who go astray. With emphasis on righteous living as the only condition to secure eternal bliss in the life hereafter, Christians are expected to separate themselves from the world (unbelievers) while trying as much as they can to take the goodnews of salvation to as many unbelievers as they can. This is what Christians see as the "great commission" – the obligation to persuade sinners to accept Christ and follow Him as members of a church.

The emphasis on the person as the most important variable in our understanding of the meaning of the church is meant to dispel the tendency to see the church entirely as the building or meeting place where Christians go to worship. While in ordinary parlance, the word "church" is literally used to refer to the place of worship.

Theologians and Christians often see the meaning of "church" as going beyond the physical structure to include the worshippers themselves as members of the church. It is believed that when our Lord Jesus Christ said to His disciple, Peter, "Thou art Peter and upon this rock I will build my church; and the gates of hell shall not prevail against it" (Matthew 16:18), He was not referring to the physical common place building or structure. The sense which our Lord Jesus Christ wants us to understand this passage is that He saw in Peter, the qualities that made him capable of leading the body of early Christians. Also, when talking about the gates of hell not prevailing against the church, Jesus Christ was not referring to the building and place of worship. To think in that direction would mean to confuse two entirely different categories since "hell" as it is widely conceived in Christendom is a prepared place of eternal doom and cannot be located, pointed at and verified physically the same way we can locate, point at and verify the church as a place of worship.

The above clarification is very necessary when we consider the central place it occupies in this work. Since we intend to see the role of the church in holistic development, we cannot really achieve this aim if we overlook a conceptual clarification of an important aspect of our work as the true meaning of the word "church". A distinction has been drawn between the local and the universal church. While the local church simply refers to any particular church that the Christian worships and fulfils his religious rites and obligations, the universal church is made up of all righteous living Christians. While the local churches are marked by doctrinal differences, the universal church is to be seen as a conglomeration of all the local churches. The universal church is the church that our Lord Jesus Christ will meet with in His second coming, the world over. The universal church signifies the underlying unity in the face of doctrinal diversity – the fact that Jesus Christ is not just interested in any particular denomination but in righteous Christians the world over, brings harmony into the otherwise discordant doctrinal tunes that various churches of our time seem to be playing. On careful consideration, we see that the church has enormous functions that it fulfils in our society. Let us consider some of them

The Functions of the Church

The functions of the church are enormous. One that readily comes to mind is the moral development of the society. Are we saying that a man, for instance, cannot be moral unless he is a Christian religious devotee? No, not at all. It is very possible that one can believe in the law of karma; that we will always pay for the wrongs we do some way, some how and this principle can indeed restrain one from doing evil and encourage him to do good without necessarily committing him to be a devoted Christian. But we know that since the arrival of Christianity on our shores in the 19th century, it has enjoyed wide acceptance to the extent that recent researches have revealed that we are the most religious people in the world. Hardly would one walk through a street in the urban, semi-urban and even rural areas without seeing a church. The irony however, is that the rise in number of churches has not translated to a rise in the level of our moral development at least, not in the lines we expected. It is this consideration that makes Jakonda (1) to ask "what has caused this situation in a continent where Christianity is fast growing? Why is it that Christian values have not affected much Africa for the better?" Questions such as these are pointers to the fact that we expected widespread acceptance of Christianity in Africa to translate into moral upliftment that would in turn, serve as the conscience that constantly regulates our behaviour both in private and public life. It is the function of the church to serve as an institution of moral control through the moral instruction it gives to its worshippers.

What appears to be the most primary, most basic function of the church is what we may call the "socio-religious function". We see that religion is one of the most powerful phenomena in human life that cannot be ignored. It is not out of place to say that there is no other phenomenon which moulds and controls man's life as much as religion does. Religion is very close to the heart and affection of people the world over. This is why it is common to see that it engenders feelings of warmth, brotherhood and trust especially between individuals that share the same faith. The church is where the Christian finds fulfillment of his religious life. He goes into the church, sings, dances, prays, fellowships, shares and feels a sense of belonging in the midst of his brethren. He receives 'messages' from preachers that either leave him happy and excited or guilty and sober. The worship sessions can be very breath-taking that the Christian would leave the church happy and satisfied that he has given reverence to who reverence is due. Sometimes we may see a grown up man breaks into tears and weep like a child or he may be speaking a language that no other person understands but the speaker himself. These and other religious experiences are associated more with the church. This is why we can say without fear of contradiction that the church fulfills the socio-religious function for Christians. We are sure to find many other functions of the church if we dig deeper, but let us now turn our attention to the question of holistic development and see what it is about since this is more central to our discourse.

What is Holistic Development?

Development theorists have defined 'development' in various ways. While some see it as an overall progress, others see it as a gradual growth of a thing in the sense of its being stronger or more advanced. It is in this sense that we can meaningfully talk of economic, political, social, cultural, educational, moral and spiritual development. This shows that development can be seen in different dimensions and dealt with in different respects. Walter Rodney (9-10) was right when he wrote that "development is a many-sided process". A nation can be considered 'developed' when she is able to improve the quality of life of its inhabitants. Lower cost of living, industrialization, economic stability, political stability, sound system of education, availability of gainful employment, social security for the disadvantaged and so on are some of the indices that distinguish the developed from the developing nations of the world. Development is both a physical reality and a state of mind which society has through some combination of social, economic and institutional processes, secured the means of obtaining better life (Enoh, 88). The most remarkable thing about this definition is that it sees development as a physical reality and also as a state of mind. This means that apart from the improved social amenities and state-of-the-art infrastructure that can be seen in the developed nations, development can also be mental and spiritual. This brings us to asking the question "how can development be holistic?" There have been complains from many quarters about the backward drift in our development impetus. Some ponder and wonder about what should be at the centre of our strive for development, vitiating the efforts we make at development. Lack of development spills over and is evident in everything around us. Etuk captures this succinctly when he writes that:

> Each successive administration in the country leaves us worse and poorer than where it met us and I mean "worse" in an all round sense in employment opportunities, in job creation, in industrialization, in the provision of infrastructure, in housing and accommodation, in food adequatecy, in healthcare delivery, in education (13).

This shows that in the different aspects of our social life, the rot, decay and breakdown are evident. At this point, development ought to go holistic and become concerned with the development of an aspect of the whole. Let us not be occupied with the parts of the problem to the extent that we lose sight of the unity and the interrelatedness to the whole. At the individual level, just as we need to have food, shelter and clothing, we must not ignore the needs of the mind, the mental and the spiritual and immaterial dimensions of our existence. This is where we see the church playing an enormous role – whenever we talk of development in a holistic sense. Let us throw more light on holistic development with this example of recent development in the medical practice. Before now, medical practice was all about curing of physical ailments. But the breakdown which goes with physical ailments penetrates and affects the ailing patient as a whole and this is why illness and wellness with regards to the human person should be treated as a whole. The human person is made up of three elements – the body, mind and spirit and his illness cannot be completely tackled if we ignore other realities which are different aspects of his makeup for just one of them – the body. In their *Love and Health*, Etuk and Etuk (20) write that "there has been a concern even within the medical practice to expand the notion of health beyond the mere healing of physical infirmities or ailments to take in what is known as wholeness, or holistic health-care" This explains why, for the Christians, one may be healed of a physical ailment miraculously, but whether the person is 'saved' is another issue altogether. Let us look at the theological perspective of holistic development.

Theological Perspective of Holistic Development

In the theological context, Jakonda (49) sees holistic development as "the transformation of a people to what God intends them to be". This is why holistic development should be of concern to the church and all Christians just as it is to the governments and many non-religious organizations. A look at the theological perspective of holistic development yields a very important insight because the church has often narrowly seen its role as limited to that of spiritual work to the neglect of the physical needs and concerns of the people and the society. Jakonda writes again:

> The scriptures however, from Genesis to Revelation, show that God is holistic and does not dichotomize His action as has been the case with much of His church. The church therefore should have a holistic approach to the world towards redeeming it to the kingdom of God. The whole universe belongs to God and we should not simply dichotomize it into spiritual and physical and assigning unto God, only the former and leaving then latter unto Satan. This is a wrong theological reflection (49).

There is need for a holistic theological education that will imbue those that pass through it with the ability to minister to al people, in all aspects of the lives of families, communities and congregation. Dickson (205), for instance, observes that 'theological training in Africa has resulted in the social background into which they had been born and into which they work'. To make for holistic development, church leaders need to be trained in ways that will make them to properly grasp and understand what it means when we say that there is totality in development. The church should approach holistic development in a way that is comprehensible to the church members. It should seek ways of catering for both the spiritual and physical needs of its members since man although he has a physical body that has needs, also has a spiritual dimension. In seeking to uplift man, it is proper for us to take adequate steps to cater for his spiritual needs, his physical needs and his soul salvation. Anything short of this would represent a narrow, partial and inadequate solution to the problem that man faces.

Technologies in Holistic Development

Technology is often seen as the application of science and other forms of organized body of knowledge towards the solution of practical problems. This view is very adequate because technology is a problem-solving process developed by man to control his environment, harness its resources and produce goods and services with the goal of improving the quality of human life. This distinction between technology and science apart from others is that science together with its rise and development can be traced to the 16th century, whereas technology is much older than Western science and it is as old as man himself.

Since man has been solving the practical problems he faces from time immemorial, then technology is as old as man himself. The modern state-of-the-art products of technology is possible because technology has been perfected and gradually updated – latest inventions and innovations of science's partnership with technology have been responsible for the exponential growth and advancement in the products and process of science and technology all for the good of humanity. By now may be wondering what is the place of technology in holistic development? But the answer to this question can be made obvious when we consider the debate whether technology is serving man or has assumed the role of his master. When we look at the gains we see from present day information and communication technology together with all other technological innovations that have improved the quality of human life significantly from where it was even fifty years ago, we may be tempted to see technology as the greatest blessing that has happened to mankind. But when we consider that technology has in some important respects, made man more miserable than he would have been we see that technology is a mixed blessing. If there is another world war, it would be fought with weapons of mass destruction that weaponry technology has placed within man's reach and the world would be obliterated in a few hours. Information technology has come with the upsurge in computer based crimes such as cyber pornography, cyber terrorism, fraud and so on. Medical biotechnology has shown an unending desire to tinker with human cells and produce human clones that would be employed by industries seeking larger work force, whereas the unemployment index is on the increase.

The question has arisen whether mankind would be ready to treat the clone with the same dignity he would give fellow man since the clones are bound to have feelings and seek to express themselves just like any normal human being. Questions like these have made interested scholars to advocate for a technology with a humanistic face. Appropriate technology should be one that is holistic. Moral considerations need to be brought to bear on technology in order to make it saner and free technology from constituting a threat to national and international peace. Since technological innovations are bound to affect the Christian and the church either positively or negatively, the church does not need to keep silent on giving religious and moral insights on technologies that tend to overlook holistic development. This is why we want to consider the role of the church in holistic development. This is why we want to consider the role of the church in holistic development.

The Church and Development

When we consider the fact that all Christians are also members of either one society or another and also when we consider the wider acceptance that the Christian religion has with particular reference to Africa, it cannot be denied that the church has an enormous role to play in the holistic development of the human society. Even though the prevalence of churches has not translated into an ethical or moral revolution along the lines we expect, this goes on to show that majority of the churches we see, have lost sight of the virtues that our Lord Jesus Christ taught and lived out while he was here on earth some 2000 years ago. In my part of Africa, some churches are more like social gatherings where the filthy rich go to church every Sunday to show their affluence and make a shameful display of ill-gotten wealth. It is the rich who fund church projects that receive special 'anointing-filled' prayers of bountiful blessings from some preachers who have passion for material development than they do for moral and spiritual development. To such preachers, the morale of the true Biblical story of the widow's mite does not make meaning. There is an urgent need for today's church to assert itself and perform its role which entails its catering for the spiritual needs of man which at the same time, doing what it can, in the area of his material needs. The brotherly love, the observed self control, humility and moderation in action and speech that made early believers to be called Christians in Antioch should be brought back. The role of the church in holistic development can be discerned in individual development teaching, intercession, participation in community development, participation in politics, reconciliation and peace making, and the church and the kingdom of God. Let us discuss these points piece-meal.

Individual Development

It is the place of the church to ensure that their members become Christ-like in both their private and public lives. Since religion is very close to the heart and affection of the religious devotee, the church should use this advantage to place emphasis on the righteous living of its members. The holistic development of any human society is a sum-total of the holistic development index of the members of such a society. But rather than concentrate on developing people and preparing them for an enhanced social and spiritual life, many churches have selfishly chosen to strengthen the church as a social institution. Jakonda (135) is not at home with this at all. He complains that 'very often many churches have equated development to putting up structures or projects instead of focusing on the people. Thus, structures or projects are developed and after many years of the existence of these structures, the people have remained the same'.

If all Christians that worship in churches are true to their name, if they were to seek righteousness and heed the call of reason to desist from evil, our society would be better and more morally developed. It is the failure of the church and its members to be true to their calling that makes the sad observation that the crimes perpetuated in the society today, are done by persons who claim to be Christians. Some Christians in Africa remain faithful for as long as the problems of life do not show up. They reconsider their Christian status and give to Caesar that is Caesar's. Whenever calamity strikes as in sickness or death of a loved one, we see such ceremonial Christians behave in ways that are contrary to every Christian doctrine – some go diabolical.

Teaching

The church has a role to play in teaching the gospel. And the gospel is understood to mean the good news declared to man, as a way of salvation. For Etuk, Jesus' idea of salvation was not to give temporary relief from sufferings, want or persecution but to save man from sin and eternal damnation for eternal life (*The New Humanism*, 155), Jesus of Nazareth, the son of God is the major proponent and source of this gospel otherwise known as the Good News. This explains why Etuk says, in his *The New Humanism* that:

> this whole gospel is seen as coming not from man but from the realm of the supernatural and the hope it holds before man is not the hope of a better organized society guided by science and the principles of democracy here in this present world. Rather its abiding hope is the hope of eternal life in heaven. The naturalist and the materialist may hold such beliefs in contempt. Nevertheless they remain the solid foundation on which men have built their lives here, and the one sure thing which gives them the necessary courage to face death (157).

The gospel or Christian doctrines all over the world admonish man to love his neighbour as he loves himself, and to do unto others what he would want them to do unto him. This is the Golden Rule Human. The church has the responsibility to teach the whole gospel so that people start to put into practice the holistic gospel of transformation. The Jews were enjoined to impress God's commandments on their children and they did teach their children accordingly (Deuteronomy 6:7). They were extremely successful at making it an integral part of life. The reason for their success was that moral and even religious education was life-oriented, not information-oriented. Idang (154) writes that the Hebrews "used the context of daily life to teach their children about God, to follow God, to make God part of their everyday experiences". The teaching should be such that the converted individual seeks to transform his society as a whole. Teaching in the church should be on spiritual and physical matters that affect the individual in his daily life. In African societies, for instance, the church should go into dialogue and make its position known and what the scriptures say on issues of politics, economics, poverty, ecology and technology, besides the moral ones on corruption, work ethics, market ethics, self-reliance, birth control and certain cultural practices that are not in tandem with the scriptures. Areas that still demand clarification include the church's position on tribalism, racism, human rights, and environmental pollution, economic inequality between the rich and the individuals and nations and so on. Jakonda who has done an extensive research on how the church can aid holistic development through teaching observe thus:

> when a society is rotten economically or socially, the blame should be on the church because it has not adequately taught the Christians to be the light and salt of the society in the economic, social and political issues facing them (136).

Intercession

The egoistic desire that makes man to seek his personal gratification in his daily dealing may sometimes push the Christian to become increasingly self-centreed. In this way, their prayer life is affected and the Christian tends to pray for himself, family, relations and close allies. The Christian ought to intercede for all and should not only pray for those things which are perceived to be spiritual in nature or that are affecting their spiritual lives. He should also intercede that the will of God be done on earth. It is in this sense that we see that the church has a responsibility of praying holistically for the social, political, economic, environmental and cultural lives of the society. Church leaders often call for prayer and fasting on issues that they perceive to have adverse effect on Christians. However, whatever affects the peace and upliftment of the society ought to be of concern to the church. Situating it in the African context, the deplorable moral, economic and political problems of African nations should challenge the church to rise to its responsibility and fulfill its intercessory role.

Participation in Community Development

One of the main reasons why many development projects are not sustainable in our societies is because they were done without the participation of the beneficiaries of the projects. The early Missionaries must have seen the need for community participation if holistic development was to be attained when they sought the participation of the local church in establishing hospitals, schools and other social services. Sadly, Jakonda (140) writes that "the indigenous Christians had no sense of identification with the projects to the extent that "the members of the church that owned a hospital or school referred to it as a 'mission hospital' instead of 'our hospital". Our holistic development impetus can be greatly vitiated if the community participation and people centredness of the development process is ignored. The church can sensitize its members and encourage them to participate in any community building effort. Udo and Umoh (14-28) for instance, have noted the role that Qua Iboe Church of Nigeria has played in an attempt to curb the menace of HIV in Nigeria. In a bid to challenge other Christian denominations to join in this crusade, they advise that churches should include HIV/AIDS contents in pulpit instruction, encourage television and radio awareness programmes, train and assign prevention officers in local church congregations, build a relationship of love between the infected, affected and not-yet-infected persons. This is an instance where community participation of the church is really needed.

Participation in Politics

Since Christianity is not reserved about the glorification of such Christian virtue as to meekness, self-denial, humility and so on, some persons may be tempted to misinterpret this to include staying out of political participation. This view is very erroneous. In a *Foreword* on the book: *Reflections on the Christian Condition* written by Usen J. Umoh, Udo Etuk (VII) raises a fundamental question about Christian participation in politics and he ask: "If good Christian people with high ideals must stay away from politics perpetually, who, then will sanitize and rid the system of the stench and rottenness which have marred it in our nation?" Etuk reminds us of the affairs in the province of Babylon which were upturned when

God-fearing men were put at the helm of affairs. Great philosophers like Aristotle and St. Thomas Aquinas, tried to show that the good life for man is best lived in the political setting. The principles of the good life which inform the individual life are the same as those which inform the political man and the society (*The New Humanism*, 169). And we may wish to add: who will straighten the system and lead men to the fullest realization of holistic development in line with God's plan and purpose? Who will speak the truth, live by the truth and defend the truth? While it is true that the Christian should not give his consent to anything evil, it is the responsibility of Christians as members of the human community to make their voices heard right from the families to their communities, states and nations. It was Socrates that opined that good people should go into politics because if they don't, bad people would hijack the system, make bad laws and govern them. The political process, from the family through the village council to the local government council and the state, is too vital to be surrendered to evil. In his *Religion and Cultural Identity*, Etuk is of the opinion that:

> The Christian is called out by his Lord and Master to come out from among them and be separate. But by that same call, he is promptly sent back to go and serve as the salt of the earth and the light of the world. What this means, I believe, is that it is high time that the Christian voice be heard in family, village, local council and state decisions. Christians must take their rightful place and work for the demolition of structures of injustice, exploitation and intimidation by power of evil (147).

Christians and men of virtue should not keep mum on issues that shape their life's chances and fortunes just to be seen as apolitical. When this happens, men of lower moral and intellectual standards hijack pervert and abuse the political system. For most African countries, this is the stage we are in.

Reconciliation and Peace Meeting

Holistic development must include reconciliation and peace making. Peace making is itself a core Christian value and Christians are supposed to be peace makers anywhere they find themselves. Christ urges us to love, to love even our own enemies and persons that despitefully use and abuse us. The truth is that peace and reconciliation have a way of overcoming hatred and conflicts. Disagreements, rivalries and disputations can be destructive. They can engender feelings of distrust that may sometimes breakdown to open confrontation, shame, ridicule and abuse. The peace-making virtue of the Christian church ought to be brought to bear on anywhere and time that conflict can be observed, be it real or imagined. Cases of conflicts in the families of its members and even up to the armed conflicts on national scale can be properly handled if the church is ready to appeal to the ministry of forgiveness, reconciliation and peace making which is the reason why Jesus Christ died. The church should carry on this message and spread it to wherever they perceive or have confirmed the suspicion that there is conflict. Conflicts should be nipped in the bud with peace and reconciliation in order for holistic development to take place. We cannot talk of development in an atmosphere of conflict, strife, hate and war.

The Church and Kingdom of God

The church is often seen as the body of Christ. And as a body, it has many members or parts. Christians in the church have diverse gifts that ought to be used for the overall growth and stability of the body. All the gifts holistically meet the entire spiritual and physical needs of the body and of the community in which the church exists. The church ought to evangelize and ensure that the kingdom principles of love, freedom, justice and peace are established. Ladd writes that:

> The church is the custodian of the kingdom; instead of Israel, who gave up the custody to the church. Therefore, there can be no kingdom without the church, nor can there be a church without the kingdom, although the two remain distinguished concepts - the rule of God and the fellowship of men (Jakonda, 126).

The kingdom of God is where true Christians aspire to be. It is the destiny of all true Christians and it is the hope that gives them courage to endure even the worst conditions. The church has to point at it and see it as the true model of holistic development – a safe place to store one's treasures through righteousness and virtuous living.

Evaluation and Conclusion

Webster seems to have spoken our mind as he writes:
> If we work upon marble, it will perish. If we work on brass, time will efface it. If we rear temples, they will crumble to dust. But if we work upon men's immortal minds, if we imbue them with high principles, with the just fear of God and love of the fellow men, we engrave on those tablets something which no time can efface, and which will brighten and brighten to all eternity (57).

Webster was right to have noted that if we work on marble it will perish, if we work on brass, time will efface it, if we rear temples, they will crumble to the dust. What this means is that those who are tied to the world's system will lose everything when it collapses. What they have worked for a lifetime to build up will surely be destroyed within a brief moment. Thus, those who work only for material development will have nothing when they die or when their possessions are destroyed. Webster seemed to have thought about what will make people inherit God's kingdom. He, then, must have known that our faith in God, our Christian character, our relationship with others and our God are more important than materialism. In Colossians 3: 1-2, St. Paul advises the Colossians to set their hearts on things above, where Christ is seated at the right hand of God; to set their minds on things above, not on earthly things. What St. Paul actually means by setting one's heart on things above is that people should strive to put heaven's priorities into daily practice. And by setting our minds on things above, he means concentrating on the eternal truths which are more rewarding rather than the temporal truths tied to this world's system. This explains why Webster prefers working upon men's immortal minds and imbuing them with high principles with the fear of God and love for fellow man. For him, this is the only way we can engrave on those tablets something which no time can efface, and which will brighten and brighten to all eternity.

The surest way to the attainment of holistic development is by loving heavenly things and being engrossed by them. It is the level of development that a nation attains that places her in a position that she commands the respect of other sister nations. With developed countries enjoying global relevance and developing ones looking with much admiration, it is clear that development is such an important ideal that can give a people pride and at the same time be a source of great concern for others. Development has many aspects and it is the constellation of these aspects that translates into what we call holistic development.

The erroneous understanding that makes development to be synonymous with merely the physical dimension of reality is what we consider to be ripe for attack. Since man has a physical body with which he moves around and is identified and also has a spiritual dimension which does not readily lend itself to the physical, any one-sided attempt at human development fails to capture the wholeness of man and cannot adequately address the human problem. While political, economic, social, cultural and technological aspects of development are meant to guarantee a high quality of life for man in the physical realm, it should be matched with an adequate spiritual development as this will make development to be holistic. It is here that the role of the church manifests. As an important social institution, the church ought to play a vital role in holistic development not only in Nigeria but in all parts of the world emphasizing on Christian virtues in its moral instruction. The church should not join the materialistic fray. It can serve as the beacon of spiritual and moral development since it has been widely accepted in the continent.

WORKS CITED

Dickson, Kwesi. *African Theology.* New York: Obis Books, 1984.

Enoh, Christian. "Proverbs, Wise Sayings and Moral Values in the Process of National Development in Nigeria: The Case of Akwa Ibom State" in I. V. O. Modo (Ed). *South-South Journal of Culture and Development.* Vol.2, 2000.

Etuk, Udo. "Aesthetics, the New Media and National Development" in *First Professor Emmanuel Akpan Memorial Lecture*. Delivered in the University of Uyo, 2009.

Etuk, Udo. *The New Humanism*. Uyo: Afangide Bros, 1999.

Etuk, Udo. *Religion and Cultural Identity*. Ibadan: Hope Publications, 2002.

Etuk, Udo. "Foreword" in Usen J. Umoh. *Reflections on the Christian Condition*. Uyo: Abaam Publishers, 2008.

Etuk, Ebong and Udo Etuk. *Love and Health: Staying Healthier by Giving Love*. Lagos: The Quantum, 2004.

Idang, Gabriel. *Ancient Philosophy: A Text for Beginners*. Uyo: Inela Ventures, 2009.

Jakonda, Sulaiman. *Your Kingdom Come: A Book on Holistic Christian Development*. Jos: RURCON, 2001.

Rodney, Walter. *How Europe Underdeveloped Africa*. London: Bogle, 1972.

The Holy Bible. *Authorized King James Version*. Tennessee: Royal Publishers, 1971.

Udo, Manasseh and Enobong Umoh. "HIV in Nigeria: The Role of Quo Iboe Church of Nigeria" in *International Journal of African Culture, Politics and Development*. Vol. 2, No. 1, 2007.

Umoh, John. *Elements of Sociology of Religion*. Ikot Ekpene: Iwoh and Sons Enterprises, 2005

Webster, D. *Truth to Live By*. Missouri: Unity, 1985.

CHAPTER 14

AFRICA'S RESTORATION: REDISCOVERING THE PLACE OF AFRICAN CULTURAL VALUES IN AN *ICHABODDED* HISTORY
By
OKEKE JONATHAN CHIMA

Introduction

> There was a time when we knew our ways, sang our own songs, layed our own bricks but such a time is long gone.
> - Jonathan Okeke on **Ukwe Ncheta**

Long time ago, before the coming of the Whiteman, Africa was home to Africans. Africans had their ways, their laws, and their lives and through the passage of time, these things remained of their own making. Their present as of their past, was theirs to shape. They created their own customs, fashioned their own tools and told their own story. As a people, they had their own culture. And their history was marked with peace and strife, ceremonies and rituals; perhaps, barbarous or primitive, but it was their own history not until the Whiteman arrived with his own did everything change! They denied Africa a place in world history. They said the African was without norms – he therefore needed to be cultured. In other words, he was like a wild beast without the knowledge of what was right or wrong, or the knowledge of which he neither was nor was he interested in finding out. He was occupied only with the instinct of daily survival from hunger and from other beasts of his kind. As a result, he needed to be tamed with religion and then domesticated with civilization, both of which he lacked.

One might argue that the Whiteman never said this much but of course he did. According to Onyewuenyi, the great German philosopher, George Wilhelm Friedrich Hegel (1770 – 1839) believed that Africa was primitive and without culture as it has no history and positive contributions to the world civilization (93 – 104). And also Karl Jaspers (1883 – 1916), a German existentialist philosopher, held that the ancient Egyptian civilization was an age of myth and stagnation and that colonization of Africa marked the beginning of African history since there were no high cultures before the colonizers (Okoro, 6). Obviously, the views of these two men show that my classification of the western conception of Africa was indeed, watered down. So misplaced and deceitful was their interpretation, that there was nothing good and memorable about Africa in their thoughts. They were to help us create history, they were to offer us a culture and indeed, they were to bring us civilization. Africans also has no religion and by extension, no idea of God. To the whites, "Nnabuchi writes", the blackman's belief is fetish, i.e. belief in inanimate objects – those things which have ears yet they cannot hear those things which have eyes yet they cannot see (54). That African gods and amulets were eventually stashed away in boxes as myths and artifacts and ferried across the Atlantic was not however, as nagging as the assumption that without the whites, the African might never learn. This was evident in the question some whites asked: how can the untutored African know …? (Nnabuchi, 54).

And so it was that the whites tutored the blackman to learn their ways, follow their religion, imbibe their culture and accept their civilization. The problem however is, that the so-called beginning of African history in actuality, marked the end of the true African history and the beginning of an *ichabodded* history - a history without glory! This is so because, the modern African history, culture and civilization are the history, culture and civilization of the Whiteman forced upon the African. They are not his own and so, there is no glory in them. A modern African therefore, and ironically too, is a man without history unlike his ancestors. He has lost his past; he has no future and therefore has no identity. Indeed, Hegel's assertion has never been as correct just as it was never as wrong when he made it. Thus, to restore the dignity and identity of the blackman has become the foremost existential exercise and philosophy in our time. How then might we begin? In what ways was Africa robbed? Indeed, in these westernized dynamics, how might we rediscover the place of African cultural values? And what are these cultural values? This paper is an attempt to return the African to his rightful place in world history, even if that place is out in the pavement and nowhere near the inside. It will be nobler for the African to raise his lowly staff than bear the so-called glorious standards for the whiteman; For, as the Igbo would say, the tortoise prayed his kinsmen to wish him life rather than growth, because the living would surely grow. An Africa restored to its rightful history, will surely grow.

The Cry for Restoration

Thus it has come to light that Africa had a history when they said she had none, and now they say she has one is actually when she has none! This is because what is regarded as the modern African history is an *"ichabodded* history" – a history without glory. When a history is not of one's making, not her"s to shape and not created with her own native instruments such as culture, and language, then such a history has no glory. It is a borrowed or an imposed history and those living through it, a people under "home captivity". They are held captive in their own land. Africans live in Africa but the type of life they live is not decided by what one may call "native framework" constituting of local ancestral customs and norms, language and culture in general. And of more concern is the possibility that the future of Africa is being shaped by influences from "foreign framework". This prospect may not look so debasing at face value after all it is a march to keep pace with modern civilization. The question is: whose civilization? It is not outlandish for one culture to borrow and integrate elements of other cultures in its system. The problem is when one assimilates a foreign culture and purges away his own as primitive and mythical, such a people begin to live in "exile in their motherland". This goes to show that territory is not all there is in marking a people. The Chinese living in America may be away from motherland but is at home in so-far-as he has not departed from his native framework. The same could be said of a few living in Germany. During the Babylonish captivity of the Jews (Daniel 1 – 6, NIV) they were said to be in exile and that was true as far as it was a matter with territory. But if the reference were directed to cultural framework, those who were in exile were those who abandoned the native Jewish ways. Incidentally, the bible make us to understand they referred to themselves as living in exile what more could be said when they even refused to sing their own native songs. This could be rivaled with the story of the Africans who were ferried to the new world to work in the plantations as slaves. We were told they carried with them the African language, gods, customs and songs. Thus even though they were in exile, they lived at home. The story is not the same with Africans back home, for since colonialism, they have continued to "live in exile at home". They have dropped as they trudge along various elements of their culture with contempt and scorn. They are now primitive, mythical or magical! Thus John Mbiti's assertion was referring to the African before colonization when he said:

> Wherever the African is, there is his religion: he carries it to the fields where he is sowing seeds or harvesting a new crop; he takes it with him to the beer party or to attend a funeral ceremony; [However, the latter part of this assertion refers to the colonized African when he says:] ... and if he is educated, he takes religion with him to the examination room at school or in the university; if he is a politician he takes it to the house of parliament (Mbiti, 2).

The point now has changed, for the African takes the culture and religion of the west with him and no longer those of his ancestors. It is in the light of the above that Africa's restoration has become the most topical issue of our time. But this precludes the questions of who has deprived or robbed Africa? How has Africa been deprived or robbed? What has been taken away from Africa? It is the argument of this movement that returning the pride and restoring Africa's cultural elements will mean not only restoring Africa to its rightful place but more importantly, it will mark Africa's return to history. The cry for Africa's restoration has never been as crucial especially now that the identity of Africans has slid down to only the "name" without anymore psychographic and psychodynamic contents. The African is an African now only in name! This is because the cultural elements of a people are the true measures of their identity. Without a peculiar culture, a people have no identity in the eyes of the world. And without identity, a people simply do not exist. Existence in this context does not mean subsistence, it means having a place in world history. The desertification of the Sahara in about 3rd millennia BC (Agbojike, 135) isolated Africa (black Africa) from the rest of the world. This left Africa without records in world history. It was the absence of Africa in the records of world history which made Hegel and other western intellectuals to state that Africa has no contribution to world history. Though partly true, this becomes only falsified because it has been proved that the desertification isolated the Dark Continent. The cultural exchange between Africa and the rest of the world unfortunately could not continue due to climatological and geographical reason resulting from the desiccation.

In archeological studies, mankind's civilization has been traced from the old stone age (paleolithic) which is divided into three (i) lower paleolithic (ii) middle paleolithic and (iii) upper paleolithic, the new stone age (neolithic), the copper and bronze age, the iron age and to the present jet and computer age. Archeological evidences show that the Dark Continent was on top of world civilization and history from the beginning until the desiccation. For example: the remains of the earliest type of man known as the australopithecine were found in East Africa (Olduvia Gorge) Southern Africa and Chad. This ape man was thought to have live some two million years ago (Agbodike, 131). Later, the pithecanthropus erectus associated with Chilean and Acheulian cultures was excavated during the later part of the lower paleolithic some half a million years ago. And these cultures have been found in places like Mozambique, Namibia, Jos and Sokoto in Nigeria (Agbodike, 132). The middle paleolithic age was the era of the Neanderthal man believed to have lived some 30 – 40,000 years ago. This age's culture has been found in some parts of Africa. In Nigeria, Agbodike writes, the Zenebi falls and Jos are examples of places where evidence of middle Paleolithic culture has been found (133). Also, the upper Paleolithic age was the era of the first true man *Homo sapiens*. He was believed to have lived some 10,000 years ago and the age is marked with microlith culture. This culture has been discovered in some parts of Africa and in Nigeria it has been found in Rop Shelter in Northern Nigeria excavated by Ekpo Eyo (1964), Meijiro cave in old Oyo and Iwo Ileru excavated by Thurston Shaw (1965) (Agbodike, 133). The new stone age which is between 8,000 and 2,000 B.C was marked with neolithic culture. Evidences of this culture have been excavated in East, South, Central and West Africa.

The copper and bronze age was when Africa lagged behind the discovery of copper at the foot of Mt. Sinai has been place to some 3,500 year B.C. It was soon after that the desiccation of the Sahara occurred. It becomes explainable why the Dark Continent skipped this age due to its subsequent isolation. Copper and bronze (an alloy of copper and tin) could not diffuse to the dark continent until the 11th century A.D following the reopening of the trans-Saharan trade routes by the Arabs (Hartle, 3). The iron age which occurred some 1,500 years B.C has its culture found in many parts of Africa; East Africa, Central Africa and West Africa. The Nok iron works have been dated to as early as 900 years B.C (Clarke, 116). Thus, we see that contrary to the preposterous assertions by western writers that Africa has no history, archeology has in the last two centuries proved that Africa contributed immensely to world history.

However, the nagging point this paper wishes to raise here is: since a people's contribution to world history at a particular age is determined both from written history and excavations, in say 20,000 years to come, when archeologists dig, what would they find in Africa to mark this our times? Would they find microchips, computers, car frames, and crashed aero planes bearing bold inscriptions, made in UK, Germany, Japan, and China or made in say Nigeria, Chad, Kenya, etc? When historians go through the libraries, would they see ideas and theories authored by Africans or the Western intellectuals, like Einstein, Turing, Maltus, Faraday, Newton, Quine, Dewey, etc? The question is: is Africa truly contributing to the history and civilization of the present jet and computer age or merely following what the West is doing? Archeology has proved that as at the time the Negro people of Nigeria (Igbo – Ukwu, Ife and Benin) produced marvelous artistic works of bronze, it is known that there was no such comparable work of art in Europe (Agbodike, 138). This shows that ancestral Africans carved a niche for Africa with a standard for exceeding what the crest could offer in those past ages of world civilization. Yet it was erroneously said that Africa has no history. Now that the

African Political Philosophy

West say Africa had a history, what has Africa to show for it? Just as the designation prevented Africa from participating in the copper age, colonization came with factors which were collectively depriving Africa from making obvious contributions to world civilization and has dovetailed into this present jet and computer age.

However, hankering and arguing over the past is not as important as doing something for the present. This is because the present will soon become another distant past and it will be yet another time to roll-call the achievements and contributions made by different peoples of the world in the jet and computer age. Now, with this type of score sheet, one cannot say Africa made any contribution to civilization in the jet and computer age. Of course, some of these things are going to be dug up in Africa but with bold inscriptions that betray where they were made. What this shows is that the history Africa fosters now is not her"s, and the culture, simply a token from the West. Everything about the African is fake. Indeed with the above score sheet, Africans of posterity are more likely going to find it difficult defending the thesis that Africans of jet and computer age did not live in caves and forests.

Deprivation

Before the emergence of the age of science, African civilizations had declined, possibly because Egyptian civilization declined. The trade routes between Africa and the North Atlantic gradually closed down. Europeans had discovered better markets in the East which traded on goods required to build the scientific age. It should be noted that developments in the west diffused to Africa via Egypt which maintained trade with Africa. And when the goods coming from Africa was no longer required by the West, Egypt simply turned away. Africa was therefore faced with two choices: retire home to tranquil communal living and live the West and its wild ideas alone or build ships and venture into the hostile Atlantic in search of the West. The later option will take years of industry, resources and a lot of troubles to accomplish, and since the Africans of that time probably did not think seriously about the future or could not agree, they took the first option. Centuries later, when the Arabians reopened the trans-Saharan trade routes, there was nothing

Africans had to sell, so they bought humans. And this was the elementary origin of the slave trade. Much later, when the West's scientific techniques had enabled it to venture further into the seas; they sought after Newlands with exotic goods. As they discovered America with great results, they thought of revisiting Africa for possibilities of trade.

However, when they landed with what looked like superior culture, they met barbarians and primitives dwelling in cluster of huts in the forests and draped in animal skin. Was this the Africa that fought the Romans and traded with the Phoenicians? It must have been difficult for them to comprehend. They did not meet merchants but primitives who sold themselves to the Arabs as slaves. But unlike the Arabs, the Europeans saw a continent rich with raw materials only the primitives were not merchants. When they went home, they resolved to come and live and then use the natives to produce the raw materials needed in Europe. Before long, the Scramble for Africa began (Rodney, 163 and 168), culminating in the Berlin conference of 1884 the result of which was the partition. Soon, Africans were been exported in thousands to the new world – the food basket of the world. Thus began the slave trade that deprived Africans of human dignity. We shall here consider the three principal areas Africa suffered deprivation namely; human dignity, history and culture.

Human Dignity: Of all the treasures lost to shipwrecks in the sojourns to the new world; of all the economic and human losses of the Napoleonic wars and of the first and second world wars; the Blackman's loss of his dignity is probably the greatest loss of modern time. In all the Europe and the Americas where the Blackman worked for hundreds of years as a slave, generations have come to see it not only as his lot but that he is also a sub-human. Lucien Levy Bruhl's assertion that Africans are prelogical (17) stems from this impression. So strong was this impression that despite declarations abolishing the institution of slavery in, in all parts of the world, over 200 hundred years after, Blackman is still a victim of contemptuous racist remarks and attacks in our time. He has since been nicknamed a nigger, a black monkey, a coloured etc all pointing towards his psychological and biological deficiency as a human. Attempts have been made at international level to stamp out racism, laws have been enacted and so much more without much success. It is therefore no doubt that the only veritable solution would have to come from Africans themselves. They created the problem when they showed the whites they were as barbarous and un-intelligent as to sell their own children, they have to solve it by posing serious challenge to the whites in all things which have to do with human intellect. This is because what demeans Africans about slavery is not that their brothers were used as slaves sometimes in the past but that it were Africans themselves who willingly sold their own sons and daughters into slavery. It is only a people who are lacking in humanity who would do such. Therefore, when the Blackman sold his son, he also sold his dignity as a human. In order to get it back, he must work for it.

History: Hegel shouted from the roof top that Africa has no history (Onyewuenyi, 59), a position dutifully disproved later on with immense archeological discoveries. David Hume on his part justified the enslavement and colonization of Africans "according to Eneh", because Africans had no ingenious manufacturers, arts and sciences of their own (3). This is a fact that history has proved even though it does not justify such in-human oppressions. But many African scholars would not want to hear that. Eneh, for instance sees western historians as prejudiced. Why would they tell stories of Africa's failures and ignore the glorious ones?:

> The westerns failed to teach us that some African emperors like Septimus Severus and his son, Caracalla were emperors in the Roman Empire. They neither taught us that an African abbot, Adrain was the archbishop of Canterbury in 710 AD nor did we know that an African, Miltiodes was a pope in the Roman Catholic Church (2).

What Eneh fails to understand and one of the focal points of this chapter is that Africa has two histories: before and after slavery. Before slavery, historical evidences abound which show that neither the blacks nor the whites looked down on each other. And the achievements Eneh mentioned above took place then. However, with the trans-Atlantic slave trade came what I have chosen to dub in this chapter "The Second Fall". This is the fall of black man from human dignity. The West beheld with great shock as humans running into millions were sold by their own parents, sometimes for a price as low as a bottle of gin for one human. If one were to consider this from an unprejudiced spectacle, it would not be difficult to reach a conclusion that only a people (possibly) lacking in full capacity of humanity who would do such. Whether the West is right or wrong depends on what Africans of this age are able to come up with to change the ugly impression – and to rewrite the ugly history. Commentators should note that the Portuguese and the Spanish explorers who first shipped slaves out of Africa in the 13th and 14th centuries AD did not sail to Africa with the intent of enslaving Africans. They had gone to buy goods and found that the only wares Africans had to sell were their children, so they bought some at first. When they found them useful, they began to buy in hundreds of thousands. The first shipment to the New World was made in 1526.

Apparently, the conditions leading to the enslavement and subsequent colonization of Africa may have prompted Hegel to say, according to Eneh, that colonization marked the beginning of African history since there were no high cultures in Africa before ... (4). Eneh like most Afroscent intellectuals found this deceptive, disgusting and loathsome. How, "they ask", can the west humiliate Africa in this way? Hegel's assertion is both false and true, despite. It is false because Africa had a history before the second fall. It is true because with the fall, Africa lost her glory and colonization which followed emancipation became an attempt to construct a new history with a new culture. Only that the new history was built on the foundation of a foreign (strange) culture or framework. It was like a garden belonging to the West while Africans acted as the gardeners. It has no glory – it was and still is an *ichabodded* history. Therefore, when the African fell, she lost everything. In order to reclaim her past, she must construct a new history on the foundation of her own cultural framework. She must speak her own language, groom her own science, develop her own people and economy, produce her own goods and be ready to stand on her own feet in the theatre of nations.

Culture: The only bad thing about colonization was the washing away of native culture. Everywhere in the world they talk about the rich African cultural heritage but we Africans know that what we show on TV and write in books and newspapers are all theatrics. In practice and in reality of everyday living, we Africans know that our cultures have been eroded. How many places in Igboland can one see the famous Nzen'ozo institution with its original credibility? Or the Ofo is still being struck on the earth with its full powers and effect? How many places in Akan, or Zulu, or Bantu or Efik and Ibibio or Yoruba land can one still see the holiness of traditional institutions or the sanctity of life and the integrity of elders? Or the moral regard for traditional values? Or even respect for those old cultural beliefs which ensure peace and remarkable communal living? All those cultural values are now symbols which point to nothing beyond the surface decorations. Indeed, in many African countries, they are now used as tourist attractions – a sun without the shine, a beautiful box without content. Many of the current generation of Africans do not as little as understand the meaning and essence of African cultural practices.

Thus, it can be argued here that the worst crime the west committed in the modern times was not the slave trade for they paid for every African shipped abroad. It is essentially the destruction and erosion of the African cultural framework. In replacing the African culture with theirs, they had isolated the African from her root thereby making it difficult (if not impossible) for the African to ever rediscover herself let alone finding her lost identity. The African would then forever be at loss in her own motherland. Her ideas of justice, right and wrong; her beliefs in life and after life, God; her views about the society, other humans, human behaviour about nature and indeed everything that made her an African have been eroded. It is not that her cultural values were fortified by those of the West, they were entirely replaced. And because these cultural frameworks are incompatible with Africans, Africans have been at conflict and confusion trying to live by them – be it in politics, education, leadership, economy and so on. This leaves Africans at the constant mercy of their western lords. As far as the jet and computer age has gone, Africa has not made any significant contributions to world civilization.

When Azikiwe was laying the foundation stone of the University of Nigeria Nsukka early in the 60s, he was quoted to have said that western education would restore the dignity of the Blackman. But he was wrong of course because a westernized approach to education cannot do an African any good beyond putting food on his table. Africa has through this method of education produced innumerable physicians and pharmacists who have not invented any new drug or diagnostic pattern, uncountable mechanical engineers who have not produced any automobile, many electronic and electrical engineers who have not invented any gadgets, many philosophers who have neither invented any ideas nor solved any problems. Everything they teach in African schools to this day is ideas of Whiteman. The system is bound to be inimical to Africa's restoration because the western logic is not African logic. Africans are not forced to learn and imbibe a reasoning process which made sense to them nor could they apply it successfully as a Whiteman could. What more, African economy become consumerist, her political structures enmeshed in confusion, her system of government becomes chaotic and dependent and indeed all things, come falling apart (Achebe, 1958), thereby making it difficult for the centre to hold. In order to fast-track Africa's restoration, it is imperative to first, rediscover the place of African cultural values in this present *ichabodded* historical dynamics. And this shall occupy this chapter presently.

The Place of African Cultural Values in Building a True African History

It is not admissible in this paper that a history built upon a foreign cultural framework, will be germane to Africans and their philosophy. And it is also difficult to see how such might translate into a veritable theoretic base and problem solving indices. Uduigwomen has contended that a philosophical problem will remain in the abstract plane except it is made to have local or concrete relevance (6). This means for instance that the existential or identity problem of an African will not make much sense nor yield any positive result unless it is discussed within the context of African cultural traits and values. One might ask: what is African culture and values? This leads us directly into defining culture. Agi however points out that there are many definitions of culture: the ethnologist's, historian's, the mixture of the two, etc, which makes it a bit difficult to generate a consensus definition (141). Thus, in harnessing the elements of the three conceptions we may perhaps come nearest the mark by saying that the cultural conception we are now trying to grasp aims to embrace in; good and evil and set parameter for general human behaviour in the society before colonialism (Mbon, 101; Ekeoparo, 1; Sogolo, 119). Thus, African cultural values roughly a single term those general attitudes, views of life and specific manifestation of civilization that give a particular people its distinctive place in the world (Sapir, 78). The reason for so many definitions of culture, according to Bascom and Herskovits, is that culture is heterogeneous – "it refers to a single item of reality, but to innumerable items at different levels of generality: ideas, sentiments, values, objects, actions, tendencies, and accumulations" (1).

Values on the other hand is a collection of objects, symbols and norms which express a people's conception of right and wrongmean the aggregate of cultural heritage and moral principles which characterize the African and shape his life. The question now is, what are the constituents of African cultural values? This question has a philosophical underpinning which means to fully assess the content of African cultural values is a task of African philosophy Bodunrin on his part perceives this task of African philosophy as "the discovery of authentic African ideas or thought systems uninfluenced by alien accretions" (XI). This does not mean that rediscovering the place of African cultural values in contemporary dynamics implies purification or purgation of any useful foreign ideas. There is and there has always been a room for intercultural exchanges in building civilization. Oladipo explains that the reappraisal and, of course, the rediscovery of the place of African cultural values have the potential of promoting the kind of self-understanding that would provide some basis for determining the kind of socio-cultural reconstructions that would enable Africans to come to terms with the challenges of contemporary life (16 – 17) this attitude does not denigrate African cultural values as the framework of authentic African history, yet it fortifies it to be able to meet the challenges of building a true African civilization in the contemporary times.

African cultural values constitutes, according to Ezedike, the sum total of shared attitudinal inclinations and capabilities, art, beliefs, moral codes and practices which characterize Africans (455). This is continuous and cumulative thus containing both material and non-material elements that are socially transmitted from one generation to another. Concerning crimes and punishment for instance, Africans believe as depicted by Achebe, that one man's crime can "ruin the whole clan" (22). As a result, Ndubuisi writes, punishment for crime in African culture is necessary for continuous existence of the society, to correct the culprits and to deter would be ones (189). Africans believe the fates of individuals in a community have a spiritual linkage which is why one man's troubles or successes become indirectly, the troubles or successes of the entire clan. Among the Igbo, there are aphorisms which explain this well:

i. *Otu Mkpuru aka ruta mmanu, ozu oha onu* (when a finger is dipped in red oil, it spreads to the rest).
ii. *Ofeke nyuchie nsi uzo, osie onye obula* (when one miscreant deficates at an improper place, it fouls the air everyone breathes).
iii. *Otu onye gbuo agu, ndi obodo azaba ogbu agu* (when one man kills a lion, his clan will begin to answer lion killers).
iv. *Oha obodo n'azu nwa* (it takes a whole village to raise a child).
v. *Ngozi n'abiara obodo, n'esi n'aka otu onye* (any blessing that come to a clan, comes through one man).

Thus, we can see that African communalism as an element of culture is based on the spiritual connections existing among the individuals of a given community. Concerning moral codes, African ethics like those of Hanumrabi the wise, are put forward by the gods. This gives it basis in the African religion; a point emphasized by Mbiti (2), Iwe (13), Idowu (16) and Esomonu (183). This means that in African culture, religion and morality are intertwined. The moral codes are therefore derived from the spirit world and its divinity means that the gods have the ability to punish any deviation from or violations of the moral law.Apparently, it can be generalized that every aspect of African culture has the element of the spiritual. Idoniboye relates that spirits are the one entity that remains constant in all African belief systems (84). Thus, the African ontology consists in both the physical and the spiritual (Unah, 249: Ijiomah, 76). Her art, objects, identity, craft, symbols, etc have both the human and the metaphysical dimensions. The extent to which this type of culture and worldview are going to be instrumental in her quest to rediscover her place in history in an arching scientific world is immaterial, because there is room for cultural exchanges, there is metaphysics in science and all sciences do not have to follow the same method. Thus, building the authentic African history through the instrumentality of African cultural framework involves:

i. Teaching and learning in African languages.
ii. Raising children and operating an educational curriculum which coheres with African logic or reasoning pattern.
iii. Building a scientific world view which corresponds to African ontology and realities.
iv. Developing research methodologies which will view reality and nature from the African perspectives.
v. Building a mentality of originality and cooperation rather than dependence towards other civilizations, with the one goal of making African contribution to world history and civilization something that would come to stay.

This is a far cry from what obtains in the current *Ichabodded* history that Africans live through. Agi has explained that the colonizers left the post-colonial Africa in the hands of western groomed African elites who have internalized western culture as a true framework (146). Firstly, Africans are told that their culture is uncivilized and therefore inferior to the Europeans (Agi, 145). Then western civilization is presented to Africans as a "necessary good" which should be accepted without further questions. Thus, using civilization as a banner, Nwokeji argues, cultural displacement and conquest proceed with the corroboration even of the colonized peoples, who now accept what is coming as "civilization" (153). Nwokeji goes on to say that by the time they proclaimed independence for generations who had been psychologically battered and sedated for over sixty years (1900 – 1960) the people had only a disastrously tattered picture of their people's culture, ways of life, and everything (157). Thus, the independence period elites, given their past, necessarily were a lost generation as one can see. Nothing good, for these lost people, can come from Africa.

According to Agbo, Jeremiah Abalaka was asked to shut-up when he said he had found both preventive and curative vaccines for

HIV/AIDS through traditional means (238). He goes on to say that slavery and colonialism are part of the wreckage of African history, a fact that needs to be understood and overcome. This is a challenge to African philosophers to embrace the culture of social thinking. The existential situation of Africa should not become a mere subject of constant lamentation. Philosophy should address the African situation (238). Nnabuchi in his prodigious book, *In Defence of Igbo Belief System*, states:

> with due respect to the whites who brought to us what is regarded as civilization, one thing has constantly been my views as it concerns the use of teaching or religion as an instrument of colonization and that is that the belief of our ancestors was deliberately misinterpreted, debased or 'murdered' so as to have a firm control of our people. My disappointment is not with the actions of foreigners but with those of our kiths and kins who with the same zeal and enthusiasm catapulted the destruction of our belief, culture, and historical heritage by holding brief for the colonizers. To dismantle our beliefs, different and foreign beliefs were introduced and perpetuated by our own sons and daughters (58 – 59).

Nnabuchi bemoans a current situation where Africa rides on a fake history and suggests that education and religion of the West which were instrumental to it, be dismantled and replaced with their African versions. Nwokeji opines that the "goal of colonialism is the cultural subjugation and overmastering of those colonized" and suggests that the process of successful decolonization must, therefore involve the rejection of these foreign symbols of 'colonial civilization' (153). In his book, *The Principles of Western Civilization*, Benjamin Kidd identified brute force and imposition of European culture as the principle of the so-called civilization. In his word as captured by Nwokeji, western civilization aims to build,

> … a universal empire in which a particular belief has become absolute; in which it is again conceived that the rule of religion should, in the last resort be a rule of civil law; in which it is considered that the state itself exists now for no higher end than that all

its machinery and purposes, and powers should be devoted to establishing and maintaining throughout the world the sway of one accepted and authoritative interpretation of absolute truth ... (151).

In another of his book, *The Science of Power* Nwokeji quotes Kidd as saying that "... the blinding vision of which the west has caught sight has been that there is but one class, and but one colour and but one soul in humanity (the Whiteman) and this shall be preserved with force and power (152). Buckle in his "The History of Civilization in England" surmises that the history of the world has been in Europe to elevate the Whiteman to a godly status and outside Europe to make other races his subject and worshipers (Nwokeji, 152). It is now pertinent that to free Africans from this monstrous god, recourse to African cultural framework is imperative. Nwokeji had noted that the traditional culture and ethics were left to decay. African religions were discredited and European colonial religions enthroned. The African religions allowed Africans to appeal to God directly. The European one ended that, and established that Africans can only appeal to God through Jesus Christ, Mary and the European (Whiteman) saints. This meant that the distance between Africans and their God has increased and Jesus, Mary, the saints and the angels, were introduced in-between (157).

The inference here is that the African now rides on a culture that is both strange and fake to her. As a result, Agi suggested that the traditional African cultural values and their institutions be restored. He says that the traditional education for instance laid a premium on discipline, moral integrity, family and community solidarity, social responsibility, industry and integration (149). It is therefore feasible that by modernizing and fortifying the African cultural values, a new and authentic African history and civilization might be created based on the framework. Macaulay advances similar suggestion when he states that:
> China, North Korea and India are making great strides in the scientific world because their technological development is anchored on the modernization of traditional technologies and the

adoption and adaptation of imported technologies to their cultural systems (348).

This means like China, North Korea, India and other races of the world who are currently mounting stiff challenge to the West in all areas of human development, Africa will be able to create her own history and thus, forge her own civilization should she retrace her steps. Retracing her steps involves going back to her cultural heritage, dusting up the old kiths and tools, and may be freeing the gods from the boxes. This is merely symbolic but calls for a significant drive to modernize whatever Africa had and invent what she had not following a peculiar pattern. It is only in the light of the above, when the place of African cultural values is rediscovered anew, amidst the confusions, intricacies and complexities of an inglorious history and a fake culture, that Africa as a continent and as a people might be fully restored back to world history.

Conclusion

I have speculated earlier in this chapter that because of some changes in the commercial life of the West, Egypt turned away from the Dark Continent thereby severing the line of cultural exchanges between Africa and the rest of the world. (Note that throughout this chapter, I have treated Africa as only the areas occupied by Negroid [black race]). In the grime reality of this isolation Africans had two choices: the first "I said", would be to build ships and venture into the hostile Atlantic Ocean in search of direct contact with the West and East. The second would be to settle for tranquil communal living. I speculated that Africans of the time chose the second choice because:

i. The first option would require the organization of a huge manpower, industry, time and resources which were either too bogus for the capacities of those moderate kingdoms or that agreements were not reached among the lords.
ii. Again, it could be that Africans of the time never fully understood the importance of maintaining contact with the rest of the world. In other words, they never thought seriously about future.

African Political Philosophy

Whatever be the case, they did not venture out to the seas. Years later, the following implications must have ensued:

i. Increase in taxation for the up keep of the palace whose income dwindled as trade with the Egyptians and Arabians stopped.
ii. The kings employed greater force for their benefit and comfort.
iii. Internal strife followed leading to mass uprising.
iv. Disintegration of kingdoms – here, families and clans migrated further and established small communities inside tick forests.

This final stage isolated such communities from the high culture of their time. They lost contact with the cities most of which now laid in ruin. As a result, they had to develop crude tools and implements for their survival. The Phoenician fabrics were no longer available, so they had to resort to animal skin and plant leaves for clothing. And for their shelter, they erected shabby huts to serve in the interim for they were not sure environmental and climate concerns would not force them to move the next season. But the stern reality was that they were building a "forest civilization" with paleolithic cultures again. A stage they had passed thousands of years ago. Death, soon took the elderly ones and the younger generation born in these forests were raised under this civilization knowing nothing of the existence of the rest of the world and the high cultures. Their instincts were to survive and the only external culture and civilization they had contact with was those of the brutes or beasts. And they must have learnt a few things from the beats. They saw for instance, how the male ones took the female ones with rashness and domination; the man of the forest civilization in turn took his women likewise. He was the owner of his women and could sell off their children if he wished. It showed his power and superiority, a fact the women must have accepted as normal. So strong was the influence of the beast culture that the Igbo of that time named their children after the character or aesthetics of any beast they admired. Below are examples of such names:

i. *Agu* - Lion (masculine)
ii. *Odum* - Tiger (masculine)

iii.	*Enyi*	-	Elephant (masculine)
iv.	*Akwaeke*	-	python's egg (feminine)
v.	*Ugo*	-	Eagle (feminine)
vi.	*Eneh*	-	Antelope (unisex)
vii.	*Oji*	-	Iroko (masculine)
viii.	*Obiagu*	-	Lion heart (masculine)
ix.	*Ugonma*	-	Eagle's beauty (feminine)
x.	*Oduenyi*	-	Elephant's tusk (feminine)
xi.	*Ugoloma*	-	Peacock (feminine)

It is no doubt that a people whose only external interaction was with the beast would depreciate in rationality. This is made evident by their willful selling of their children later on, sometimes for a price as low as a bottle of gin. If Africans are to rediscover their true identity, this is where the inference has to begin. To cut open a leaking goard, "Igbo aphorism has it", it is important to discover the point where water entered it. This means that to solve any complex problem, it is most efficient to trace its origin. African culture and civilization at a time declined so terribly that the rationality of the Africans was affected because of their cultural exchange with the beasts. It was the reopening of the trans-Saharan trade routes which brought them in contact with the Arabs and subsequently with the European tradesmen and colonizers that began to tune-up the African man's rationality. This is a truth Afroscent scholars have deliberately excluded from their writings. However, a great damage was done by the colonizers who chose to displace the culture of Africans with theirs, thereby making it difficult for the Africans to ever discover their true identity. Of course, and painfully too, making it impossible for the Africans to ever contribute anything to world history and civilization. A strange culture has been forced upon them which has a different reasoning process (logic) with theirs, thus creating on top of it, a fake history – in a way an extension of the western history. The analysis of this civilization in some 20,000 years to come, will reveal a domination of a terribly inferior human race by a superior one, whose sincere goal it was to tutor, train and make them rational. This, I think, is the biggest battle Africans have to fight now, at least for posterity's sake. Thus, rediscovering the place of African cultural values in this our time, will do well to displace the fake, fictitious, distorted and undermining history built upon a strange and incompatible culture.

In this way, the centre may yet stand again and Africa may yet be restored to its rightful place among other races of the world.

WORKS CITED

Achebe, Chinua. *Things Fall Apart*. London: Heinemann Educational Books, 1958.

Agbo, Joseph. "Globalization and African Philosophy" in A. F. Uduigwomen (Ed) *From Footmarks to Landmarks on African Philosophy*. Lagos: OO Publishers, 2009.

Agbodike, C. C. "Archaeology and the Reconstruction of the Nigerian Past" in Emeka Oguegbu (Ed). *The Humanities and All of Us*. Onitsha: Watchword, 1990.

Agi, S. P. I. "Unity and Diversity in Nigeria Culture". Emeka Oguegbu (Ed) *The Humanities and All of Us*. Onitsha: Watchword, 1990.

Bascom, W. R. and Herskovits, M. J. (Eds) *Continuity and Change in African Cultures*. Chicago: University of Chicago Press, 1970.

Bodurin, P. O. *Philosophy in Africa: Trends and Perspectives*. Ife: University of Ife Press, 1985.

Buckle, Henry Thomas. "History of Civilization in England" in Humphrey Milford (Ed). London: OUP, 1857.

Clark, Grahame. *World Prehistory - An Outline*. Cambridge: Cambridge University Press, 1962.

Ekeopara, Augustine. "Traditional Ethics and Social Stability" in *Sophia: An African Journal of Philosophy*. Vol. 9, No. 1, 2006.

Eneh, Joseph. *An Introduction to African Philosophy and Thought*. Enugu: Satellite Press, 1999.

Esemonu, L. E. *Respect for Human Life in Igbo Religion and Morality*. Ronie: Topographical, 'Lebent', 1981.

Ezedike, E. U. "Moral Problems in Nigeria: The Relevance of Traditional Ethics to Contemporary African Society". A. F. Uduigwomen (Ed) *From Footmarks to Landmarks on African Philosophy*. Lagos: O O Publishers,, 2009.

Hartle, Donald. "Archaeology East of the Niger: A Review of Cultural – Historical Developments" in Unpublished Monograph, Department of History, U. N. N., March 1972. Quoted from Donald Hartle: "Stop Press, Radio-Carbon-Dates" in *The West African Archaeological Newsletter*. No. 9, May, 1968.

Idoniboye, D. E. "The Idea of an African Philosophy: The Concept of Spirit in African Metaphysics" in *Second Order*. Vol. 11 No. 1, 1973.

Idowu, Bolaji. African Traditional Religion: A Definition. London: SCM, 1973.

Ijiomah, Chris. "Some Epistemological Tools With Which Africans Relate To Their Realities". *Ultimate Reality and Meaning*. Vol. 28, No. 1. March, 2005.

Iwe, N. S. S. *Socio-Ethical Issues in Nigeria*. Obosi: Pacific Publishers, 1991.

Kanu, Macaulay. "Towards a Philosophy of Indigenous Technology" in A. F. Uduigwomen (Ed) *From Footmarks to Landmarks on African Philosophy*. Lagos: O. O. Publishers, 2009.

Kidd, Benjamin. *Principles of Western Civilization*. London: Macmillan, 1902.

Kidd, Benjamin. *The Science of Power*. London: Methuen, 1918.

Levy-Bruhl, Lucien. *Primitive Mentality*. Paris: University of France Press, 1947.

Mbiti, John. *African Religions & Philosophy*. Oxford: Heinemann, 1989.

Mbon, F. M. "African Traditional Socio-Religious Ethics and National Development: The Nigerian Case". Jacob, Olupona (Ed). *African Traditional Religions in Contemporary Society*. New York: Paragon House, 1990.

Ndubuisi, F. N. "Crime and Punishment of an Ancient African Morality" in A. F. Uduigwomen (Ed) *From Footmarks to Landmarks on African Philosophy*. Lagos: O. O. Publishers, 2009.

Nnabuchi, Nwankwo. *In Defence of Igbo Belief System: A Dialectical Approach*. Enugu: Life Paths, 1987.

Nwokeji, Orizu. "Cultural Decolonization and Cultural Revival: Problems and Prospects" in Emeke Oguegbu (Ed) Onitsha: Watchword, 1990.

Okoro, C. M. *A Course Text on African Philosophy: Question and Debate* (BK One). Enugu: Paqon Press, 2004.

Oladipo, Olusegun. "Issues in the Definition of African Philosophy" in *Core Issues in African Philosophy* Olusegun Oladipo (Ed) Ibadan: Hope Publishers, 2006.

Onyewuenyi, Innocent. *The African Origin of Greek Philosophy: An Exercise in Afro-centrism*. Nsukka: University of Nigeria Press, 1993.

Rodney, Walter. *How Europe Underdeveloped Africa*. Abuja: Panaf, 2005.

Sapir, E. "Culture, Language and Personality: Selected Essays". D. G. Mendelbaum (Ed.). Berkeley: University of California Press, 1956.

Sogolo, Godwin. *Foundations of African Philosophy*. Ibadan: Ibadan University Press, 1993.

Typhoon International. *The New International Webster's Comprehensive Dictionary of The English Language*. (Encyclopedic Edition). Florida: Trident Press, 2004.

Uduigwomen, Andrew. "Philosophy and the Place of African Philosophy" in A. F. Uduigwomen (Ed). *From Footmarks to Landmarks on African Philosophy*. Lagos: O. O. P. Publishers, 2009.

Unah, Jim. "Ontologico-Epistemological Background to Authentic African Socio Economic and Political Institutions" in A. F. Uduigwomen (Ed) *From Footmarks to Landmarks on African Philosophy*. Lagos: O. O. Publishers, 2009.

SECTION TWO

CHAPTER 15

SENGHOR'S NEGRITUDE
By
ODUORA OKPOKAM ASUO

Introduction

In the introduction to his book, *African Religions and Philosophy*, J. S. Mbiti posits that philosophy of one kind or another is behind the thinking and acting of every people (1). It is in line with this assertion that African nationalists' leaders pursued their aspirations for self actualization with the guide of philosophies, most of which were carved out of the experiences of their people. Such were the principles behind Nkrumah's "consciencism", Nyerere's "ujamaa" and the "negritude" of Leopold Senghor. Senghor's "negritude" was an attempt at self realization, actualization and the restoration of the hitherto bastardized image of the African personality. Of all genres of literature, Senghor chose poetry as the most penetrating mode of transferring the African experience to other Africans in particular and the world at large. Being taught to live and express oneself in another man's language and custom tacitly or openly affects his mode of thinking, and this is most often to the benefit of the colonizer. This was the major pitfall of the Senghorian Negritude, which though sought to paint a uniquely African picture, ended up using a French brush on African canvass.

The Person of Leopold Senghor

Leopold Sedar Senghor was born on October 9, 1906, in the small Senegalese coastal town of Joal. His father was a prosperous peanut farmer and trader who had 20 children. His mother was a Roman Catholic and she had him educated at a nearby Catholic mission and seminary. When he turned 20 however, he abandoned his calling to the priesthood and transferred to secondary school in Dakar. In

1928, he won a partial scholarship that permitted him to study at the Lycee Louis-Le-Grand at the Sorbonne in Paris (*New York Times*, 1). It was during his Sorbonne years that Senghor discovered the uniqueness of the African art and the contribution of the African to "the civilization of the universe". In his studies of philosophy, he originated, with Aime Cesaire of Martinique and Leon Damas of French Guiana, the concept of negritude, in part as a protest against French rule and the policy of assimilation. He espoused the ideals of negritude through his love poems which condemned the "soulessness" of western civilization and maintained that only African culture has presented a mystical means of reviving "the world that has died of machines and cannons" (2).

At the Sorbonne, Senghor was recognized as one of the most brilliant students, and upon his graduation in 1935, achieved the distinction of becoming the first African *agrege*, the highest-ranked teacher in the French school system. He taught French to French children in Tours. He was later drafted into the French Army in 1939 and was captured by the Germans in 1940 and he spent two years in Nazi camps where he wrote some of his best poems, collected in a volume in 1945, titled "*Chantesd' Ombre*". In 1945, he became deputy for Senegal to the French Constituent Assembly. He was elected to the National Assembly and became the first president of Senegal in 1960. He was re-elected in 1963, 1968 and 1973 and remained president till 1980. He married Ginette Eboue, the daughter of a Guyanese. They had two children before they divorced nine years later. He later married Colette Hubert, a Frenchwoman from Normandy. The couple had a son who died in an accident in the 1980's. Senghor died on December 20, 2001 at 95 years of age in Normandy.

The Philosophy of Leopold Senghor

Senghor's philosophy is aptly called negritude. Negritude is more of a movement that was conceived and formed by Senghor, Aime Cesaire and Leon Damas. It is a French word meaning blackness and is aimed at dissuading Africans from imitation of European styles, traditions and values, which were often imposed on Africa during colonial times. African tradition, culture and expressions were considered to be uncivilized and primitive, and were often neglected

(Kajubi, 364). This is why Omoregbe advised that Senghor's philosophy of negritude should be seen against the background of the French colonial policy of assimilating Africans into the French culture and citizenship (33). Nwokereke summed Senghor's philosophy of negritude thus:

> A philosophy of re-discovery and cultural emancipation aimed at giving the African people a sense of pride and dignity in their culture as distinct from French culture and identity as Africans (34).

In a way therefore this philosophy is reactionary, seeking to war against such tendencies as expose the African to mental enslavement. In the words of Senghor himself, as quoted by Markovitz,

> Negritude is the whole of the values of civilization - cultural, economic social, political - which characterize the black peoples, more exactly, the Negro-African world. It is essentially instinctive reason, which pervades all these values. It is reason of the impressions, reason that is "seized". It is expressed by the emotions through abandonment of self and a complete identification with the object, through the myth of the archetype of the collective soul, and the myth primordial accorded to the cosmos. In other terms, the sense of communion, the gift of imagination, the gift of rhythm - these are the traits of negritude that we find like an indelible seal on all works and activities of the black man (41).

The presupposition of Senghor here is that all black men share similar existential positions and that negritude arises first from the singular racial characteristics of the black. Looking at the historical antecedents of negritude, Markovitz posited that:

> At different times in the history of its evolution as an ideology, negritude stood for a number of things. A critique of imperialism, a revolutionary African development distinguished from the proletariat revolt, the birth of a new black civilization, a philosophy of life; an ideology for African unity, a methodology for

development; a justification for rule by indigenous elites; a defense of the dignity of cultured blacks (42).

It is worthwhile to explain here that negritude was both a revolutionary and a reactionary philosophy: revolutionary in its attack on the French colonial myth and reactionary in its adoption of the past glory of Africa as a working tool for the asserting of the prowess of the black race. Senghor saw colonialism as an evil that erodes or will ultimately erode the black personality and leave only the colour. So negritude became a weapon of reappraisal of the dignity of the black man. Markovitz, in his own definition saw Negritude as a "black is beauty" doctrine originated by black intellectuals in pre-world war II Paris to assert the unique contributions, values and characteristics of black men and black civilization. It is an attempt to kill the old Negro, the invention of a meaning so that the world can be seen with fresh eyes and turned inside out by men working to improve it and themselves. This attempt at re-orientation was the main objective of the new African elite. The re-orientation must have been considered necessary to the emancipation course of the elites who considered themselves and their potentials stifled or endangered by the bigotry of racism.

Evolution of Negritude

The philosophy of negritude was a brain child of Paris based black-skinned students notably Leon Damas and Aime Cesaire, who were concerned about the position of the black race in the world of the whites in the pre-world war II era. Senghor, at the time also a student in France, adopted the ideas of the other students and joined in the agitations for the acknowledgement of the black race. Negritude, even in the hands of Senghor, underwent some fundamental changes. Beginning from pre-war Paris, when theories of negritude first took shape, Negritude had some of the characteristics of revolutionary potential which many commentators still ascribe to it. Negritude came closest to being an ideology of racial superiority - a militant racism accompanied by a stance of withdrawal and an attitude of total non-cooperation which could possibly have barred communication and accommodation with the French. According to Markovitz, negritude at the beginning had been an anti-racist racism (50). This reaction, for so it was, by the founders of negritude was unavoidable for they had to buy or make dignity for their devalued race. They had to build a cascade against the burden, the unfairness of being judged by so superficial a characteristic as one's skin colour. The morality however, of matching racism with an equal or even higher degree of racism at this point of movement is what raises a discordant note. This radical racist response must have prompted Markovitz to posit that negritude found its origins in passion, not political contribution (53). It should be stated that white superiority and racism are not a product of subtle intellectual consideration. In fact all racist acts do not stem from academic debates but from passions and emotions, neither do they get resolved by inviting the offender to a round table intellectual deliberation. Reactions to them are most times spontaneous and in similar passion-laden manner.

The next stage in the evolution of negritude did not have as much militant racism as the formative stage of negritude. While the theories of innate racial differences were never dropped from Negritude, Senghor began to moderate them with increased emphasis on cultural differences. By the outbreak of the war (II World War), he had reached the position that although innate racial differences exist, they do not necessarily involve the questions of racial superiority or inferiority, and that, further, the main task at hand was the cultural regeneration of the black man. This was in fact the birth of the cultural assimilation that hid the African in the cloaks of French men. In spite of this policy of assimilation which was hitherto accepted by both black and white alike as the only legitimate goal for the members of the black elite, Senghor mildly rejected assimilation on the basis of the fact that the African culture was essentially different from that of the French. According to him,

> ... a racial reaction of man on his milieu tending towards an intellectual and moral balance between man and his milieu. As the milieu is no more immutable than race, culture becomes a perpetual effort towards a perfect balance, a divine balance. Education ... is the instrument of culture. It consists for the child of the acquisition of experience accumulated from previous generations under the form of concepts, ideas, methods and techniques (Markovitz, 55).

By this, Senghor posits that though education is important, such as has been given to the black elites, yet it (the French brand of education) cannot and should not change the culture of the African which is entirely unique and makes a unique people. To Senghor, Africans differ from Europeans because of the experience of generations spread over centuries. Those blacks who later became intellectuals in France were raised in a distinctly African environment; Africans cannot therefore be treated simply as black French men. It was on the basis of this that Senghor urged the black intellectuals to work towards the restoration of "black values in their truth and excellence". In summary, this period of the evolution of negritude saw a shift from the exposition of racial differences to cultural differences. It was a period that saw to the calling of the European to dispassionately and understandingly look at the uniqueness of the culture of other lands, "the sweetness of being different and together" (56).

In the period after the war, Senghor further developed those theories and aspects of negritude that facilitated dialogue and accommodation with the colonial powers. Although independence was readily granted as a consequence of this 'accommodation', yet the colonialists were granting independence to an assimilated people, a people whose personality had been fundamentally tampered with, like Markovitz averred, their assimilation was to the extent that they used French categories of thought and were never to be true Africans (57). It was on the basis of this that Frantz Fanon advised that for any positive action to be taken for Africa, those taking it must themselves be a living part of Africa and of her thought (166). The evolution of negritude from a radical, supposedly revolutionary doctrine to that of accommodation, assimilation, association and synthesis suggests many things, the most important of which is the fact that its proponent showed a loss of focus in allowing a dilution of its ideals. This was so bad that Senghor in helplessness appointed French as the irrevocable language of the "French African". According to him in a newspaper article "Esprit" quoted by Markovitz, French has made it possible

> ... to communicate to our brothers and to the world the unheard of message which only we could write, it has allowed us to bring to universal civilization

a contribution without which the civilization of the twentieth century could not have been universal (63).

By this declaration, Senghor has gone ahead to deny a purely African worldview but accepts one which exists only because others exist. He also posited his theory of "universal civilization", by which be beggarly showed Africa as an almost insignificant contributor to the "universal civilization", hence the need to give her a place in the scheme of things. This "civilization of the universe" is defined by Markovitz as the ultimate which incorporates the special and unique aspects of all cultures (68), became the central point of negritude in the post-independence era. It is a conscious effort to justify or rationalize not just forced accommodation but colonialism. Senghor fashioned this theory after the position of Teilhard de Chardin that the "foyers of human development" always coincide with points of meeting and synthesis of several races (36).

According to Senghor, Chardin's position was a justification for negritude and advocated a synthesis since each civilization has some unique element, which can contribute to the universal civilization. Colonialism, he averred has actually aided in hastening the civilization of the universal. Senghor emphasized the benefits of colonization and urged the importance of encouraging this cultural intermingling, so that all peoples can help in the creation of the civilization of the universe. Senghor's advocating the civilization of the universal was tantamount to a denial of the uniqueness of a purely African worldview. During the early years of independence and national development, wherein Senghor was concerned with how to enhance economic development of the country, negritude was formulated into a practical philosophy which espoused communal life and work. So the philosophy of negritude was allied with the task of nation-building. This buttresses the fact that Senghor's conception was generally loose to make it able to rationalize or give backing to whatever it is called upon to defend. This looseness leaves one only to imagine what the substance of negritude truly was.

Critique of Negritude

One of the most critical points raised against Negritude is perhaps the one by Markovitz which was buttressed by Fanon that until now, negritude has been neither an ideology of, nor for, the masses. The audiences to which it spoke were either the members of the various French establishments, or black intellectuals. This points to the fact that negritude was not of the people but was a weapon aimed at serving the purpose of the educated elite. It was in a bid to avoid this that Fanon held that in order to achieve real action, you must yourself, be a living part of Africa and of her thought; you must be an element of that popular energy which is entirely called forth for the freeing, the progress and the happiness of Africa (166). The intellectual most times takes up the personality of the colonial country and losses the personhood of the oppressed. This cannot cultivate a healthy contest for freedom. He gives too much concession which at the end gives rise to incomplete freedom. Adding voice to this W.E. Abraham writes:

> In order to set their nations on a course of progress most African rulers, under goading of their passion for western achievements, have tried, at times injudiciously, to import the palpable fruit of that achievement, and, more uncertainly, the mechanical and social technology which was the active means to that achievement. With the least success, they have also tried to import those institutions believed to facilitate the technological society, and have tragically overlooked what could not be imported, what indeed must be supplied by the African societies themselves, namely the inner dynamism, the unspoken but knowing adjustment indispensable for the growth and endurance of the western institutions which they sought to borrow (295).

The philosophies of some African nationalist leaders including that of Senghor are guilty of this, as they lift western ideas and try to 'Africanize' them without in-depth consideration of what might be the reaction of their native lands to such superimposed hegemony. This has been a problem not only in the political scene but in lack of growth in critical areas like science and technology. The "Asian

Tigers" were able to develop technologically and scientifically because they did not just lift the technological ideas of the West but localized these ideas to suit the dynamics of their indigenous know-how. Similarly, nations of the world that have prospered from the political ideals of the West or the East as the case may be, have not attempted to imbibe and practicalise these ideals "hook, line and sinker", but have taken time to delete such aspects as threaten the continued existence of such local ideals and inputs as make their home nations unique and workable; hence Chinese socialism differs in practice from that of the U.S.S.R and the capitalist ideals of Japan have adaptations that bring their culture through to the fore and encourage growth that is different and not necessarily identical to that of the West.

Senghor, however, proved by his words and deeds, to be more of a French man than an African, hence he only helped to perpetually lead his people into the bondage of eternal Frenchification. This was voiced by Chinweizu, in his book, *The West and the Rest of Us* when he advised us not to be carried away by the error of considering Senghorian negritude as a champion of african cultural identity, autonomy and artistic renaissance (364); According to him, "by the middle of the 1950's, the Senghorian strand of negritude had become a handmaid of French imperialism" (364). This could be the reason why former French colonies still have themselves tied to the placenta of their master - France. The latter variants of negritude showed us a picture that was in no way an African worldview. A worldview that recognizes the African reality and the attendant problems which cannot be shared by any other people and which seeks to solve them for Africans and from a distinctly African perspective, rather Senghor saw the African reality as tied to that of the colonizer - the French, and felt the African makes meaning only from the perspective of a Frenchman.

Senghor was consistently pushing the African into adopting a French personality, identity and nationality. His civilization of the universal points to this fact as it attempts to hide the African civilization or give it relevance only as a contributor to the universe, which is unarguably moulded on European paradigms. Adding flesh to this, Ezekiel Mphalele accuses Senghor of oversimplification and romanticizing of African life and history. According to him, negritude tells only half, and often a falsified half, of the story of Africa. In his words,

> Who is so stupid as to deny the historical fact of negritude as both a protest and a positive assertion of African cultural values? All this is valid. What I do not accept is the way in which too much of the poetry inspired by it romanticizes Africa - as a symbol of innocence, purity and artless primitiveness. I feel insulted when some people imply that Africa is not also a violent continent. I am a violent person, and proud of it, because it is often a healthy human state of mind; some day, I'm going to plunder, rape, set things on fire; I'm going to cut someone's throat; I'm going to subvert a government; I'm going to organize a coup d'etat; yes, I'm. going to oppress my own people I'm going to hunt down the rich fat black men who bully the small weak black men and destroy them; I'm going to become a capitalist, and woe to all who cross my path or who want to be my servants or chauffeurs and so on; I'm going to lead a break away church. There is money in it, I'm going to attack the black bourgeoisie while I cultivate a garden, rear dogs and parrots; listen to Jazz and classics, read "culture" and so on. Yes, I'm going to organize a strike. Don't you know that sometimes I kill to the rhythm of drums and cut the sinews of a baby to cure it of paralysis? (624-625).

Whereas, we can be justified in accusing Mphalele of savagery and in some cases, exaggeration, yet the truth should be told that these are realities in Africa, just like they are anywhere else in the world. The advocates of negritude however, carefully downplayed these realities while praise-singing the black man, hence making the outside world to have a distorted view of Africa which makes the outside world not to respect Africa. It was this situation that made Paul Niger and Guy Tirolien, as quoted by Markovitz, after a pilgrimage to the "ancestral sources", to criticize the contents of negritude thus:

> We had lived an unreal negritude, made out of the theories of ethnologists, sociologists, and other scholars who studied man under glass. They have injected the Negroite with formaldehyde, and pretended it was a type of happy man (58).

Apparently their on-the-spot assessment of Africa had revealed more awful truths than they had seen in the tablets and speeches of negritude. Negritude in its operation and concession has made African culture subservient to that of the French. According to Nathan Hare, culture is supposed to be an ideological weapon which gives consciousness to its people. On, the contrary however, negritude collaborated with colonialism to rip the people of their culture and left the issue of "oppression and liberation in the realm of mystification", which is hostile to the cultural development of Africa (48). This was contrary to the thought of Fanon in his *Black Skin, White Mask*, where he posited that a people cannot have a culture when they are still with the fetters of the oppressor (187). That culture, if any, will definitely be subsumed under the worldview of the oppressor. Negritude was not *prima facie* advocating the distinctness of the African but tended to work on the premise that the African was completely cultured only in his place as a French citizen. In summary, I will use the words of Markovitz that negritude as defined by Senghor spoke to alienation and not to exploitation, to the individual and not to the mass, to the intellectual and not to the illiterate, to the modern and not to the traditional (45), to say that negritude failed as a liberationist or revolutionary philosophy because of its cultural separateness from the people it purported to be wanting to serve and its collaboration with the imperialists. Ijiomah, in his contribution to *Sophia* says that each philosopher has to be inspired by his immediate worldview as he goes into a critical inquiry (47). By this it can be averred that what makes a person's thought or philosophy indigent is its adherence to the worldview of his people.

In terms of worldview and reality, Senghor's negritude was primarily aimed at resolving or giving voice to a uniquely African reality - the reality of slavery, colonialism, imperialism and racism. In spite of the fact that "negritude, from its origins, was conceived within the scope of the French colonial myth" (Markovitz, 42), it cannot be deprived of its Africanness, since it seeks primarily to proffer solution to an African problem - the problem of an erosion of the African personality with his culture by the forces of white supremacy. These inconsistencies do not completely erode this aim. An issue that is intricately tied to the position that negritude is an African philosophy on the basis of the fact that it seeks to solve an African problem is the question of whether a philosophy that is conceived and written in another man's language can genuinely convey the worldview of the people writing it. This difficulty is conveyed by Leon Laleau a Haitian poet, when he asked this question:

> Do you feel this suffering and this despair equal to no other; of being trapped with the words of France? This is the heart which is come to me from Senegal (Markovitz, 33).

This poet was painting a picture of the near impossibility of asserting the totality of one's worldview when one abandons his mother tongue for that of the "mother country". According to Markovitz, a point admitted by Senghor himself, literature done in another man's language, as in black literature done in French language wouldn't know how to express "our soul". There is *a certain flavour, a certain odour, certain accent, a certain black timbre, which cannot be expressed on European instruments" (62).* To show the importance of language in African thinking, Ehusani holds that for a people who did not write, their language itself is an encyclopedia of knowledge about their history, their religion, their cosmology and their value system. It is part of the resource text from which their history, philosophy and theology could be written (105-106). So when Senghor writes in French, he has abandoned the African position of reality for a French categorization which he, being a foreigner to, cannot adequately comprehend, at least not as much as the French themselves. In his analogy of the millennium Africa, Ijiomah highlights the danger of thinking with another's language when he held that one's language is related to the metaphysics of his people, the African who is in paradigm conflict gets confused linguistically, (*A Man in Confluence*, 140). This paradigm conflict according to him arises from imhibitions of western thinking and lifestyle alongside that of native Africa which

then causes an internal warfare and confusion. Furthermore, speaking on the place of language in thought, Ijiomah holds that
> When an African who thinks in African language perceives objects or things which his Western counterpart does perceive at the same time, the African mental picture of the objects differs from that of the Western man because the two men operate from different linguistic decoding concepts. Accordingly, thinking in a particular language implies corroboration of conceptualization from a particular natural post. This natural post is the cultural milieu (*Dilemma in Language*, 84).

In the case of Senghor and his poetry, he was merely viewing reality from the French man's perspective, to toe the line of this analogy. We should however understand the helplessness of Senghor and every other "modern" African that is forced into learning and using another man's language to observe and interpret reality. It is a reality which the underlying geographical and political scenario may not easily let us to overcome. In essence, though we know, just like Ijiomah, that "we can use African language to probe into how an African understands and explains reality" (Metaphysical, 48), yet the reality of bilingualism, as articulated by Senghor, should make us fashion another means of still having a unique African epistemology, in spite of the use of foreign languages.

Conclusion

Negritude was given birth to with the aim of protecting the dignity of the Negro race in the face of white supremacist ideas. Leopold Senghor extended the use of this philosophy to the realm of government when the French granted political independence to Senegal. Whereas Negritude seeks to uncover and popularize the uniquely African personality; it has been discovered in this work that the philosophy of Negritude turned out to be more of an instrument in the hands of the colonizers for the continued subjugation of the Africans while giving the false impression that they are French citizens with black colour. This makes questionable the claim to self government and self determination by former

French colonies and exposes the collusion by the elites and intellectuals of these colonies in the fate of their states.

WORKS CITED

Abraham, W. *The Mind of Africa*. Chicago: University of Chicago Press, 1962.

Chardin, T. *Great Africans and Arabs of Negritude*. Paris: Presence Africaine, 1967.

Chinweizu, *The West and the Rest of Us*. London, Nok Publishers, 1978.

Ehusani, G. An *Afro Christian Vision "Ozovehe": Toward a More Humanized World*. Oxford: Oxford University Press, 1965.

Fanon, F. *Black Skin, White Mask*. Paris: Du Sevil, 1952.

Fanon, F. *The Wretched of the Earth: The Classics of Third World Politics*. London: Penguin Books, 1983.

Hare, N. "A Report on the Pan-African Cultural Festival" in Robert Christmas and Nathan Hare (Eds). *Pan-Africanism*. New York: Bobbs-Merill, 1974.

Ijiomah, C. O. "A Man in Confluence: An Index for the Millennium African Philosophy" in *Karunungan: A Journal of Philosophy*, Vol. 22, 2005.

Ijiomah, C. O. "The Truth-Functional Dilemma in Language - Thought Relationship in African Humanism and Isomorphism: A Way Out" in *Ndunode: Calabar Journal of Humanities*. Vol. 3, Number 2, 2002.

Ijiomah, C. O. "Metaphysical Reference in African Language: A Paradigm Shift from Western Philosophy of Language" in *Sophia: An African Journal of Philosophy*. Vol. 5, No 1, September, 2002.

Kajubi, A. (Ed). *African Encyclopedia.* Oxford: Oxford University Press, 1979.

Markovitz, I. *Leopold Sedar Senghor and the Politics of Negritude.* New York: Atheneum, 1969.

Mbiti, J. S. *African Religions and Philosophy.* London: Heinemann, 1977.

Mphalele, E. *The African Image.* New York: Praeger, 1962.

Nwokereke, E. *Trends and Perspectives in African Socio-Political Philosophy.* Abakiliki: Copycraft Publications, 2005.

Omoregbe, J. Knowing Philosophy: A General Introduction. Lagos: Joja Press, 2001.

INTERNET MATERIAL

Krebs, Albin. *Leopold Senghor Dies at 95; Senegal's Poet of Negritude.* http:nytimes.com December 21, 2001

CHAPTER 16

NKRUMAH's IDEOLOGY FOR AFRICA
By
IKS J. NWANKWOR, Ph.D.

Introduction

Kwame Nkrumah (1909 - 1972), one of the prominent figures that secured political independence for African nations, is a very controversial man. In theory, the man is rigorous and refined. In practice, he bits more than he can chew. In what follows, we shall expose the vision and mission of the man, and his ideological option for Africa, giving some critical appraisal.

Nkrumah: Vision and Mission

Few individuals enter the planet-earth, like others, simply naked and unnoticed; but live and leave, unlike others, creating indelible marks on the sands of time. Kwame Nkrumah of Ghana, born in 1909, quietly and humbly like many others, is among these few individuals, who lived and left terrestrial terrain, raising dust of recognition for all times. Concerning Nkrumah, "the record shows a person of ideas, working ceaselessly, through political activity, economic planning, and continental and international diplomacy in the prosecution of national and continental vision" (Akilagpa Sawyer, 14). In Nkrumah, we see a foresighted visionary and activist who helped to define and determine the times in which he lived. God, who has perfect arrangement of things, usually bring such men/women into existence when society (ies) suffocates from the pollution of injustice and imbalance. That is why Nkrumah, perhaps more than any of his Ghanaian contemporaries,
> ... was able to identify, focus and catalyze the major factors and players driving the struggle

for political independence in Ghana and liberation in other parts of Africa. In the process, he committed his life and work totally to a wide variety of activities and processes in Ghana, the continent and in the global Non-Aligned Movement (Akilagpa Sawyer, 14).

Nkrumah, no doubt, is the major political engineer that set Ghana on records, as the first black African nation that achieved political independence on 6th March, 1957. Not only that, he was the first serious pan-Africanist who dreamt, labored, and preached the gospel of African unity with all zeal and determination.

... Nkrumah's zeal for African unity led him at every important stage in his career – at the creation of the Convention People's Party in 1949, at Ghana's independence in 1957, and at the establishment, of the Republic of Ghana in 1960 – to insist that Ghana would be ready to surrender her sovereignty in the interest of African unity (Rooney, 10).

In Nkrumah, we notice a far-sighted visionary, who was not only concerned with the present, but with the integral implication(s) of the present in the future. Consequently, while some of his contemporaries thought political independence to be the end of the kingdom, Nkrumah looked beyond to behold autonomy, self-reliance, and self-determination of African nations as the launch-pad to true political kingdom.

He envisaged a united and self-sufficient Africa as the ultimate objective of all the independence struggles and to achieve this aim he shaped a new philosophy – Nkrumaism or scientific socialism – relevant first to Ghana and secondly to Africa (Rooney, 9).

Kwame Nkrumah, "almost alone among African leaders, saw the future in global perspective" (Rooney, 9). Thus, he labored, perhaps more seriously that all, in determining an ideological path-way for Africa. Being conscious that practice without theory is blind and theory without practice is futile, he set his brilliant mind to fashion an ideology which would be suitable for African conditions. However, in his enthusiasm to form a suitable home-grown ideology, Nkrumah, as is usually the case; reclined more on the resources of his education, drawing much vigor from his erudition in Marxist-Leninist socialism.

> From a predominantly Marxist standpoint, he saw the power of the Western industrial countries and their multinational companies as the main threat to the economic prosperity of the Third World Countries then moving towards independence (Rooney, 10).

Having had a clear vision of the horizon, his next thrust was a practical action to upturn the substructures that maintain the superstructures of oppression and injustice that weigh heavily on the masses of his nation and continent.

> He, therefore, produced an ideology in which the government would take the means of production and distribution, and use the expected profits to provide for further industrial and social development (Rooney, 10).

Such was his vision and target – a broad thinking for integral and comprehensive emancipation of African nations from their imperialist brothers. On achieving independence, Nkrumah, having seen that full political liberation is tied to economic emancipation, set in motion principles for total industrialization of Ghana, nay Africa, and a policy for agrarian revolution. Thus,

> Through the Volta River Project, he set out to make Ghana the nucleus of an industrial base for the whole of Africa, and to save the continent from the debt-creating attentions of the capitalist world (Rooney, 10).

His goal in this mission, it would seem, is to let Africa stand on her own as a proud black continent, that freely refuses the blended scores and rations, which her colonial masters may deem fit to grant. Nkrumah never wavered nor was deterred from his vision and determination to accomplish the mission of African grand liberation; However, along the line, this "… brilliant and highly controversial figure, who so nearly straddled the East-West divide", met with a number of obstacles in a bid to realize his dreams. He meant so many things to so many people: to some, he was beautiful; to others, he was ugly; he was "loved and hated, worshipped and derided, misunderstood and distrusted" (Rooney, 8). But like the biblical Joseph, those who threw him to the pit and later sold him as useless, are now missing him dearly, especially in his beloved Ghana. However, this may not imply that Nkrumah was an angel, sent on earth without blemishes; as every mortal, he has his limitations.

Despite his brilliant contributions to "national unity", "economic transformation", "total liberation and unity of Africa and its non-alignment in the Cold War between the super power blocs", Nkrumah has been rated as an exceptional visionary "whose achievements were undermined by the inadequacy of his administration" (Rooney, 10). He has been accused of "failure to address the question of corruption and the abuse of state power, particularly in relation to detention without trial" (Rooney, 15). Some have also criticized his "one-man-squad" method of implementation of his new ideology, "a task too big for any one man." But when the chips are down, Nkrumah would ever be remembered for his visionary prerogatives, and his flaws could be veritable education and sparks of wisdom for future African leaders. David Rooney's summary may not be bettered:

> Nkrumah saw all the visions, dreamt all the dreams, and made all the mistakes. These mistakes cost Ghana dear, but the mistakes he made are, in their way, as valuable as his vision to an Africa still grappling with problems of poverty, exploitation, and debt. Learning from these mistakes could still save Africa's leaders from future blunders, while the inspiration of his idealism still impels them towards the elusive goal of a prosperous and united Africa (Rooney, 11).

But if Nkrumah is (such) a controversial person in practice, perhaps an exposition of his socio-political and economic ideology would reveal the refined man of thought which he is.

Nkrumah's Ideological Proposal

Nkrumah specifically speaks on ideology. He asserts that ideology can galvanize the political, social, cultural, economic, and artistic experiences of the people. According to him:

> ... an ideology seeks to bring a specific order into the total life of its society. It displays itself in political theory, social theory and moral theory, and uses these as instruments (Nkrumah's *Consciencism*, 59).

The ideology of a people, in Nkrumah's opinion, is all-embracive. It encompasses the total life processes of the people. "It embraces the whole life ... and manifests itself in their class-structure, history, literature, art, religion ..." (Nkrumah's *Consciencism*, 59). Because the activities of ideology are integrative in nature, it is also a formidable vehicle of social control. Nkrumah argues as follows:

> If an ideology is integrative in intent, that is to say, if it seeks to introduce a certain order which will unite the actions of millions towards specific and definite goals, then its instruments can also be seen as instrument of social control (Nkrumah's *Consciencism*, 59-60).

Unlike Julius Nyerere whose ideological proposals explicitly applied to his country, Tanzania, and implicitly to the African continent, Kwame Nkrumah's views on ideology was holistic and could apply to all African nations. His main ideas on ideological option for Africa are contained in his book – *Africa Must Unite*, published in 1963. His brand of ideology is "Scientific Socialism", not "African socialism". This "scientific socialism" apes Marxist socialist theory in outlook, despite Nkrumah's contention to the contrary. In line with Marxist theory, which argues that the forces of exploitation have inherent contradictions that destroy its working principles, Nkrumah contends that imperialism has four internal factors or contradictions that work against its prosperity. These factors include:

(a) the emergence of a colonial intelligentsia; (b) the awakening of national consciousness among colonial peoples; (c) the emergence of a working-class movement; and (d) the growth of a national liberation movement (Nkrumah's *Towards Colonial Freedom*, 59).

Thus, Nkrumah's total plan for African liberation has three areas of concentration videlicet (namely):

(1) Political freedom, i.e. complete and absolute independence from the control of any foreign government; (2) Democratic freedom, i.e. freedom from political tyranny and establishment of democracy in which sovereignty is vested in the broad masses of the people; (3) Social Reconstruction; i.e. freedom from poverty and economic exploitation and the improvement of social and economic conditions of the people... (Nwoko, 219 - 220).

In the area of political freedom, the total liberation of Africa must be from both within and without. From within, Africa must fight its real enemies who are Africans by origin but westerners or foreigners by inclinations and exploitation of their respective nations. These categories of enemies can be found in the military or among civilian elites who do not have the progress and interest of Africa at heart. But from without, Africa had always had foes; who would not want her progress economically, politically, or culturally. These external foes use divergent methods in propagating their objectives. Often times, they use African compradors as collaborators in their heinous activities. To eliminate external foes that hinder African freedom, there is the necessity for "the establishment of free and people's own press to stir up true political consciousness in the people", as well as educate them "to pursue their own freedom and destiny and abhor external interference" (Nwoko, 219).

Nkrumah was keen to recognize the importance of true and proper education of the masses if true and genuine freedom of Africa was to be achieved. He utilized his energy, in speech and writing, to bring the people to the light of understanding and political consciousness.

He devoted several literary works to political liberation of Africa. Furthermore, Nkrumah recognized the importance of mass mobilization, especially, mobilizing the labour and the youth, in the achievement of political freedom. He devoted every ounce of his energy in making sure that Africa is united for political emancipation. Pan-Africanism and the Organization of African Unity (OAU) are some of the fruits of this strenuous endeavour. In the area of social reconstruction, the aim of Nkrumah's socialist advocation was to "abolish poverty, ignorance, illiteracy, and improve ... health services" (Nkrumah's *Africa Must Unite*, 118). In Ghana, the adoption of this socialist path will entail "full employment, good housing and equal opportunity for education and cultural advancement for all people up to the highest level possible". It means in practical terms that

> prices of goods must not exceed wages; house rental must be within the means of all groups; social welfare services must be opened to all; education and cultural amenities must be available to everyone (Nkrumah's *Africa Must Unite*, 119)

To be able to achieve these objectives, socialism shall assume "the public ownership of the means of production, the land and its resources, and the use of those means in fulfillment of the people's needs" (Nkrumah's *Africa Must Unite*, 119). However, to assuage people's problems, emphasis is placed on industrialization and modernization of agriculture.

The economy of state under Nkrumah's socialist guidelines is divided into five sectors "videlicet" : "(1) state enterprises; (2) enterprises owned by foreign private interests; (3) enterprises jointly owned by state and foreign private interests; (4) co-operatives; and (5) small-scale Ghanaian private enterprise" (Nkrumah's *Africa Must Unite*, 121). But he expressly warned that no exclusive rights of economic operation should be granted any single individual, and that government has the prerogative of over-seeing all economic activities within the state. Through his socialist principles, Nkrumah hoped to create "... a diversified, many-sided economy" that would be "able to supply their growing population with the basic commodities that will lessen the burden now imposed on the country by the need to import so many of its requirements" (Nkrumah's *Africa Must Unite*, 121).

From the fore-going, Nkrumah seemed to reduce the problem of authority and freedom in Africa to that of economic liberalism. His argument seems to be that if Africa is able to liberate herself from economic entanglements, she will be free indeed. He advocates for economic independence in order to be really free from colonial bondage. For him, the role of agriculture in the procurement of African economic freedom cannot be attenuated. If agriculture is transformed from subsistent to exportive, it can support Africa and thus help boost her "ego" dilapidated by long years of colonialism. Thus, Nkrumah strongly argues that:

> There must be a transformation of our subsistence farms into commodity producing farms, so that they may provide enough food for our steadily rising population, give raw materials to feed secondary industries and cash crops to help pay for our necessary imports (Nkrumah's *Africa Must Unite*, 121).

In another vein, Nkrumah advocates for the promotion of "capital formation" to enable the amelioration of the imbalance created by colonialism among the different regions. Thus, attention will be paid to investment that promotes capital formation through saving imports and increasing exports.

Nkrumah's socialist plan also incorporates "educational, social welfare, and health programmes". This is because "an educated, healthy population represents the human investment and development" (Nkrumah's *Africa Must Unite*, 122). Above all, the over-all planning is designed to discipline and unify all economic activity within the socialist state. These over-all plans will also "expand the creative spirit of the people by the task of responsibility that will be given them in management, supervision and invention" (Nkrumah's *Africa Must Unite*, 122). In all these, there ought to be control from the top to ensure that individual executives and administrators do not derail from the general plan and the co-ordinate pattern of policy and budgeting.

Nkrumah stresses the need of diversified agricultural and industrial base so as to cushion the effects of foreign investment, which has the potentiality of leading to economic servitude. He also reasons that the surpluses arriving from the rise in production would be used in financing development. In his overall economic plan, he keeps the working class close to his heart. He contends that "wages must be set at a level which will provide proper diet and maintain working energy". And as the product of labour increases, government will increase wages thereby raising the standard of living of the workers.

To realize these lofty ideals, the executives of the public and statutory organizations ought to achieve a new attitude to work, recognize that they are in service of their nation at the expense of the farmers or workers. Consequently, they ought not to be involved in "unproductive ventures" which will merely satiate their inordinate ambition for profit and leave their nation impoverished.

In Nkrumah's socialist plan, the educational system is tailored towards the production of skilled personnel ready to serve the country's needs at all levels. It also makes provision for the unemployed. They (unemployed) are to be trained in "discipline, responsibility and citizenship" to enable them find employment in agriculture and industry (Nkrumah's *Africa Must Unite*, 126).

In the envisaged socialist state of Nkrumah, the trade union work hand-in-hand with government for genuine progress. They are never in conflict with each other as this tends to retard progress. In effect, the role of African trade union movements was explicitly spelt out by Nkrumah. The African trade union movement must promote the independence and welfare of the African workers; it cannot run the risk of subordinating the safety of African independence and the needs of African development to other, non-African influences (Nkrumah's *Africa Must Unite*, 128). Nkrumah prayed for an "All-African Trade Union Federation" which will be a rallying pivot for the promotion of African interests. On this Trade Union Federation, he tied a lot of hope to the future of Africa. According to him:

> Such a dynamic force, allied to political action, is the surest means of routing out of our continent the last remnants of colonialism and exploitation, since it will stimulate the

effectiveness of the nationalist movements (Nkrumah's *Africa Must Unite,* 128).

Nkrumah believes that the objectives of socialism and economic independence could be achieved through "decisive party leadership". In his socialist state, there is no friction between authority and freedom for "the people exercise control of the state through their will as expressed in the direct consultation between government and them" (Nkrumah's *Africa Must Unite,* 129). In fact, in this socialist state, true democracy is in operation.

For the onerous task of bringing socialism to be, there is the need to be socialist teachers and leaders. Like Plato, Nkrumah enlisted the types of educational training, physical and mental, which the would-be socialist propagators are to undertake. Indeed all, including members of the Central Committee, Ministers, high party officials, farmers, factory workers, et cetera have to undergo special educational training "to broaden their political knowledge and ideological understanding" (Nkrumah's *Africa Must Unite,* 131). Nkrumah maintained that these facilities and opportunities of socialism are not meant for his country – Ghana alone, but for the whole Africa and indeed "the world who seek knowledge to fit themselves for the great freedom fight against imperialism, old or new" (Nkrumah's *Africa Must Unite,* 131). In all these, Nkrumah seems to mimic the Marxist socialist theory or philosophy, although he argues that his is entirely Ghanaian content-wise and African in outlook.

One cord that seems to run throughout Nkrumah's ideological position is the emphasis on economic vibrancy as the sustainer of political freedom. His earlier assertion somewhere that we should first seek the political freedom seems to have its concomitant follow-up in the advocacy for economic emancipation. His "scientific socialism" for Ghana and Africa, he has no doubt, will lead to complete freedom for the continent. In this ideology, he does not envisage autocracy or illiberalism since the interest of the masses is close to its chest and, as it were, the bedrock of its proposition.

Critical Remarks

Much as we recognize the pious contributions of Nkrumah in proposing an ideology for the solution of the socio-economic and political quandaries that faced African countries immediately after political independence, we need to point out that African peculiarities make it imperative that we decipher foreign ideologies (in whatever garbs they may appear) before we can swallow them line, hook and sinker. Even though Nkrumah emphasizes the peculiarity of his *"Scientific Socialism"* for Ghana and African nations, there is no doubt that the thinking pattern, analysis and linguistic emblems of this ideology are foreign. Specifically, it is an African resurrection of Marxist-Leninist socialist theory and ideology. However, the major problem of this "Scientific Socialism" may not necessarily be its "foreign identity" but its ontological presuppositions and epistemological oversights. Nkrumah must have presumed, as Marxists - Leninists theorists, that matter is the supreme determinant of all realities. The emphasis on political liberation and economic emancipation speaks this point loudly.

There is no doubt that "Marxist-Leninist Socialism" is downright materialistic. The specific harm of absolute materialism is the oversimplification of being and reality under the one and supposed "category of matter".

This oversimplification and ontological disposition ignore the multisided and complex features of existence and existential problematic. Not only that, it identifies the essence of existence with an existential problematic. If materialism, expressed in any of its substructures, like political institutions and economic establishments, is the underlying principle of existence, how is it that the so-called affluent and developed nations of the world are still battling with human-related problems and global changes and challenges posed in our terrestrial and aquatic habitat and ecosystems. One would have thought that given their practice of democracy for some precious time now, and given their giant leaps in scientific and technological developments, the developed nations would have turned into heaven on earth. But the reality that stares one in the face is the helplessness of man even with his imposing ideologies and developed environmental substructures and superstructures. This goes to confirm our claim somewhere that:

"Science and technology can lead us to life or death, if they are able to lead us to both, then we should be wary about them" (Nwankwor's *Sparks of Wisdom,* Vol. 1, Cat. 4: 228, p. 104). When all is said and done, man still yearns for spiritual fulfillment; and not only material prosperity.

Furthermore, Nkrumah's "scientific socialism", whether he calls it African or universal, apart from ontological set-backs, is bemused by some epistemological difficulties. One may still wonder why Nkrumah, despite his fine "scientific socialist theory" was not altogether a success story, even in his beloved Ghana? One could ask: why is a man, of such ebullient vision and knowledge, not able to administer the affairs of a sovereign state as Ghana, without side murmurings. This immediately introduces us to the wide chasm between epistemological know-how and ontological reality. Even though Prof. G. O. Ozumba, taking cue from Hegel, would write: "the African must know that the mind is supreme, the mind thinks its own idea, and every idea is rational and what is rational should be real and the real is the actual" (36). Still some questions may persist such as: how real are ideas, especially in influencing the action(s) of their originators? It may not be doubted that some idealists practice what they think and propagate; but, it is also a truism that some think in one way, and act the opposite way.

This is an internecine combat in man which St. Paul, the Apostle, describes in the Holy Writ (Romans 7: 14- 25): "... For I do not do the good I want, but I do the evil I do not want..." *(The African Bible,* 1896). Nkrumah may have originated fine ideas and philosophies like: Consciencism, Scientific Socialism, Pan-Africanism, Unity and Love among men, still all his actions did not speak so eloquently and beautifully as his fine thoughts and ideas; So one may still doubt whether ideas always influence actions as Ozumba (37) seems to conclude: "As you think, you idealize, you conceptualize and then, incubate the idea and what follows is fabrication and creation". However, the position may still be tenable if Nkrumah was thinking the right and its opposite at the same time, and then incubating both concurrently.

While advocating for philosophical consciencism as the lee-way out of the labyrinth of African socio-political and economic quandaries,

Nkrumah also advocated the revolutionary path for this transformation, arguing that: "It is out of tension that being is born. Becoming is tension and being is the child of that tension of opposed forces and tendencies" (Nkrumah's *Consciencism,* 108). While this line of thought concurs with those that maintain that if you want to have your right, you fight for it, it did not critically distinguish between the ends and the means; neither did it speak specifically about the justification of the means to an end. Assuming the end is the "political kingdom", as Nkrumah is wont to say: "seek ye first the political kingdom, and everything else shall follow"; can we agree with him at all times, and in all respects? Is the "political kingdom" actually the end or is it human happiness and fulfillment? Can we, on this token, justify the colonial masters and the imperialists who may have sought their political kingdoms, found and harvested in Africa?

Again, assuming the political kingdom is a good end/goal can't the means of arriving at it be questioned? If we justify revolution as a means, can't we, on the same token, justify slavery, oppression, intimidation, tyranny, autocracy, dictatorship and a litany of such vices (or do we call them virtues?)? When we think and act or pretend to act as if the "means" is indifferent in the consideration of the "end", we may be guilty of making room for recurrent succession of chaos and anarchy.

Summary and Conclusion

The socio-political and economic environment under which African nations operated during the close of 19th- century is, to say the least, oppressive, exploitative, and dehumanizing. That Ghana, the gold coast, got her political freedom before any other nation in Africa is a tribute which she got through the sweet and brow of her visionary, foresighted and mission-oriented leaders such as Nkrumah. This reinforces our earlier claim that: "A nation is as great as the vision, mission, and readiness for service, which her leaders possess" (Nwankwor's *Sparks of Wisdom* Vol. 3, Cat. 3: 340, p. 66).

Nkrumah understood his national role in the gold coast Ghana early enough that he wasted no time to prepare himself academically and intellectually for this national call. The outcome of his intellectual development was his thorough grooming in the science of colonial and post-colonial thesis and anti-thesis. This intellectual "risorgimento" led to the birth of his *Philosophy of Consciencism*, which following the Marxist-Leninist socialist tradition advocates among other things: "the conscientization and education of African nations" to live above "the ideological disintegration consequent upon colonialism"; the spearheading of a "unitarily based economic planning, a unified military and defense strategy, and a unified foreign and diplomatic policy" (Iroegbu and Izibili, 68); and finally the use of revolution to achieve African communalism and *Scientific Socialism* (which he believes would guarantee African integral development). For Nkrumah:

> The development form of communalism is socialism; hence by adopting socialism, African nations would not only be going back to their roots but would be adopting it in its developed form (Nkrumah's *Consciencism*, 94).

We have seen the limitations of Nkrumah's reductionist ideology which was couched mainly on materialism. The fact that Nkrumah's epistemological ambition, so fine as it looks, did not stand the test of time, is a vindication of its ontological shortsightedness. God and His influence on politics and meta-politics of existence were totally ignored by Nkrumah. His advocacy of revolution as the last resort to all political quandaries smacks of hopelessness. As we wrote elsewhere: "When a nation (individual) abandons God, calamity becomes his/her next neighbour" (Nwankwor's *Sparks of Wisdom*, Vol.3, Cat. 3:398, p. 72). Thus, by that his advocacy, Nkrumah was inadvertently writing the epitaph of the demise of his administration, which was to be read by the military coup plotters who ousted him from power. He went into exile and later died there in 1972. Such then is the strength and weakness of Nkrumah's socio-political and economic ideology for Ghana and Africa.

WORKS CITED

Akilagpa Sawyer, "Forward" in David Rooney Kwame *Nkrumah: Vision and Tragedy*. Ghana: Sub-Saharan Publishers, 2007.

Iroegbu, P. O. and M. A. Izibili, *Kpim of Democracy (Thematic Introduction to Socio-political Philosophy)*. Benin City: Ever-Blessed Publishers, 2004.

Nkrumah, K., *Towards Colonial Freedom*. London: Panaf Books, 1962.

Nkrumah, K., *Consciencism*. London: Panaf Books. 1964.

Nkrumah, K., *Africa Must Unite*. London: Mercury Books, 1965.

Nwankwor, I. J., *Sparks of Wisdom*, Vol. 1, Onitsha: Tabansi Press, 1999.

Nwankwor, I. J., *Sparks of Wisdom (Divine Love and Mercy Edition)*, Vol. 3, Uyo: IMK Prints, 2008.

Nwoko, M. I., *Basic World Political Theories*. Owerri: Claretian Institute of Philosophy, 1988.

Ozumba, G. O. (Ed.), *A Colloquium on African Philosophy*, Vol. 2, Calabar: Jochrisam Publishers, 2004.

Rooney, D., *Kwame Nkrumah: Vision and Tragedy*. Ghana: Sub-Saharan Publishers, 2007.

Zinkuratire, Victor, *et al.*, *The African Bible*. Kenya: Paulines Publications Africa, 2010.

CHAPTER 17

FANON'S PHILOSOPHY OF DECOLONIZATION
By
MESEMBE ITA EDET

Introduction

One of the major themes of contemporary African socio-political philosophy is African decolonization. Decolonization is a critical response to the pseudo ideology of European colonialism. Throughout human history, nations and peoples have continuously colonized and been colonized. It is said that when a foreign colonial or imperial power is too strong to be effectively resisted, the colonized population often has no other immediate option than to accept the rule of the foreigners as an inescapable reality of life. As time progresses, the colonized indigenous people, the natives, would perceive the differences between the foreigners and themselves, between the foreigners' ways and the natives' ways. This would then sometimes lead the natives to mimic the foreigners that are in power as they began to associate that power and success with the foreigner's ways. This eventually leads to the development of a colonial mentality. Colonial mentality refers to institutionalized or systemic feelings of inferiority within some societies or peoples who have been subjected to colonialism, relative to the ways, mores or values of the foreign powers which had previously subjugated them through colonization.

The colonizers' ways, culture or doctrines begin to be accepted by the colonized as intrinsically better, more worthy or superior. The colonizers' ways are held in higher esteem than previous indigenous ways. This is the African experience. Consequently, African decolonization is a deconstructive ideological response to European colonialism. If European colonialism is taken aesthetically, African decolonization becomes antithetical. Famous examples of the African decolonial anti-thesis, counter ideological to the European colonial thesis include Kwame Nkrumah's, "consciencism", Leopold Senghor's "negritude" and the idea of "African socialism" of Julius Nyerere and Kenneth Kaunda. One other leading anti-colonial thinker of the 20th century was Frantz Omar Fanon, a French psychiatrist, philosopher, revolutionary and author. Fanon has often been portrayed as an advocate of violence in revolution. It is our view that this characterization of Fanon's work and philosophy is reductionist because it ignores the subtlety of his understanding of the colonial system. Our task in this essay is to position Fanon's work in his own time and draw out its implications for contemporary African socio-political philosophy and the philosophy of decolonization. Our thesis is that Fanon was never an apologist of violence or a revolutionary, but a "thinker of violence".

The Life and Times of Fanon

Frantz Fanon was a black man born on July 20, 1925 on the Caribbean Island of Martinique, which was then a French colony. He was born into a mixed family background: his father was the descendent of African slaves, and his mother was said to be an illegitimate child of mixed race, whose white ancestors came from Strasbourg in Alsace. Fanon's family was socio economically middle class, and they could afford the fees for the Lycee Schoelcher, which was then the most prestigious high school in Martinique, where the writer, Aime Cesaire, was one of his teachers. The young Fanon conceived of himself as French, a consequence of the French "assimilationist" policy, but his encounters with racial prejudice later in life decisively shaped his attitude to colonial racism. The first was in 1940, after France fell to the Nazis. Vichy French Naval troops were blockaded on Martinique. Forced to remain on the island, the French soldiers began to segregate, oppress and abuse the Martiniquan people. There were many accusations of harassment and sexual misconduct. The abuse of the Martiniquan people by the French army was a major influence on Fanon as it generated feelings of alienation, disorientation and disgust at the realities of colonial racism. At the age of eighteen, Fanon fled the island of Martinique and traveled to the then – British colony, Dominic to join the free French forces.

Fanon subsequently enlisted in the French army and joined an allied convoy that arrived in Casablanca. He was later transferred to an army base at Bejaia on the Kabyle coast of Algeria. He left Algeria from Oran and saw military service in France, notably in the battles of Alsace. In 1944, he was wounded at Colmar and received the *Croix de Guerre* medal. When the Nazis were defeated and allied forces crossed the Rhine into Germany, along with photo journalists, Fanon's regiment was "bleached" of all non-white soldiers and Fanon and his fellow Caribbean soldiers were sent to Toulon province instead. Later they were transferred to Normandy to await repatriation home. This experience reinforced his feelings of alienation and his disgust of colonial racism. In 1945, Fanon returned to Martinique and worked for the parliamentary campaign of his former teacher, friend and mentor, Aimé Césaire who was running as a parliamentary delegate from Martinique to the first National Assembly of the fourth republic.

Aime Cesaire would subsequently be the greatest influence in Fanon's life. Fanon stayed long enough to complete his Baccalaureate and then went to France for further studies. He studied in Lyon and graduated in medicine and psychiatry. He also studied literature, drama and philosophy. In Lyon, he experienced racial segregation. Writing on the ordeal of the black man in *Black Skin, White Masks*, Fanon reports that at various times he was described as "dirty nigger?" or simply, "look, a nigger!". He writes,

> The evidence was there, inescapable and implacable. And my blackness was solid and indisputable; it tormented me, pursued me, perturbed me, and exasperated me. Negroes are savage, bestial, illiterate. But I knew that, as for me, these accusations were false. There was a myth about the Negro that had to be disproved and demolished regardless of the cost ... Neither my polished manners, nor my knowledge of literature, nor my understanding of the quantum theory found favour or ensured my acceptance (BSWM, 130).

It was Fanon's experiences in Martinique, his service in France's army and his encounters in Lyon that influenced his first book in 1952, *Black Skin, White Masks* (BSWM), an analysis of the effect of colonial subjugation on humanity. This book was originally his doctoral thesis submitted at Lyon and entitled, "The Disalienation of the Black Man". The rejection of the thesis led Fanon to seek to have the book published. It was the left wing philosopher, Francis Jeanson, leader of the pro-Algerian independence, Jeanson Network, who insisted on the new title and also wrote an epilogue for the publication. Fanon left France for Algeria. He secured an appointment as a psychiatrist at Blida – Joinville Psychiatric Hospital. Following the outbreak of the Algerian revolution in November 1954, he joined the FLN Liberation Front (Front de Liberation Nationale). He traveled extensively across Algeria working clandestinely for the FLN.

In the course of the struggle, he was expelled from Algeria in January 1957. Fanon left for France and subsequently, traveled secretly to Tunis. He was part of the editorial team of *El Moudjahid* and continued to write for them to the end of his life. He also served as Ambassador to Ghana for the Provisional Algerian Government (GPRA) and attended conferences in Accra, Conakry, Addis Ababa, Leopoldville, Cairo and Tripoli. Many of his short writings from this period were collected posthumously in the book, *Toward the African Revolution*. While in Ghana, Fanon developed leukemia and though encouraged by friends to rest, he refused. He completed his final and most fiery indictment of the colonial condition, *The Wretched of the Earth* in 10 months and the book was published by Jean-Paul Sartre in the year of his death. Frantz Fanon died on December 6, 1961 at the National Institute of Health in Bethesda, Maryland, where he had sought treatment for his cancer. At his request, his body was returned to Algeria and buried with honours by the Algerian National Army of Liberation. He was survived by his wife Josie, their son Oliver, and his daughter (from a previous) relationship, Mireille.

The Philosophy of Fanon

Frantz Fanon's relatively short life yielded two potent and influential statements of anti-colonial revolutionary thought, *Black*

Skin, White Masks and *The Wretched of the Earth*. These works have made Fanon a prominent contributor to post-colonial studies and particularly to the thesis of African decolonization in contemporary African socio-political philosophy. We shall rely on these two works to highlight Fanon's philosophy. In *Black Skin, White Masks*, Fanon presents his personal experience as a black intellectual in a whitened world and elaborates the ways in which the colonizer/colonized relationship is normalized as psychology. With his medical and psychological training he sought to articulate the psychodynamics of colonialism and racism. As a psychiatrist, he explored the psychological effect of colonization on the psyche of a nation as well as its broader implications for building a movement for decolonization. African colonial pathology became a key issue. Part of Fanon's thesis is that a racist culture prohibits psychological health in the black man. He revealed the understanding that racism generates harmful psychological constructs. Fanon writes in *Black Skin, White Masks*,

> As long as the black man is among his own people except on the occasion of minor internal struggles, he will have no need to put his own being to the test for someone else's benefit... for the black man has no further occasion to be black, but is only such when confronted by the white (BSWM, 116).

The point Fanon makes here is that "black" and "white" are psychological constructs. He insists that the category "white" depends for its stability on its negation "black". None exists without the other, and both come into being at the moment of imperial conquest. According to Fanon, colonialism is made of African pathological cases of intimidation, lack of self-esteem and inferiority. Fanon laments,

> The black man cannot withstand the white man's gaze. Overnight, as it were, Negroes had two frames of reference in terms of which they had to adjust themselves. Their metaphysics or, less pretentiously, their customs and the procedures relating thereto, were abolished because they were found to be in contradiction with a civilization of which Negroes had no knowledge and which imposed itself upon them (BSWM 125).

Fanon identifies other complexes of colonized Africans. These are: being withdrawn, deviated, escapist, and schizophrenic. They suffer from the morbid feelings of alienation, confusion, agitation and restlessness. Fanon expresses his exasperation in the following words:

> Shame, shame, and contempt for myself, nausea when people like me, they tell me they like me in spite of my colour. When they hate me, they hasten to add that it isn't because of my colour... whether here or there, I am a prisoner of this vicious circle (BSWM, 129).

Part of the colonial strategy included massive misinformation, deformation and defamation of the African. Fanon laments "... my eardrums were shattered by the sounds of cannibalism, mental retardation, fetishism, racial defects, slave-traders... the Negro is an animal. The Negro is evil. The Negro is nasty. The Negro is ugly-look! A Negro!" (BSWM, 121; 123). The mission of the white world is clear in Fanon's mind,

> The white wants control of the world. He wants it for himself alone. He regards himself as the fore-ordained master of the world. He bends it to his will. There is established between him and the world a coercive form of possessiveness (BSWM, 134).

The challenge before the black world was obvious and decolonization was inevitable. Fanon states it thus:

> An unfamiliar and oppressive weight settled down upon us. The real world was challenging our rightful share in it. In the white world the coloured man encounters difficulties in establishing the schematic elements of his physical being (BSWM, 124).

Fanon then proceeded to espouse a Black Race Philosophy. In nauseating disgust, he challenges colonialism and provokes black consciousness in his statement that,

> What? How's that? While I was the one with every possible reason to hate and despise, it was I who was being rejected? Whereas I should have been pleaded with and implored, I was refused all recognition? Since it was impossible for me to act from any "innate complex", I decided to assert myself, to affirm my existence on the basis of my colour – as Black. Since the other was reluctant to recognize me, there was only one solution left: to make myself recognized (BSWM, 147).

The situation had become untenable. Fanon had come to the realization that all the racialism, the slavery and the oppression of colonialism, the ambiguity of attitudes on the part of both whites and blacks was the cause of the psychological and cultural alienation, the personal estrangement and the loss of collective identity of the Africans. Fanon identifies one supreme cause of all colour prejudice: hatred;

> Colour prejudice is nothing more than the unreasoning hatred of one race for another, the contempt of the stronger and richer peoples for those whom they consider inferior to themselves, and the bitter resentment of those who are kept in subjection and so frequently insulted. As colour is the most obvious manifestation of race, it has been made the criterion by which men are judged, irrespective of their social or educational attainments. The light skinned races have come to despise all those of a darker colour, and the darker skinned peoples will no longer accept the inferior position to which they have been relegated (BSWM, 133).

A very important aspect of Fanon's philosophy, which is never given adequate attention, is the role of language and how it molds the position of natives or those victimized by colonization. For Fanon, being colonized by a language has larger implications for one's consciousness. He states, "To speak the language of the colonizer means above all to assume a culture, to support the crushing weight of a civilization" (BSWM, 17). Speaking French means that one accepts or is coerced into accepting the collective consciousness of the French, which identifies blackness with evil and sin. In an attempt to escape the association of blackness with evil, the black man dons a white mask, or thinks of himself as a universal subject equally participating in a society that advocates equality supposedly abstracted from personal appearance. The cultural values of the colonizer are internalized into consciousness, creating a fundamental disjuncture between the black man's consciousness and his body. Under these conditions, the black man is necessarily alienated from himself. His consciousness is whitewashed. *The Wretched of the Earth* is undoubtedly Fanon's most famous work, written during and regarding the Algerian struggle for independence from colonial rule. A controversial introduction to the text by Jean Paul Sartre presents Fanon's thesis as an advocacy of violence. A part of Sartre's preface to the book reads "There is one duty to be done, one end to achieve: to thrust out colonialism by every means in their power" (WE, 18). Furthermore, Sartre writes,

> They would do well to read Fanon, for he shows clearly that this irrepressible violence is neither sound and fury, nor the resurrection of savage instincts, nor even the effect of resentment: it is man re-creating himself. I think we understood this truth at one time, but we have forgotten it - that no gentleness can efface the marks of violence; only violence itself can destroy them. The native cures himself of colonial neurosis by thrusting out the settler through force of arms...(WE, 18).

Fanon does not help matters as he devotes the opening chapter of the book to "Concerning Violence" which is a caustic indictment of colonialism and its legacy. In his opening statements he says,

> National liberation, national renaissance, the restoration of nationhood to the people, commonwealth; whatever may be the headings used or the new formulas introduced, decolonization is always a violent phenomenon (WE, 27).

Fanon contends that to overcome the binary system in which black is bad and white is good; an entirely new world must come into being. This utopian desire to be absolutely free of the past requires total revolution, "absolute violence". The opening chapter discusses violence as a means of liberation and catharsis to subjugation. For Fanon the colonial situation is an inherently violent one and needs to be resisted with violence. According to him, "… it is obvious here that the agents of government speak the language of pure force" (WE, 30). Here again, we see the relevance of language in the philosophy of Fanon. Some reviewers and critics of Fanon have focused on this aspect of his theory and then characterize him mostly as a promoter of violence, especially with relation to violence in revolution. We consider this understanding of Fanon, reductionist and limited as we shall argue subsequently that Fanon was never an apologist of violence or a radical revolutionary. Indeed, a further reading of the *Wretched of the Earth* reveals a thorough critique of nationalism and imperialism which also develops to cover areas such as mental health and the role of intellectuals in revolutionary situations.

Fanon goes into great detail explaining that revolutionary groups should look to the *lumpenproletariat, peasants*, for the force needed to expel the colonists. The *lumpenproletariat* in traditional Marxist theories are considered the lowest, most degraded stratum of the proletariat, especially criminals, vagrants, and the unemployed, who lacked class consciousness. Fanon uses the term to refer to those inhabitants of colonized countries who are not involved in industrial production, particularly peasants living outside the cities. He argues that only this group, unlike the industrial proletariat or urban proletariat, has sufficient independence from the colonists to successfully make a revolution against them. This emphasis on the rural underclass obviously highlights Fanon's disgust with the greed and politicking of the comprador bourgeoisie in new African nations. The brand of nationalism espoused by these classes, and even by the urban proletariat, Fanon contends, is insufficient for total revolution, because such classes benefit from the economic structures of imperialism. Fanon claims that urban proletariat revolutions end when these urban classes consolidate their own power, without really remaking or overhauling the entire system.

The point Fanon makes here is that total revolution can only be effected by the African peasants.

Reflection on Fanon's Philosophy

It is an indubitable the fact that political thinkers are products of their social milieu. Their thoughts and writings are profoundly affected by the complex nature of the various social influences and forces to which they are exposed and subjected. In the case of Fanon, his entire philosophy was rooted in the socio-economic and political milieu created by French colonial rule in Martinique and Algeria. The logic of French colonial rule, reflected in the French colonial policies of assimilation, and association is based primarily on the assumption of the superiority of French culture and civilization, an assumption that rests on the denial of the authenticity of the indigenous culture. This was unacceptable to Fanon. Fanon's experiences in Martinique and France clearly showed hypocrisy expressed in the theory and practice of assimilation. Although he had "assimilated" French values in Martinique, he discovered later in life that colonialist society was a rigidly stratified racist society in which the colour question was an overriding one that precluded his admission to, and mobility within, French society on equal socio-economic and political terms with the white Frenchman.

The portrayal of Fanon as an advocate of violence is in our view a simplistic and reductionist vision of Fanon's work. What we see in Fanon is a total condemnation of the violence inflicted on the colonized by the colonizer. He believes that such violence is not conducive to the self-realization of the colonized. Of course, he recognizes the instrumental value of violence as a means to a desirable end when socially organized and ideologically directed to achieve the liberation of the colonized because violence is the *language* that the colonizer understands. In this sense, Fanon regards violence as the praxis of decolonization. In this regard, we consider Fanon, not as an apologist of violence, but as a "thinker of violence".

Fanon's theory of the psychodynamics of colonialism and racism provides illuminating insights into the enduring legacy of colonialism on the psychics of the colonized which is very relevant today, as such social diagnoses has broader implications for the present. We must note that for Fanon, liberation struggle ought not to end with decolonization but must manifest in the well-being of the people, freed from all forms of domination, alienation and most importantly neo-colonialism. The portrait of Fanon that should be promoted is that of a powerful intellectual, moralist and humanist who expressed a passionate concern for, and commitment to humanity, freedom and the human condition. He was basically dissatisfied with a hypocritical world where mere lip service is paid to the ideals of social justice, equality and freedom.

WORKS CITED

Fanon, Frantz. *Black Skin, White Masks*. New York: Grove Press, 1967.

Fanon, Frantz. *The Wretched of the Earth*. London: Penguin Books, 1982.

CHAPTER 18

KING'S PAN-AFRICAN VISION
By
KINGSLEY CHRISTOPHER SOLOMON

Introduction

A society where law and order exist is principally and basically fashioned for the purpose of establishing justice. But when this fails in its responsibility, it adversely becomes "dangerously structured dams" potent enough to obstruct the flow of social progress. Man exists in a socio-political environment with the intent of maximum utilization of such setting for his highest good and the derivation of the joy of being. It is therefore disheartened to note that where socio-political setting is devoid of crucial elements like justice, equality, love and respect for human worth and dignity, such is bound to nurture coarse, confusion, crises, turbulence and trauma. Martin Luther King Junior, fashions out properly articulated philosophical positions, meant to enhance a proper formulation and structuring of a peaceful society, in other to enhance equal opportunities, and advantages of co-existence of citizens in a well defined civil society. The problem of man in a society begins where proper things are not adequately done, and good laws made to checkmate the excesses of human activities in a given setting. The purpose of this chapter therefore is to picture Martin Luther King Junior's concept of justice, civil disobedience and non-violence as is encapsulated in his political philosophy of pan-African vision.

Early Life and Influence

Born in Atlanta, Georgia on January 15, 1929, the son of Reverend Martin King, and Alberta Williams king grow up to develop a unique and formidable philosophy potent enough to restructure the African-American society, and to overthrow the thrown of segregation which delineated the Black populace. King attended the

Booker T. Washington High School, from where he moved to the Morehouse College at age fifteen. In 1948, he graduated from Morehouse College with a Bachelor of Arts degree in Sociology. He further enrolled in Cozer Theological Seminary in Chester Pennsylvania from which he graduated with Bachelor of Divinity degree in 1951. In order to fulfill the family demands of becoming a Baptist minister, King decided to further equipped himself by undergoing a doctoral studies in systematic theology at Boston University where he received is Doctor of Philosophy on June 5, 1955, with a dissertation on "A Comparison of the Conceptions of God in the Thinking of Paul Tillich and Henry Nelson Wieman". At age twenty-five, King became the pastor of the Dexter Avenue Baptist Church in Montgomery, Alabama, prior to social instability and the denial of the Black (African) rights consequential to the segregation in the United States. The clergyman and activist became the prominent leader of the African-American civil rights movements. As an activist, his main legacy was to secure progress on civil rights in the United States. This led to the establishment of the Southern Christian Leadership Conference established in 1957, which he served as its first president.

The philosophy of Martin Luther King Junior received an oceanic flow of inspiration from the philosophy of Mahatma Gandhi. As every philosophy is a child of its circumstance, and is meant to solve the problems of human existential situation, Martin Luther King Junior found himself in a society where the tide of racial discrimination and segregation was at its full rage. The blacks suffered grievous humiliation at pubic places, police brutality, and inequality which were incited by the 'unjust' laws promulgated by the whites. For every action, there must be an equal reaction at the opposite direction. Therefore, to tackle this monsteric situation which brought the blacks to a zero point, King saw the imperative of developing a substantial philosophy whose therapeutic effects will supersede the 'sick' situation of his country. While studying at Crozar, King came in contact with Mahatma Gandhi's philosophy of non-violence, and how it was used by the Indians to fight British governance. Martin Luther King Junior became quite intrigued by Gandhi's philosophy, and saw in it a life force which could be systematically utilized by the black Americans and adequately channeled it to break the back of segregation.

King's Political Philosophy

Martin Luther King Junior's political philosophy accelerates by painting the picture of a society where justice reigns supreme. An ideal society suitable for a peaceful co-existence of humans must be that where the sovereignty of justice is allowed to have its course. For King, justice which could simply be seen as consistent and permanent will to render to everyone his due becomes an indispensable element of a peaceful society. It is a necessity for social progress. Any society where injustice prevails is that whose basic features includes uproar, turbulence, conflict, clamour and social backwardness. For him, justice must be pictured in the actions of the citizenry, and particularly in the law of the land which serves as a pivot to the human society. All laws made for governance must be 'just laws' meant to maintain order, and the dignity and peaceful co-existence of the citizens.

According to him, "law and order exist for the purpose of establishing justice, and when they fail to do this they become dangerously structured dams that block the flow of social progress" (King, 221). Justice for King implies equality before the law, equal standard devoid of segregation and humiliation. It is the formulation of good and just laws which runs in line with the moral or natural law. Justice is a situation where all men respect the dignity and worth of human personality. Injustice therefore is all forms of inequality and unfair treatment arising from racial, sexual and religious segregation or discrimination. A just society, for King, must necessarily experience peace through the adequate provision of equal economic, social, religious and political opportunities for all its citizens devoid of any atom of segregation. In re-echoing Iwe, Uduigwomen states:

> Justice is so essential to the survival of a state that it has often been acclaimed as the foundation of peace among men, as the basis of law and order, as the foundation of the state and its constitution (73).

Martin Luther King Junior's concept of justice could be further explained through John Rawls theory of justice. For Rawls as with King, justice could be described as fairness and equality. He states "each individual is to have a right to the greatest equal liberty compatible with a like liberty for all" (Honderich, 745). According to him:

> Justice is the first virtue of social institutions, as truth is of systems of thought. A theory however elegant and economical must be rejected or revised if it is untrue, likewise laws and institutions no matter how efficient and well-arranged must be reformed or abolished if they are unjust. Each person possesses an inviolability founded on justice that even the welfare of society as a whole cannot override. For this reason, justice denies that the loss of freedom for some is made right by a greater good shared by others. It does not allow that the sacrifices imposed on a few are outweighed by the larger sum of advantages enjoyed by many. Therefore, in a just society the liberties of equal citizenship are taken as settled; the rights secured by justice are not subject to political bargaining or to the calculus of social interest (Valasquez, 666).

For Rawls as with King, the most essential question to ask about a society is: is it just? Laws and institutions of a society must embody justice, or they must be reformed. Martin Luther King Junior points out that there are two types of laws, the just laws and the unjust laws one would readily ask what the differences between these two are. And how does one determine when a law is just or unjust. In answering this question, King posits:

> A just law is a man-made code that squares with the moral law or the law of God. And unjust law is a code that is out of harmony with the moral law. To put it in the terms of saint Thomas Aquinas, an unjust law is a human law that is not rooted in eternal and natural law. Any law that uplifts human personality is just. Any law that degrades human personality is unjust. All segregation status are

unjust because segregation distorts the soul and damages the personality, it gives the segregator a false sense of superiority, and the segregated a false sense of inferiority (King 219).

Certain laws are promulgated out of selfish desires to protect the interest of the few, against the interest of the majority. The masquerading faces of such laws are made open through intent of implementation which is meant to inflict pain and victimize the *hoipoloi*. Unjust laws constantly infringe on human freedom. It withdraws the natural rights of the citizens with the intent of subjecting the citizens through some traumatic conditions. In fact, without gainsaying, unjust laws dehumanize. The presence of these sorts of laws necessitates the absence of liberty, property and peace. Not only does the unjust positive law hinder the presence of peace in the society, it also runs in conflict with the natural law. The natural law according to Augustine is the reason and will of God which commands the preservation of the natural order and prohibits its disturbance (Omoregbe, 12-13). This law, he says, is the highest reason, and ought to be always obeyed. The natural law is the foundation of morality, which all positive laws must imbibe. For Augustine therefore, any positive law that runs not with the natural law and the moral foundation of justice is automatically null and void: there is no law except it is just." Any positive law that is unjust is in conflict with the law of nature and is *ipso facto* null and void. Such laws could be described as nothing than tyrannical command. "Remove justice," says Augustine, "and what are kingdoms but gangs of criminals on a large scale" (Omoregbe, 13). Accessing the delineating pictures of unjust laws, King agrees with Augustine that "an unjust law is no law at all (219).

Civil Disobedience

The state is the sole authority and custodian of the law; it has the final say in the implementation of these legal codes (laws). The mandate to make laws for the state is the sole responsibility of the legislature. It makes laws in consonance with the natural law to protect the interest of the citizenry. The citizens in turn are obliged to obey the laws of the land implicitly, but where the law is seen as the instrument of mal-treatment and denial of natural rights, what do the citizens do? Martin Luther King Junior advocates an outright disobedience of all unjust laws. Laws are made to protect the interest of the citizens, but where hardcore draconian laws are imposed on the citizens, contrary to the natural law, the citizen are not obliged to obey such laws, they are to directly obey the natural laws and flout any unjust positive law. King takes into cognizance the natural attributes of human beings. He presents that "there comes a time when the cup of endurance runs over, and men are no longer willing to be plunged into the abyss of injustice where they experience the blackness of corroding despair" (King, 219). Even if men initially obey the unjust laws made by the state as postulated by Socrates, yet there comes a time where their vessel of patience and endurance will be filled, and they realize that they have to kick against such laws. Civil disobedience is a conscious violation of unjust laws and policies through the application of non-violent and peaceful measure, with the intent of appealing to the conscience of the promulgators of such laws and the society in general, for adequate change. Adeigbe sees it as:

> A non-violent disobedience of at least a presumptively valid law or some policy or decision of the government generally thought to have the force of law, it is conscientiously committed, (that is, as a last resort) and yet politically motivated (Uduigwomen, 146).

King pictures the hierarchy of laws. As earlier stated, the natural law as the law of God supersedes the positive or civil law. The natural law as moral imperative, describes what happens in human relationship. It is the moral law from God, which appeals to humans, and is best appreciated through human reason and conscience. The natural law as the basis of moral obligation is built into the very nature of humans in the form of various inclinations, such as preservation of life, the propagation of the species, search for property, satisfaction, dignity, etc. The human mind and reason are fashioned and adequately equipped, as to discern the right course of conduct. This natural light of perception illuminated through the natural law enables man to tailor his own rules and regulations, codes of conduct, or law, depicting and enforcing the moral, or natural law. Human law therefore is no law, where it fails to implement the divine or natural law. Martin Luther King Junior in his popular letter from the Birmingham Jail postulates that all laws which violate the divine and moral principles are unjust laws. These laws degrade human personality and must be done away with. He advocates a non-violent break of such laws. Citizens could break such laws through a peaceful, non-violent demonstration and resistance carried out in love and patience with the intent of appealing to the conscience of the society, and throwing naked the evil intentions of each law. One who engages in non-violent 'direct action' is not a creator of tension, but one who brings the already existing tension to the surface to be seen and dealt with, according to King:

> We merely bring to the surface the hidden tension that is already alive. We bring it out in the open where it can be seen and dealt with. Like a boil hat can never be cured as long as it is covered up but must be opened with all its pus-flowing ugliness to the natural medicines of air and light; injustice must likewise be exposed, with all of tension its exposing creates, to the light of human conscience and the air of national opinion before it can be cured (221).

Injustice must not be hid in a corner of the society, but it must be exposed through a peaceful non-violent break of any law which depicts injustice. A persistent break of such laws enacts a cure through a positive change. Anyone who breaks obnoxious laws with the intent of facilitating a positive change may likely be attacked or punished. King stresses that such should be willing to accept the punishment in patience and love. He stresses further that one who breaks obnoxious laws and is willing to accept the penalty, expresses the highest respect for law.

> One who breaks an unjust law must do it openly, lovingly... and with a willingness to accept the penalty. I submit that an individual who breaks a law that conscience tells him is unjust, and willingly accepts the penalty by staying in jail to arouse the conscience of the community over its injustice, is in reality expressing the highest respect for law (King, 220).

The search for justice through the principle of non-violence must be rapped up in love. Love, for King, is an essential element of the non-violence method and approach for justice. Anyone who is involved in a non-violence search for truth must guide his or her self with the weapon of love. It is through love that the oppressed overcomes the hate of his oppressor. King asserts: that hate cannot quench hate just as fire cannot be used to quench fire. Love of the oppressed must be used to suppress the hate of oppressor. This must be the weapon applied through non-violence to quail the problems faced in the society. King asserts "non-violence" is the answer to the crucial political and moral questions of our time – the need for man to overcome oppression and violence without resorting to violence and oppression (Jakoubek, 12). He cautions:

> If you will protest courageously, and yet with dignity and Christian love, when the history books are written for future generations, the historians will have to pause and say, there lived a great people – a black people who injected new meaning and dignity into the veins of civilization (Jakoubek, 8).

Love is the principal weapon of non-violence. It is the extinguisher of hate and oppression. The principle of non-violence brings justice into the front line of the society. It quails oppression and facilitates unity. Where there is peace in the society, there is bound to be unity, and progress characterizes such society. A general disposition to engage in justified civil disobedience introduces stability into a well-ordered society" (Omoregbe, 104). Martin Luther King Junior's philosophy is therefore a pivot of justice in contemporary society. It injects into the vein of Black African thought a systematic consciousness and criticality. King's philosophy is a revolutionary and reformative philosophy meant to shape the African (Black) populace into a refined nature of consciousness. It facilitates a thought provoking inspiration fashioned to equip the Blacks against all forms of suppression, maltreatment and bad governance. The intent therefore is to structurally elevate properly organized societies devoid of dangerous draconian laws. Enhancing adequate joy and peaceful co-existence of African citizens with equal privilege and opportunities is one among these great principles of Martin Luther King Junior's philosophy.

WORKS CITED

Jakoubek, Robert. *I Have A Dream. Martin Luther King Junior Civil Rights Leader*. New York: Chelsea House Publishers, 1989.

King, Martin Luther. "Letter from Birmingham City Jail" in Warburton Nigel (Ed). *Philosophy Basic Reading*. London: Routledge, 1999.

Omoregbe, Joseph. *An Introduction to Philosophical Jurisprudence*. Lagos: Joja Educational Research and Publishers, 1994.

Uduigwomen, Andrew F. *Studies in Philosophical Jurisprudence*. Calabar: Jochrisam Publishers, 2005.

Velasquez, Manuel G. *Philosophy: A Text with Readings*. Belmont: Wordsworth Thomson Learning, 2002.

CHAPTER 19

ACHEBE'S CONCEPT OF AN AFRICAN PHILOSOPHER
By
GODWIN C. S. IWUCHUKWU, Ph.D.

Introduction

Many people in Nigeria, Africa and African Diaspora as well as the entire world at large could readily affirm that Chinua Achebe is among the best literary icons the world has produced. However, not many could subscribe to the fact that Achebe is not only a (great) philosopher, but an avowed crusader, campaigner and promoter of African philosophy even after reading his classical novel *Things Fall Apart*. The authenticity and validity of African philosophy tend no more to be in doubt even though there are still controversies and debates over its rightful methodologies postulated and the vibrancy of the debate as canvassed for by the proponents rather than being viewed as weakening the validity of the concept of African philosophy, much more rather is a consolidation of its authenticity and validity. There could not be much controversy on the methodology of analyzing the existence of vacuum or nothing. This does not presuppose that there are not still some voices of dissent from some western philosophers as well as some African exoglosic scholars who believe that any school of thought or theory that did not emanate from the West cannot be authentic.

Oruka (112) defines African philosophy as "the work dealing with a specific African issue formulated by indigenous African thinkers or by a thinker versed in African cultural and intellectual life". Azenabor (70) on his own part defines African philosophy as "the reflections of an African or non African, on how Africans (whether ancient or modern) make sense of their existence, condition and the world in which they live in, based on the African cultural experience, history, tradition and reality". This according to him implies that African philosophy is embedded in both the oral and written traditions of Africa. The challenge to demonstrate the authenticity, validity, viability, acceptability and relevance of African art, philosophy, literature, linguistics, history, technology as well as African theories and scientific postulations in the opinion of the present writer, tend not only to be overstretched but also proven beyond all reasonable doubts; the only difference between the two (the rest of the world and Africa) only lies in their perception of space, time and motion. Animalu (10) states that "The difference between Renaissance Europe and 1950 Biafar (Igbo) becomes evident, not in the physical and the spiritual dimensions of being but it is in the abstract dimension of the triangle of being".

A number of African societies including Nigeria and the Igbo, for example, operate on a cosmological framework where time is conceived as cyclical and space in organized in three compartments; The heavens above, the earth below it and the underworld beneath the earth, all of which are contiguous and continuous. He reduced the Igbo perception of motion as cyclic changes of space and time to a mathematical precision comparable to that of several scholars, scientists and philosophers. For example, he compared the perception of motion by the Igbo in the period of the renaissance to be in line with various others perceptions of various other scholars at the same period. Kepler's perception was that if one squares the year of a planet, one gets a number which is proportional to the cube of its average distance from the sun. Copernicus who is reputed to have "stopped the sun and moved the earth" perceived that the orbit of the planets would look simpler if they were viewed from the sun. This was different from Ptolemy's view that it would be better viewed from the earth and Descate's aphorism "give me space and motion and I will give you the world". Galileo claimed that even the earth was moving while Isaac Newton propounded laws of motion which he applied to the motion of the heavenly bodies in accordance with the law of gravitational attraction between the bodies. The sum of the argument here is that there is no one way of looking at reality. The Igbo law of motion which is no less fundamental than Newton's law of motion is the basis of the recurrent motif in various forms of

Igbo and African artistic, linguistic, literary and philosophic expressions. According to Achebe himself:
The traditional attitude of Europe or the West is that Africa is a continent of children. A man as powerful and enlightened as Albert Schweitzer was able to say, "The black people are my brothers but my junior brothers"; we are not anybody's junior brothers" (Animalu, 36).

Profile

Albert Chinualeumogu Achebe was born on November 16, 1930, at Ogidi in Idemili Local Government Area of Anambra State, of East Central Nigeria. He had his primary education at the Church Missionary Society (CMS) Primary School, Ogidi. From there, he attended Government College Umualuia, Nigeria in 1948. On completion of secondary education, he was admitted to Nigeria's "Premier University, the University of Ibadan, to study medicine but after one year, changed to English Literature and History. He graduated with a BA (Hons) in 1953. After this, he joined the Nigerian Broadcasting Corporation and while he was on a training course at BBC in London, his manuscript *Things Fall Apart* which has made him one of the most widely read authors of the 20th century, leading founder of Modern African Literature, a recent nominee of the Prospect and Foreign Affairs magazine as one of the world's top 100 public intellectuals, was published. The book *Things Fall Apart* translated into about fifty (50) languages of the world and a recently celebrated fifty (50) years anniversary is said to be probably the most widely read book by black Africans. More than twelve million copies of the book have been sold. Achebe is married to Christie Chinwe Achebe (Nee Okoli) and the marriage is blessed with four children two sons (Ikechukwu and Chide) and two daughters (Chinelo and Nwando). HIs career includes Editor, Heinemann African Writer's Series; 1971 founding Editor, Okike, 1985-Emeritus Professor of English, University of Nigeria, Nsukka; 1990-Charles P. Stevens Professor, Bard College, New York. Some books by Achebe: **Fiction:** *Things Fall Apart* (1958), *No Longer At Ease* (1960), *Arrow of God* (1964), *A Man of the People* (1966), *Girls at War* (Stories, 1972), *Anthills of the Savannah*. **Poetry:** *Beware Soul Brother* (1971), *Another African* (1998). **Essays:** *The*

Trouble with Nigeria (1983), *Hopes and Impediments* (1988), *Home and Exile* (2000). **Edited Books:** *African Short Stories; Don't Let Him Die; The Umuahian; Aka Weta; Egwu Aguluagu Na Eqwu Edeluede; Africa* and *The Drum and the Flute.*

Awards: Commonwealth Poetry Prize (1979), more than twenty honorary doctorates; refused Nigeria's highest honour in 2004 and 2011 in protest against her sordid democracy, a member of the American Academy and Institute of Letters, United Nation's Special Ambassador; Fellow, Modern Language Assocaition of America (1975); Fellow, Royal Society of Literature, London (1981); The Margaret Wong Prize; The New Statement Jack Campbell Prize; 2007 Man Booker International Award and Deputy National President, People Redemption Party (PRP), 1983.

Achebe as a Philosopher

According to David and Marianna Fisher (2010), the global significance of Chinua Achebe is not only in his talent and recognition as a writer, but also as a critical thinker, Achebe is a philosopher of no less comparison to the world's ancient and modern philosophers like Aristotle, Plato, Oruka, etc. Nnaji (11) recognizes Achebe not only as a thinker but also as a legend. Plato and Aristotle were legendary Greek philosophers because they gave thought and made sense of almost everything around them then. Most of their thoughts are still relevant to their fields in contemporary times. For example, Nwankwor (1) showed how Plato's influence, theories and saying like the advocacy for philosopher-kings still have patronage even in our 3rd millennium A.D not minding that the man lived in the 3rd century B.C. In linguistics, Plato is said to be the first to have taken the subject of grammar seriously and treating it as a specific topic. He introduced a fundamental division of the Greek sentence into nominal component which he referred to as 'onoma' and a verbal component which he identified as 'rhema'. It must be pointed out that most subsequent linguistic descriptions bordering on syntactic analysis was based on Plato's work. Aristotle had a mastery of almost all fields including ethics, politics, logic, physics, biology and natural history. In linguistics, he added a third class of syntactic component refrred to as *'Syndesmoi'*. Thus, class covered what is later identified to be conjunction, articles and pronouns. He further gave a formal definition of the word as a linguistic unit and a component of a sentence, having a meaning of its own which he said cannot be further divided into meaningful units. This his view of the indivisibility of the word remains the major inadequacy of his description presently since it is now known that the 'word' can be further sub-divided into smaller meaningful units known as morphemes.

Since philosophy is not just the exercise of one's curiosity or intelligence merely as an aesthetic disposition but a critical inquiry and intelligence which produces knowledge useful in solving problems. The philosopher then becomes the theoretical visioner whose vision guides human actions in multiple fields of human endeavour. Achebe like Plato, Socrates and other world philosophers has employed his critical thinking and intelligence to initiate a course of action for reasonable part of humanity. It has equally helped in providing solutions to a myriad of societal problems. For example, his thought, theories, and sayings some of which are expressed through his literary pieces was a source of strength and consolation to the renowned Nelson Mandela while serving twenty-seven (27) years jail term. It has helped to free Africa from its past, fought for Africa's freedom, altered the unicentric view of the world. Also, it solved with "deceptive" ease difficult technical question such as how you represent the language of one society in the language of a very different one and creating a third position out of the tension between African language (Igbo) and English (Ngugi Wa Thiongo, 2010). These areas mentioned above cut across politics, culture, history, literature, philosophy, education as well as language. We therefore, acknowledge the unarguable membership of Achebe as an indisputable member of the world "Academy" of philosophers.

Achebe as an African Philosopher

While we recognize Achebe as a philosopher of world repute, it must be stated that Africa is the centrepiece of his philosophical pontification. This is why we shall examine Achebe as an African philosopher and his concept of Omakalili Onye? This we shall do under three sub-headings of culture, politics and ethics after defining the concept. *Omakalili Onye?* Is a rhetorical phrased question in Igbo language, literarily meaning "Who is self-sufficient?" This statement is a reflection of the Igbo worldbview variously expressed as "Uwaezuoke", Onyeekaozuru?

Culture

It is this concept self-sufficiency that Achebe, an ardent lover of African culture projects to the whole world. It is his central theme in *Things Fall Apart*. He projects the world (Africa and West) as a theatre of war where there is neither winner nor vanquished. His protagonist and hero, Okonkwo and the coward and weakling, Unoka or even the white missionaries were exempted from having a fair share of life's infirmities, incapacitations, limitations and inconsistencies. They all shopped from the market of Nnamdi Azikiwe's truism that "No condition is permanent". They shared moments of rising and falling, joy and sadness as well as sorrow and happiness. It is indeed a world of complimentary as captured by Asouzu's (2008) Igbo philosophy of *ibuanyindanda*. Achebe has unequivocally declared that African culture is of no less significance with any other culture of the world. He holds that there is no absolute in anything. The world is a world of dualities. By holding that "The coward holds the life of the brave" (*onye ujo ji ndu ya na onye ike*). In Igbo culture, it is acknowledged that the brave and the coward exist in complimentarity. He has fought with his literary pieces and in public speeches and conferences; any reference to African culture including her languages as savage or barbaric. The ensuing cultural conflict triggered by this one-sided view of the western/European missionaries was demonstrated by Achebe using his trilogy – *Things Fall Apart* (1966), *Arrow of God* (1969), and *No Longer at Ease* (1981).

According to Animalu (37) "There is no analogy of thought between Kepler in the *mysterium cosmogra phicum* and the young Christian convert, Oduche, in Achebe's *Arrow of God* (70): a new and exciting thought came to him (Oduche) then, he opened the box which Moses had built for him...and locked the python inside. He felt a great relief within. The python would die for lack of air, and he would be responsible for its death without being guilty of killing it".

In like manner, Kepler locked the rectangular model of the universe in the Copernican shphere, so that the rectangular model would die without his being guilty like Galileo of killing it. Animalu believes that this analogy can best be understood as a method of thinking about conflicts in geometrical terms. Achebe made a painstaking observation of the snake totem of his homeland among the Idemili riverine Igbo, and tried in *Arrow of God* to fit it into a pattern from which he deduced the empirical laws of thought governing its confrontation with the invading European rectangular totem. In the same way, Kepler made a painstaking observation of the planetary system and tried to fit it into a pattern, showing that the planets moved in elliptical units round the sun as the motto on the great seal of the United States of America, and the symbolic appearance of the inscription "In God we trust" on their coin.

Achebe not only shows the confinement of African culture by the western culture but has gone further to advertise and project the culture in her languages including its literature to the whole world thus ensuring its survival. He maintains that Igbo and many African cultures were well-ordered and self-sufficient where things only began to "fall apart" with the arrival of the Europeans. Furthermore, Achebe has made a substantial and weighty investment in the building of literary arts institutions. As the founding editor of the Heinemann African writer's series, he edited more than one hundred titles. He was also the founding editor of *Okike*, a Nigerian journal of new writing. He edited the University of Nigeria's *Nsakka journal*, *Nsukka Scope* and assisted in the founding of a publishing house, Nwamife Books - an organization responsible for publishing other ground-breaking work by award winning writers. He is still continuing his longstanding work on the development of institutional spaces where writers can be published and develop creative and intellectual community. An assessment of Achebe by other international African writers could best describe how much Achebe accomplished as an African cultural cum literary ambassador through his works.

The Kenyan writer, Ngugi Wa Thiongo believes that Achebe made 'a whole generation of African people believe in themselves and in the possibility of their being writers'. On his part, the Somalian novelist, Nunedin Farah, admits that he learned his craft from

Achebe, "He taught us a way of integrating what we know from being African with what we've become, hybrids of a sort". For Achebe, "while colonial education was saying that there was nothing worth much in my society, I was beginning to question that, to see there were things beautiful even in the heathen". He could thus be described as a cuiltural nationalist with a revolutionary mission to help his society regain belief in itself and put away the complexes of the years of denigration and self abasement.

Ethics

It is also pertinent looking at the morality of Achebe's ideas and actions both in Africa and the world. Achebe has not only stood in defense of African culture but has stood for the downtrodden, the oppressed people in Africa and Africans in the Diaspora. He had also deployed all the weapons at his disposal: public speeches, literary works, etc, to fight and change the course of the liberation of the people from victimization, oppression and corruption. His concept of omakalili onye in ethics is anchored on justice and fair play. He believes that the poor and the vulnerable group have a right to survive alongside the rich, the governed have the right to live and survive alongside the governors and rulers. Africa and the developing nations have a right to survive alongside the developed and advanced nations. The basis of the relationship that should exist among these groups in his view must be equality and complimentary rather than that of master-servant. Achebe's novel, *A Man of the People,* published in 1966 was a satire on corruption and power struggles in a fictitious African country. It was his way of expressing his disdain and that of many Africans about the disappointment and collusive swindle that independence turned out to be for them.

Then central characters are the minister of culture, Nanga, the man of the people, and teacher Odili, an African lucky Jim, who tells the story. Odili stands against the government, but not because of ideological reasons. He has personal interest: Nanga has seduced his girlfriend. Their political confrontation becamre violent, Nanga's thugs inflict havoc and chaos, and the army responds by staging a coup. He is still criticizing post colonial African leaders who have destroyed their economies by stealing the people's money and not rendering the services for which they were elected into the positions. During the despotive regimes of Sanni Abacha, Achebe left Nigeria several times because the regime was brutal against her critics. The Nobel Laureatte, Wole Soyinka, acknowledges Achebe's moral standing when in Achebe's 70th birthday he said "Achebe never hesitates to lay blame for the woes of the African continent squarely where it belongs".

Achebe's values are moderation, integrity, simplicity, and zero tolerance for corruption. In a country where praise singing is almost being raised to an art, and people are ready to do anything for political and ethnic based patronage, he risks his life by daring the corrupt leaders in order to identify with the masses who he represents. He is simple and non-flamboyant considering his intellectual, political and economic accomplishments in the society. Some years after his accident that confined him to a wheel chair as he returned from the USA, he publicly declared his first impression about Lagos. He saw Lagos as looking deserted and not well looked after, potholes even in the landing strip. According to him, he decided to return unrecognized, not wanting a red carpet reception because he wanted to see the country as it is. The sight of beggars camping out by the roadsides made him conclude that Nigeria was sicker than he "feared" In 2004 and 2011; Achebe refused Nigeria's highest honour offered by former Nigerian presidents in protest of the sordid democracy and sanity. Even in literary works, Achebe has never spared any piece, local or international that he judges to be morally bankrupt. It was for this reason that he criticized Joseph Comrade's novel as one that dehumanizes a portion of the human race and so could not be regulated as a great work of art. Speaking further, Achebe said concerning Comrade's prose,

> it would have been better if the beautiful prose were used to unite the human race, rather than separate it. The best works seem to me to have an intrinsic morality; it is not Sunday school morality, but I have not encountered any good art that promotes genocide (Jaggi, 1).

Such strict moral demand or expectation by Achebe is sometimes misconstrued as censorship. To this he replies that he is not

Ayatollah Khomeni (who bans books e.g. Salman Rushdie's books) but he believes that books should be read carefully. He is simply saying that books with moral burden should be read only by mature minds and any such work of art limited in readership could hardly be adjudged to be great. This goes a long way in demonstrating the height of Achebe's moral standing and ethical values. He is still among those few whose consciences have not been sold out for filthy lucre. He dropped his English name 'Albert' in protest of the racist view and utterances about Africa.

Politics

Achebe's moral and ethical crusade is extended into politics. Achebe is not only a political thinker but a freedom fighter and emancipator as well as anti-racial campaigner. It needs to be pointed out that Achebe played a strategic role in the abolition of the obnoxious apartheid and racist regime in South Africa and subsequent enthronement of majority black rule as well as subsequent independence of that country. According to Jaggi (1), quoting Nelson Mandela, the former South African president, and anti-apartheid crusader as saying that during his 27 years in jail, he drew consolation and strength from a writer "in whose company the prison walls fell down". That writer is no other than Chinualumogu Achebe. For Mandela, the greatness of Chinua Achebe, founding father of modern African novel in English, lies in his having "brought Africa to the world while remaining rooted as an African. He maintains that Achebe used his pen to free the continent from its past. According to Mandela, both of us (Mandela and Achebe in our differing circumstances within the context of white domination of our continent became freedom fighters".

Mandela's tribute was videoed in honour of Achebe's 70th birthday which he celebrated at the Leafy Bard College in Upstate, New York; where Achebe is professor of language and literature. Other world leaders in their tributes to Achebe in that occasion included the then United Nations Secretary-General, Koffi Annan, three Nobel Laureattes: Tony Morrison, Wole Soyinka and Nadine Gordimer all acknowledge Achebe's political sagacity through literature. In his humorous and politically loaded response to the tributes on his 70th birthday, Achebe said that he was pleased to hear such concerted singing of praises which was only given to third world electorate. He had fought and resisted dictatorship not only in Africa, third world nations and every part of the world. Achebe has suffered for challenging such strongmen in Nigeria. He condemns all forms of electoral rigging and is an advocate of transparency and good governance. In March 1990, only weeks after attending a gathering that anticipated his 60th birthday in the Eastern Nigerian town of Nsukka, a car crash on the country's lethal roads left him paralyzed from the waist down, and in a wheel chair. He was air lifted to Britain for surgery, and later moved over to USA for therapy. He criticized the home government for not only addressing the infrastructural decay that led to the road mishap but also promoting a failed medical system that could not guarantee an effective and efficient health and medical care.

According to Achebe, "But home has simply got from bad to worse in terms of hospital facilities. I've had severe infections, and you need proper antibiotics, not fakes. When you say a country has broken down, that's what it means Jaggi, 1).

Achebe was criticizing the despotic military regimes in Nigeria at that time that denied Nigerians the dividends of good governance. The annulment of Nigeria's elections in 1993 by President Ibrahim Babangida (military ruler) militated against his return because he was among the few voices that spoke and condemned the criminal act. He also stood against the subsequent coup by General Sanni Abacha which brought even harsher dictatorship – marked by the hanging of the writer, Ken Saro-Wiwa in 1995. In his book *The Trouble with Nigeria*, Achebe insists that Nigerians are what they are only because their leaders are not what they should be.

In 1966 when Nigeria suffered ethnic violence which culminated in the civil war that broke out in 1967 with the Igbos of the eastern region attempting to establish an independent republic of Biafra. During the three-year struggle, Achebe sought to publicize the plight of his people. His collection of poems about the war, *Beware Soul Brother*, was published in 1971, appearing in the United States as *Christmas in Biafra* and other poems. His political philosophy encapsulated in *omakalili onye?* could be said to be his people, their well being and good governance.

According to him, "My people deserve better things than they've had by a long chalk". This is comparable to the *ujamaa* political philosophy of some other African philosophers like Julius Nyerere of Tanzania. *Anthills of the Savanna* which was published in 1987 and short-listed for the Booker Prize of that year, was used to describe the failure of contemporary African politicians and intellectuals to meeting the needs of their people. He has been a voice for the emancipation of his people, the Igbo, Nigeria, and Africa, the black race as well as the entire world. Using his literary pieces, and every available opportunity, he contests against their oppression, victimization, colonization dehumanization and exploitation: Achebe lampoones Joseph Comrade's *Heart of Darkness* "as reinforcing a racist view of Africa". He believes the book emphasizes the continent's image as a place of negation that makes Europe's spiritual grace manifest". In his view, the whole purpose of African literature is to change the perception of the world as far as Africa is concern. Iwuchukwu (10) has postulated Achebe's role in the dynamics of power relationship between English language, on the one hand, and African languages on the other hand. Iwuchukuw's submission is that, "Achebe and a host of African literature writers, have through the English language, taught the world more about African languages, history, values, cosmology, traditional religion, ethnic values as well as Africans themselves.

In a 1998 lecture to the World Bank, Achebe urged the cancellation of Third World debts. In an earlier lecture to the western bankers in Paris a decade before, he criticized them for talking about structural adjustment in such a way as depicting Africa as some kind of laboratory, when Africa is a people. There is no doubt to say that such voices as that of Achebe would have, in no small measure contributed to the recent partial cancellation of the debt burden of some African nations and prepared a ground for the possibility of Nigeria's recent exit of the Paris Club of creditors to which she was a debtor and a possible buy back of her debts from the western countries. The recent global economic meltdown which began from the west particularly, the United States of America tend to have proved Achebe's *omakalili onye* in politics, a reality. Neither the superpowers, developed economies nor the emerging/powerless and powers/poor economies are immuned from the vagaries of economic meltdowns". Both must survive in complimentarity. He extends this concept to his gender sensitivity. From his work, he promotes the mutual reprocity that should exist among the male and female gender in Africa and outside Africa.

Conclusion

This work has set out to highlight Achebe as not only a philosopher but an African philosopher. Anchoring on his concept of *omakalili onye* which views everything in the world from a bipolar dimension, we have amply shown Achebe as an African thinker, spokesman, defender, and fighter and in fact, the conscience of the people. He is a politician, social critic, writer, publisher, educationist, liberation fighter and anticorruption crusader, all aided at a better life for his people and humanity at large. Through the captainship or mastery of his literary endowment, he navigates through different worlds of politcs, culture, ethics, morality, etc without missing his direction. However, only an indepth analysis and contrast between these different worlds in which Achebe navigates with expertise, will reveal the 'world' that acts as the engine upon which he rotates to others. For example, on the eve of the Nigerian civil war of 1967 – 1970, Achebe had an audience with President Leopold Senghor of Senegal, founder-poet of the francophone negritude movement. Achebe was sent by the government of Biafra because he was a writer, in the hope of stopping the war. However, according to Achebe, "We talked about Biafra for ten minutes and literature for two hours". This is an insight into the relationship that exists between Achebe's world as a philosopher, navigating through the fields of literature, arts, culture, language, politics, ethics and morals with literature leading the way.

WORKS CITED

Achebe, Chinua (Ed). "Moyer's A World of Idea" in *Betty Sue Flowers*. New York: Doubleday, 1989.

Achebe, Chinua. *Odenigbo Echi Di Ime taa Bu Gboo*. Owerri: Villa Assumpta, 1999.

Animalu, Alexander. "Ucheakonam: A Way of Life in the Modern Scientific Age" in *Ahajiaku Lecture*. Owerri: Ministry of Information and Culture, 1990.

Appia, Kwame. in Jaggi, Maya. http.www.storyteller of the Savannah. Net on 21st March, 2010.

Asouzo, Innocent. Address Presented at the 19th Annual International Conference on African Literature and the English Language (ICALEL). University of Calabar. May, 7 – 10, 2008 (http. www. fraouzo. com).

Azenabor, Godwin. "Odera Oruka's Philosophic Sagacity: Problems and Challenges of Conservation Method in African Philosophy" in *Sophia: An African Journal of Philosophy.* Vol.10, No.2, 2008.

Okonkwo, Jerome (Ed). "Element of Igbo Traditional Religious Practice" in *A Paper presented at the 2002 Aliajioku Lecture: Onugaotu Colloquium*. Owerri: Ministry of Information and Culture, 2002.

Fisher, David and Fisher, Marianna. (http.www.University Professor. Professor of African Studies). Net on 21st March, 2010.

Iwuchukwu, Godwin. "Dynamics of Power Relationship English vs African Languages: A Cross Current of a Sort" in *A Paper Presented at the Biennial International Conference on Mapping Africa in the English Speaking World held at the University of Botswana* on 2nd – 4th June, 2009.

Jaggi, Maya. (http.www.storytellerontheSavannah). Net on 21st March, 2010.

Ngugi, Wa Thiongo in Jaggi, Maya (http.www .storyteller oftheSavannah). Net on 21st March, 2010.

Nnaji, Batholomew. "Ka ihe Di: The Power of Light Energy as a Fundamental Instrument for Socio-economic Development" in *Ahiajioku Lecture*. Owerri: Ministry of Information and Culture, 2009.

Nwachukwu, Michael. "Beyond Technuzu Reflections on Igbo Perception and Practice of Technology" in *Ahiajioku Lecture*. Owerri. Ministry of Information and Culture, 2003.

Nwankwor, IKS. "Plato and the Art of Leadership and Citizenship" in *Sophia: A Journal of Philosophy and Public Affairs*. Vol.10, No.2, 2008.

Oruka, Odera. *Trends in Contemporary African Philosophy*. Nairobi: Shirikan Publishers, 1990.

Robins, R. *A Short History of Linguistics*. England: Longman, 1979.

Weiss, Jennifer (http.www.AuthorProfile).Net on 21st March, 2010.

CHAPTER 20

IROEGBU'S OHACRATIC PHILOSOPHY
By
ELIJAH OKON JOHN, Ph. D.
&
ANTHONY RAPHAEL ETUK

Introduction

This chapter undertakes an exposition of Iroegbu's ohacratic philosophy. It begins by highlighting Iroegbu's historical background through which major influences that shaped his thought are spotted. This is closely followed by his figurative analysis of the problems of African vicious triangles as well as his ohacratic option. The relevance of Iroegbu's ohacracy to the contemporary African situation is also taken up in this chapter. Later on, some evaluatory remarks which appraise his position are critically considered. In conclusion, Iroegbu is reputed for proposing the ohacratic theory which can greatly assist in the domestication of democratic ideals in Africa. Having said that, let us also observe that in the present an African appears to be situated in a concrete condition of a continent in great turmoil. For many decades after most African nations gained independence, the socio-political and economic situation of the continent is simply chaotic. Although every political political system and ideology found in the East or West has been tried out in the continent, yet none seems capable of moving Africa forward on the wing of progress. Today, the post-colonial Africa has virtually become a battle-ground of competing ideological movements, most of which are alien to the African disposition, and which have only deepen the already battered socio-political crisis in the continent.

Consequently, for more than fifty years after independence of most African countries now, not one of them can yet boast of political stability. Governments seem to exist principally to protect and advance the interests of particular individuals, groups or sections of people in the society. And they enact laws in their own interest, punish coerce those who do not obey and conform simply because they have the power to do so. Hence, as one country launches a return to democracy, another reverts to military dictatorship; as one country begins a national reconstruction after a bitter civil war, another declares a war of one kind or the other; as the workers of one country return to work after a period of total strike, the students of another country go on violent rampage.

Besides, majority of African today are living in abject poverty and reduced to a state of destitution by the combined forces of political subterfuge and economic profligacy. After the holocaust and the historical harrassment of colonialism, what remains of Africa's material resources is now being selfishly appropriated by an autochthonous club of corrupt, selfish, greedy and callous elite, who have arisen in the wake of independence to further the emasculation of the continent.

The religious climate is no less cataclysmic. Africa has not only been the dumping ground of all religions systems, sects and movements from the East and West but has also been their battleground, as they serially confront each other in pitched battles. And like the Bulgarian bear at bay, tormented and cut into pieces by a thousand bloodhounds, the African continent has been split almost into smithereens by a dramatic upsurge of religious violence.

The situation calls for serious attention and reflection, without which, as Kenneth Kaunda put it, "with the way things are going, Africa may be the last place where man can still be man" (Ehusani, 25). Such reflection must be practically orientated, based on a well-articulated and organized thought that can bear the brunt of a concrete action that can lead to Africa's true and authentic socio-political development and success. Over the years, attempts have been made by notable African socio-political philosophers and thinkers to suggest the way forward for the realization of the best form of government for the African people. Iroegbu's political philosophy is one of such modest efforts.

His political thought, flowing from the conviction that responsible governance and democratic ideals are realizable in Africa, is a systemic etiological delineation of the socio-political problems in African life. His theory of ohacracy modeled in line with the African political roots, is a synthesis of his political thought, bequeathed to the African philosophy as the best form of governance that can achieve the set of objectives of governing the African people with reasonable success.

The basic thrust of this chapter, therefore, is to expose Iroegbu's political thought and the labyrinth of his ohacratic political option. We shall identify too the major influences on his political thought which persuaded his ohacracy theory, as well as discuss the relevance of this theory to the contemporary socio-political situation in Africa. It is a well known fact that every philosophy is a child of circumstance. Be that as it may, it would be necessary to begin our work with Iroegbu's historical background, through which major sources of his influences could be identified.

Iroegbu's Profile

Pantaleon Osundu Iroegbu, a reverend minister of the Catholic order and a professor of philosophy, was born on October 31, 1951 in Umueze-Umunumo, in Ehime Mbano Local Government Area, Imo State of Nigeria. After his primary education at St. Charles' School, Umunumo in 1965, he moved to the Immaculate Conception Seminary, Umuahia, for his secondary education, which he completed with distinction in 1971. Having had the strong desire to serve God as a Catholic priest in his life, Iroegbu was admitted into a priestly formation and philosophical studies at the Bigard Memorial Seminary, Enugu in 1973. In 1976, he bagged a Diploma in philosophy, as the Seminary did not offer a degree programme in philosophy then. He was later sent back to his Alma mater, for his theological studies, which he completed in 1980 with a first class honours in Bachelor of Divinity (B.D).

He served the church in different capacities after his priestly ordination in July 05, 1980. Between 1985 and 1991, Iroegbu underwent intensive and integral further studies overseas, done mainly in the prestigious University of Louvain-la-Neuve and the

Catholic University of Louvain, Belgium. He acquired various degrees within this short period, which greatly boasted his academic profile. For example, in 1987, he bagged Masters of Arts in philosophy (M.A). In 1980, he also got his Masters of Arts in Ecclesiastical Sciences. In 1989, he bagged his Doctorate in philosophy (PhD). In 1990, he acquired his Masters in Theology (M.Theol) He later enrolled for his Doctorate programme in dogmatic theology on the topic: "Theology and Community: Through Narrative Theology to an African Ecclesiology". This research was later published in Nigeria with the title: "Appropriate Ecclesiology: Through Narrative Theology to an African Church" (1996).

Iroegbu was a distinguished philosopher-theologian of international repute. He had wide-ranging research interest in social, philosophical and theological issues. His life was one of outstanding personal feat and of continuous highly regarded intellectual, scientific and community service. As an accomplished writer and publisher, he had over twenty-five books and sixty-four articles to his credit. He died in February 24, 2006 in his sleep after the day's priestly and academic work. Some of his publications include, *Nigerianism: Philosophical Foundation for Nigeria* (1984), *When all is said and Done, Retreat Reflections* (1984), *Enwisdomization and African Philosophy* (1994), *Metaphysics, The Kpim of Philosophy* (1995), *Communualism: Towards Justice in African Political Culture* (1996), and *African Vicious Triangles - A Plea for "Ohacracy": The Socio-Political Leeway* (1997, unpublished Public Lecture).

While a graduate-student at the University of Louvain in Europe, Iroegbu started building up a mindset to invest in teaching, research and publication to provide envisdomised knowledge to issues bordering on societal problems, especially those in Africa. Iroegbu was heavily influences by his Christianity background, some western political thinkers such as John Locke, Jaen-Jacques Rousseau and from many African philosophers and political thinkers such as Julius Nyerere and Kwame Nkrumah. These influences dovetail into many of his works in socio-political philosophy. As a Catholic theologian, for instance, Iroegbu believes that a just society can become a reality only when it is based on the respect of the transcendent dignity of the human person created in the image of God. This is implied in his theory of humanization of governance, which he defines as giving government a human touch (2004, 135). Hence, for him, the social order, and its development must invariably work for the benefit of the human person. Here, Iroegbu is being faithful to his religious formation, because the Catholic Church teaches that:

> the order of things in the society is to be subordinate to the order of persons, and not the other way round. (*Gaudium et Spes*, 26).

In the Church's teaching, every political, social, scientific and cultural programme must be inspired by the awareness of the primacy of each human being over the society (*Catechism of the Catholic Church*, 2235). Drawing from his conception of man in society, Iroegbu (2004, 135) writes, the social order exists for "the provision of morally valid and legally justified needs of the people". Thus, "man in government...is to be considered an image of God, thus one deserves respect even in governance" (Iroegbu, 2004, 136). In no case, therefore the human person to be manipulated for ends that are foreign to his own development, or subjected to unjust restrictions in the exercise of his rights and freedom. All these is based on the Christian vision of man as a person, that is to say as an active and responsible subject of his own growth process, together with the community to which he belongs – a vision of the human person, which Iroegbu so faithfully embraced.

From John Locke, Iroegbu borrowed the concept of the ideal principles of democratic governance and of the rulership of law in the society. In his *Two Treaties of Government*, Locke (160) maintains that wherever any numbers of men so unite into one society as to quit everyone his executive power of the law of nature and to resign it to the public, then and there only is a political and civil society. On this platform, Locke as against Hobbes and Hegel (both of whom argued for absolute monarchy), dismisses all forms of monarchy as being no form of civil government at all (Iroegbu, 2004, 103). Rather, in a decent or civil society, every man, by consenting with others, makes one body politic under one government and thereby submits to the determination of the majority. This is not such that no member of the community, including the sovereign is above the law, nor can any man in civil a society be exempted from the laws of the land. Locke also argues that the essence of a democratic set-up is the ability of the people to creatively participate in government, in one way or the other, since power lies with the people.

Iroegbu's political thought is highly shaped by this Lockean political theory. Hence, he agrees with Locke that "the success of the rule of each individual is guaranteed by the rule of law, like the equal basic liberty of each person" (Iroegbu, 2004, 104). He further maintains in line with Locke's position that sovereignty lies with the people when he writes: "power lies with the people and that is the basis of democracy. That the rulers or better the leaders are basically accountable to those who choose them" (Iroegbu, 2004, 105). Hence, for Iroegbu (2004, 104-105), true democracy is "any system of government in which the governed have the power to decide on the governing forces that determine their destiny. This power, he stresses, is exercised both at the beginning of government, that is, during the choice of those to govern through the people's exercise of the power of franchise, during the actual governance through consultation, free expression, contribution to laws and policies that rule their lives, because the government must be accountable to the governed; and in the end changes government when necessary. One would notice that there is an affinity between Iroegbu's position and Lockean concept of a democratic set up, namely: the ability of the people to creatively participate in government, in one way or the other. For Iroegbu, and Locke, the ultimate end of government and the bottom line of true democracy is the realization of the common good, which he generally called "essential liberty" (Iroegbu, 2004, 105).

However, as a true son of Africa, Iroegbu is moved by the plights of his fellow Africans who are dastardly enmeshed in deplorable socio-political conditions to seek for an alternative form of governance to the western liberal democracy; one that is truly democratic and yet African, which can definitely lead Africa on the path of progress. His pan-African belief, which is highly motivated by Julius Nyerere's philosophy, persuades his conviction for Africa to return to their communal roots and build from there a political system that will work for contemporary Africa. This is the genesis of his ohacratic theory. This theory, for Iroegbu, is indebted to Nyerere in some ways as his mentor. Like Kwame Nkrumah and Leopold Senghor, Julius Nyerere of Tanzania believed that the traditional African society is communalistic and that capitalism and individualism are foreign to Africa (Omoregbe, 2001, 34). His philosophy of "ujamaa" (family) of which Iroegbu borrows most elements from is based on the communalism of traditional African society. Traditional African society, Nyerere, argued is not based on conflict, struggle or tension in "familyhood", that is family relationship (Nyerere, 70).

Ujamaa is a political theory constructed on the model of a family as its foundation. Nyerere envisaged a society made up of atomic family units, a country made up of ujamaa villages, a kind of "family villages", with mutual co-operation and collaboration. Such a nation would be basically family units extended to embrace the whole society. The capitalistic spirit of acquisition, individualism, and exploitation of man by man, class struggle and conflicts will all be excluded from that society. Inequality will be eliminated and everyone will be prepared to work for the good of the community in any capacity. Nyerere (70) had argued that this is to be achieved in an egalitarian and communalistic society based on familyhood. To a great extent, Iroegbu identifies with Nyerere's philosophy of ujamaa, in his construction of ohacracy. Although he has certain reservations over the practicability of Nyerere's ujamaa, he admires Nyerere's ingenuity and "determination to base his political ideology on this extra-ordinary ideal of familyhood" (Iroegbu, 2004, 177). He puts the merit of Nyerere's political theory in sharp focus in this summary:

> It is a theory based on the African sense of family as a centre of love, affection and care for one another. Ujamaa is to inspire people to love and care for one another and not to brute to one another (Iroegbu, 2004, 176).

Iroegbu further affirms the affinity between his political thought and Nyerere's ujamaa y when he asserts in his paper entitled: "African Vicious Triangles - A Plea for Ohacracy: The Socio-political Leeway", that "ohacracy has a close semblance with Nyerere's ujamaa" (Iroegbu, 5). For him, ohacracy etymologically defined means rulership by the oha, the community members. And community is an *oha-umunna,* with one father, God Himself, and one mother, a geo-cultural mother, like Nigeria. Like in the case of ujamaa, the community of ohacracy according to Iroegbu has one general destiny: the conviction and action of all as brothers and sisters (umunna) working together for the well-being of all in the community (Iroegbu, 5). This now leads us naturally to a fuller exposition of Iroegbu's political theory of ohacracy.

Iroegbu's Theory of Ohacracy

Iroegbu's political theory or ohacratic philosophy was first set forth in a public lecture delivered at the University of Lonvain, Belgium on the topic: "African Vicious Triangles: A Plea for Ohacracy - The Socio-political Leeway". Iroegbu began his discourse of the paper with the analysis of the root causes of the socio-political crisis that bedevil the contemporary African societies. These he figuratively presents in the form of three successive and interwoven triangles, which he calls African vicious triangles (Iroegbu, 1994, 2). His choice of the image of triangles and not circle is quickly explained to imply that a triangle creates an impossible situation: "the inability to identify the starting or closing point" (Iroegbu, 1994, 3). On the other hand, a triangle has a linking hook, detachable and therefore historically identifiable in problematic situations. He states, "in Africa's vicious triangles, take-off points for solution are possible, which means we can make it" (Iroegbu, 3). What now are these triangles? The three vicious triangles of problems which form the root of Africa's socio-political malaise, according to Iroegbu, are: the macro-triangle, labeled "r,m,h", representing religious, moral and human problems, respectively; the median-triangle, labeled "p,e,s", representing the political, economic and social problems, respectively; and the micro-triangle, labeled "i,p,d", representing ignorance, poverty and disease problems respectively. He observes that the micro-triangle (ipd) lies within the median-triangle (pes), which in turn lies within the macro-triangle (rmh); and though these triangles are separate from each other in terms of their problematic nature, yet those that lie within others have causal influence from their mother-triangles and there is a general osmosis of influence of on triangle on the others, which suggests that the problems are foundational (Iroegbu, 1994, 3).

Iroegbu's interpretation of this network of African vicious triangles is as follows: our "religious disintegration" in Africa naturally leads to our "moral inauthenticity", which eventually leads to our "little human integrity", which includes the very low mentality we have of ourselves both as individuals and as a people. Secondly, "our political numbo-jumbo irresponsibility" leads to our "economic morass", which eventually gives rise to our "social cannibalism". Commenting on Iroegbu's point here, Nwankwor (182) observes that "this is very evident in the activities of most of our politicians who always look outside or overseas for blueprints of their actions, choices and political decisions". Lastly, Iroegbu (3), maintains that, because we are ignorant, uneducated and therefore culpably wanting on essential developmental knowledge, we are condemned to gruesome poverty, which eventually leaves us helpless in the face of disease.

Having so thematically diagnosed the root of Africa's socio-political problem, Iroegbu (3) then proposes an ethico-political theory called "ohacracy", which he believes "will solve the long years of African predicament", which "will succeed in building a just society" (Nwankwor, 8). Ohacracy is what Iroegbu (5) calls "democracy in an African context", which is a practical conception of the social order and governance in which the community determines the praxis of the socio-political life of the people, while taking into account basic individual and group peculiarities (Iroegbu, 5). Ohacracy as a term is a product of two conjoined words "oha" (Igbo term, meaning, community, assembly), and the suffix- "cracy" (which is Greek word, meaning to rule, govern, organize). Hence, etymologically viewed, ohacracy means "rulership by the *oha*, the community members" (Iroegbu, 5).

Like Nyerere, Iroegbu envisages a society made up of a community of brotherhood, an *oha-umunna*, with one father, God Himself and one mother, a geo-cultural mother (the society), where the members act with mutual co-operation and collaboration for the good of all in the community. For Iroegbu (5), the members of such a community have one general destiny: the conviction and action as *umunna* (brothers and sisters) as foundation stone.

In ohacracy, fellowship is as important as leadership, which itself must never be a one-man show, not a matter of hierarchical or aristocratic imposition. Rather, leadership must be a collaborative effort between the leaders and the led. In other words, the rulers will identify themselves with the masses and work with them. Here, we notice the influence of the Christian moral tradition, Lockean concept of democratic set-up as well as Nyerere's political thought playing out in the labyrinth of Iroegbu's ohacratic society. He further stresses that in the ohacratic society, there is solidarity of decision and implementation of decision by the members in matters that affect them (Iroegbu, 1994, 5). In all these, the *oha* (community) is the central focus; for the individual exists as individual not in isolation but in the community. "The *oha* is a community of individuals and the individuals are individuals in oha" (Iroegbu, 1994, 5). Iroegbu's view is a true reflection of the traditional African mind-set, which has no room for "social dualism" between the individual and the community. For the traditional African, outside the community, there is no life (Musonda, 86). At the same time, the community cannot constitute a threat for the individual for it is precisely in community that individual existence is affirmed, as the saying goes, "I am because we are, and since we are, therefore I am" (Elusani, 220). John is quite familiar with African mood and concept of the communal spirit when he succinctly declares that every African:

> passionately understands and exercisesd in practical terms a symbiotic relationship between man and man, man and society, man and his ancestors and man and everything (both the seen and unseen, the perceived and unperceived objects around him). This kind of ontology is one with a complete unity, which nothing can destroy. To take away anything or tamper with one aspect of these categories is to destroy the whole existence and possibly the existence of the Supreme Being, the ultimate creator (2006: 230).

Again, Iroegbu states that in the ohacratic society, the mandate of the people is the determinant factor; for power belongs to the people. Hence, all forms of dictatorship, military rule or domination by a group, class or region will all be excluded from the society (Iroegbu,

African Political Philosophy

1994, 6). The basic individuality of persons will be respected as well as particular talents and group values such as language, cultural artifacts and socio-moral values. These, however, must not threaten the existence of the community as an entity. The individual will grow and develop but in the community. Iroegbu builds his theory of ohacracy upon this understanding, which he calls, "the principles of a just ohacratic society" (Iroegbu, 1994, 7).In relation to democracy in general, he considers ohacracy as the African model (of democracy), or rather, democracy in the African context, which takes into account the African identity and values, building also on the African experience - its history, circumstances and contemporary situation. Having examined the meaning and mechanics of Iroegbu's political theory of ohacracy, let us now examine his therapeutic application of this theory to three vicious triangles he identifies in Africa.

Ohacracy and the African Vicious Triangles

To resolve African religious, moral and human problems symbolized in the first (macro) triangle, Iroegbu averrs that ohacracy maintains that any religion in Africa today must see her neighbour first and foremost as a member of the community (7). In line with the pristine African world-view which sees the individual person as belonging to the community, this leads to mutual acceptance of all as well as a fair chance given to all to develop in equal substantive liberty. The end product of this in Iroegbu's view will be the development of moral authenticity and the genuine human flourishing.

To address the problems associated with the political, economic and social conditions of the African continent, as depicted in the second (median) triangle, Iroegbu maintains that ohacracy insists on "strong political will of the people to choose who will lead them" (Iroegbu, 1994, 7). This choice of leadership made without any coercion will be followed up by the necessary co-operation from the followership in form of reasonable obedience, open dialogue and critical loyalty inspired by the spirit of communal solidarity. This will lead to the building up of a viable economy, which will in turn lead to social stability (Iroegbu, 1994, 8). To facilitate this set-up, Iroegbu insists that a fair chance in the fundamental structure for all to participate in both the productive and distributive justice will be created; and this will ensure a continuity of the good order obtained in economic and social life.

About the problems of ignorance, poverty and disease represented in the third (micro) triangle, Iroegbu maintains that ohacracy will address these through a sustained and massive education of the masses, since "education is the bedrock of development. Through functional education, diseases will be avoided and inevitable ones cured, and so our healthy living will be ensured. With good health assured, the problem of poverty will be addressed, since we will be able to work and get our means of livelihood. What this means is that, if ohacracy breaks the chain of ignorance through functional education, the ones of disease and poverty will naturally collapse.

Having theoretically exposed the steps to be taken within the ohacratic arrangement to remedy the three African vicious triangles, Iroegbu undertakes a discourse on the practical steps to be followed so as to perfectly and decisively dismantle each triangular joint. However, before going into this, he includes the following as integrating values in the ohacratic arrangement, which he equally regards as "deep African values". These are: the centrality of the human person, respect for life, the extended family system, solidarity, hospitality, deep religiosity (or transcendence), the sacredness of nature, high moral standard, dialogue and communication, openness in political discussion and frankness in communal decisions (Iroegbu, 1994, 9). Iroegbu opines that these essential African values must be "structurally built into the African society in view of reaching integral development in the ohacratic manner" (1994, 9).

Iroegbu's Ohacratic Praxis

To the question of how ohacracy can in concrete terms, help in dismantling the three vicious triangles which he identifies as the root of African socio-political problems, Iroegbu maintains that there are two majors way this can be done; namely, the micro or individual wave, and the macro or communal wave (Iroegbu, 1994, 9-10). The micro wave is made mainly of the individual constructive and virtuous action aimed at benefiting the *oha* (community). Hence Iroegbu insists here that:

> Each person must decidedly light a candle in the vast darkness. To light a candle is to undertake some concrete exemplary action that will promote the religious, political and educational life of the people. Such a candle will lead to moral, educational and welfare survival of our people (1994, 9).

Iroegbu drives home his point here with an example of a contractor, whom he insists must fully utilize the fund given to him by the state or company and do the job contracted to him. This, he says, will also bring about the human, social and health welfare to all. Iroegbu is convinced too that several individual lights of devotedness to duty whatsoever, will not only bring a leap forward in the ohacratic society, but will blossom into a mighty light of life and success in the society (Iroegbu, 1994, 10). For Iroegbu, one can put one's light to effective concrete action from any of the triangular joints, beginning with either religion, politics or ignorance for the collective wellbeing. In his articles on "Iroegbu's Ohacracy", Nwankwor (174,) adds that in such coordinated actions, we shall be our brothers-keepers and not wolves to each other. Leadership then would gear towards global human existential excellence not sectarian profit-oriented enterprise.

On the macro wave which concerns mainly communal actions, Ireoegbu argues that ohacracy "demands a concrete, massive and intensive conscientization process (1994, 10). This involves a systematically organized and functional education/formation programme. The aim is to re-orientate the public mind, create general awareness of the wrongs within in the present status quo, so that all may now see, judge and act more sanely and morally. To handle this task more functionally, Iroegbu, proposes the formation of "ohacratic groups" to undertake this conscience moulding, awareness, creation and sensitization process, and such groups will constitute the fulcrum of an internal revolution that will transform societal vices such as corruption, greed, etc into virtues such as honesty, patriotism, etc.

Finally, Iroegbu (10) argues here that, since distribution is in principle consequent on contribution, in ohacratic society, one cannot have the right to distribution, that is, to share in the communal goods of the society, if one does not fulfill one's responsibility of contributing to societal good. And any wealth not based on fair wage or equitable exchange must be revisited in justice. With this analysis of the African socio-political dilemma and the choice of the ohacratic political option of governance, Iroegbu believes he has found the way out of the African predicament. Iroegbu's political theory of ohacracy has expectedly excited the attention of many contemporary African philosophers and has won the approbation of not a few social scientists. However, the merit of Iroegbu's theory can better be appreciated always against the background of its liberating potentials on the contemporary African socio-political crises.

Relevance of Iroegbu's Ohacracy to Africa

The relevance of Iroegbu's ohacratic option on African crises cannot be overemphasized. Ohacracy appears to be a better political option when its therapeutic lenses are beamed on African problems. It is not merely accidental that Iroegbu begins his thematic analysis of root causes of African problems with religion. By so doing, Iroegbu perhaps acknowledges the fact that man is essentially a religious being and that "there is no phenomenon which moulds and controls man's life as religion does" (Omoregbe, 1993, xiii). But depending on how it is applied, religion can be a liberating reality for the realization of man's true dignity and ultimate goal or man's cyclonic destructive force.

From historical antecedents, it does appear that in Africa, religion has constituted the greatest bane of progress in the society due to its misapplication. Here in Africa, the various religious movements and affiliations have metamorphosed into huge monolithic entities, pitching brothers against brothers in bitter rivalry (Etuk, 29). Indeed, in Africa, religion has constituted itself into God's military agent on earth that must hound other beings like mad dogs, and put into force the type of laws and practices which jeopardize human lives, properties and legitimate businesses of thousands of people; That Africa has been made a pathetic caricature of her lofty hopes and aspirations because Africans have turned religion into a deadly epidemic that swoops on us at will, leaving behind its trail, destruction of lives and properties, is a bitter fact confirmed by our daily experience (Odey, 1996, 17). Hence, to have started his argument from the backdrop of religion in the analysis of African problems is ingenuous of Iroegbu. His ohacratic solution is no less significant.

To stem the tide of religious fanaticism and violence, which leads eventually to the frightening moral and human decline in Africa, Iroegbu has proposed in his ohacratic arrangement that the centrality of the human person and respect for human life must precede any religious fervour and proselytism in the continent. He has argued that any religion in Africa today must see the neighbour as first and foremost a member of the community deserving of equal respect and opportunity in matters of conscience and religion (Iroegbu, 1994, 7). All these, however, must be done in the interests of all in the community.

It goes without saying that nothing short of this reformed attitude is expected of Africans if we must reap the gains of religions, and consequently experience authentic moral and human development and progress. It is time we learned to tolerate and respect each other's freedom of conscience and religion. The right to religious freedom is based on the very dignity of our human person as known through the revealed word of God and bylogical reasoning. This is why faith in God is not only logical but lack of faith is also illogical (Schaeffer, 15). It expresses what is unique about the human person, for it allows us to direct our personal and social life to God, in whose light the identity, meaning and purpose of the person are fully understood.

Therefore, man's response to God in religion must be free (*Dignitatis Humanae*, 10). Freedom of this kind and within the context of our problem, means that all Africans are to be immuned from coercion on the part of individuals or of social groups and of any human power, in such a way that in matters of religion no one is to be forced to act in a manner contrary to his own beliefs. Nor is anyone to be restrained from acting in accordance with his own beliefs, whether privately or publicly (Peschke, 627). This right of

Africans to religious freedom must be definitely recognized in the constitutional law of the African societies and must thus be made a civil right.

It is the duty of the government to protect this right for all African citizens. The government is not to act in arbitrary fashion or in an unfair spirit of partisanship as it seems to be the case in Nigeria. Only in the case of where a religious group commits abuses on the pretext of freedom of religion has the state the right and duty to intervene. For this reason, no religion may tolerate violence; much less preach it in Africa. Rather, religion must work together to remove the causes of violence and promote friendship among people (John Paul II, 1). In Nigeria as well as other African nations, the government must, therefore, rise up and defend the constitutional right of Africans to religious freedom. The perpetrators of religious violence must be brought to the full wrath of the law. Religious leaders must stand and work for the unity and peace of their communities in accordance with the ohacratic demands. They must not sow seed of violence, acrimony and discord in their activities. The ohacratic arrangement frowns at the profanation and blasphemy involved in declaring oneself a terrorist in God's name. Martyrdom cannot be the act of a person who kills in the name of God; rather it is a witness of a person who gives himself up to death rather than denies God and his love. Thus, the Muslims, Christians and other religious groups in Africa must treat each others with respect and see each other as brother and sister in the community, which they must build up with the elements of their religious faith. Truth can impose itself not with force, but only by virtue of its own authority freely sought and freely accepted.

Iroegbu's next analysis of the African predicament as shown in the median-triangle started with politics. This too is significant and its relevance to the exigencies and emergencies of the contemporary African situation cannot be over-emphasized. Iroegbu's effort here is a commendable attempt to redefine politics by its essence and to take dictatorship, callousness and oppression out of African political life. Its premise is that the political structure determines the economic and social life of the people. If we do not have it right in our political life, we cannot have it right in our economic and social lives. Hence, the principle of a just ohacratic society will demand first the fixing up of our chequered political history, and this will eventually lead to our economic and social development. Thus, he calls for responsible and accountable leadership chosen by the people free and popular will as well responsible followership defined by reasonable obedience that is opened to dialogue and inspired by the spirit of communal solidarity.

It is generally acknowledged today that Africa's problem in governance rests squarely on poor and dysfunctional leadership (John, 2009). Many African leaders subvert the people's wish and enthrone themselves on power by naked force and because they have constituted themselves into power-elite, they injuriously turn the continent into a jungle of corrupt looters of public treasury, where might is right and only the fittest survives. These leaders often manipulate the engine of electoral process to perpetuate their stay in power in order to continue their "politics of btterness" and multiply their wealth and privileges with their political offices which bring about the same degree of misery to the masses. Hence, politics is seen no longer as a call to selfless service but an opportunity to criminally impose oneself over others, abuse them at will and cart away their resources.

This explains why the economic and social situations of many in Africa today live below poverty line; many are unemployed and have practically no source of income. Many are without shelter, and so take refuge under overhead bridges, in motor parks, and in petrol stations, or they parade the streets like vagabonds, and are daily exposed to element of hardness. The educational system in Africa is virtually collapsing due to poor political leadership. And public utilities like pipe-borne water and electricity, where they are available, remain very epileptic. As a result of this crushingly imposed destitution, the Africans have lost their individual and collective pride to the excess of their indigenous power-elite conquerors, which seem to recognize no order than the one established by mammon.

Certainly, as Iroegbu observed this trend must be reversed if Africa must move forward politically, economically and socially. Power and sovereignty belong to the people. And this must be shown in the people's right and liberty to choose who they want to govern them;

how they may be governed and to effect a change of government as desired. In other words, it must be fully appreciated in line with ohacratic arrangement that all forms of dictatorship and imposition are not in keeping with the ideals of democracy. Democratic government in fact, is defined first of all by all the assignment of powers and functions on the part of the people, exercised in their name, in their regard and on their behalf (*Pontifical Council for Justice*, 190).

It is therefore clearly evident that for us to have it right in our political life, leadership must be participative. This means respect to the people's electoral right and their right to participate in public life. Accountability and honesty on the part of the leaders as well as the elimination of all those attitude that encourage in citizens an inadequate or incorrect practice of participation or that condemn them to deplorable state of existence in their political, economic and social lives must be totally eradicated from the society. Everyone must be his brother's keeper.

Again, Iroegbu assumes his analysis of the African vicious triangle with the problem of ignorance, the solution of which he considers the bedrock of African healthy living as well as the way out of poverty. Only a few will doubt that out human development depends to a large extent on our mental state or formation. To educate the mind is to lay the foundation for human growth and development.

Aware of this fact, Plato had advocated rigorous mental training for rulers, who would lead the society in his Academy. Impressed by the tremendous progress by modern science through the power of the human mind, Francis Bacon had declared that, "knowledge is power". John Paul II (8), in agreement with this writes, "in order for the full actualization of the human innate abilities to take place, it is necessary above all to provide adequate education for all...." And the Nigeria's National Policy on Education as "an instrument for national development" (6), and as "the most important instrument of change" (8) states that education cannot be over-emphasized, for ignorance is poverty, ignorance is disease.

From this standpoint, Iroegbu's theory becomes very relevant in the face of high illiteracy rate confronting Africa, for which reasons Africa continues to rank lowest in all indices of human development. It was this ignorance that made Africans to physically sell over 20 millions of their sons and daughters as slaves in history (Odey, 2000, 62). It was this ignorance that gave Africa away as booty to the colonial masters. It is this ignorance that made Africa today an easy prey to neo-colonization and imperialism by the capitalists' nations of the world. Writing on this, Oyebola maintains that because of ignorance, no country in Africa has made any breakthrough in technological and scientific achievement, great inventions and discoveries, Neither has any African country evolved any indigenous solution to the myriads of problems facing Africa such as endemic poverty, hunger, disease, lack of basic education and infrastructural facilities (10-14).

Africa has indeed been so disadvantaged in the global scene due to ignorance, and operates at the subsistence level of economy with thousands of people malnourished in addition to incurable diseases. There is the need to empower the masses through the instrument of education. Parents, who are the first educators of their children, must exercise with great responsibility this parental obligation in vigilant co-operation with civil and ecclesiastical agencies.

Government must provide affordable and qualitative education to the African citizens. They must give greater attention to the demands of the United Nations Universal Declaration of Human Rights (1948), which insist that education should be free at least in the elementary or fundamental stages. Besides, they must conform with the demand of the UN Convention of 1976 which requires that secondary education in its different forms, including technical and vocational shouldl be made available and accessible to all by every appropriate means, and that higher education should be made equally accessible to all on the basis of capacity, by every appropriate means, and in particular by the progressive introduction of free education (Article 13, Para. 2).

This mental formation must also make Africans aware of their own roots and provide points of reference which allow them to define their own personal place in the world and contribute to the development of the human family. When this is done, as Iroegbu himself stressed, the problems of poverty and diseases in Africa will be effectively addressed.

Evaluatory Remarks

Perhaps, only a few would not applaud Iroegbu for his great insights and rare acumen exhibited in his explicit analysis of the African problems in the form of triangles other than circles. By choosing the triangular figures, Iroegbu has successfully displayed his philosophical sagacity. He does not tackle a problem he is not prepared to give solution to, nor does he intend to make it seems as some thinkers would do, that African problems are beyond Africans and are therefore insoluble. This precision is a worthy impression that can be discerned in his choice of the triangular shape to illustrate the African problems, his detailed and surgical analysis of these problems and the therapeutic cure he proposes for them in his ohacracy theory. Such are the vignettes or attributes of great scholars.

Again, Iroegbu's ohacracy invites Africans to return to their communal roots which values solidarity among persons and brotherhood. Nothing can be more demanded on Africans more than this, given the frightening degeneration of the human and societal values that rock the African society today as the by-products of western civilization. Today, the characteristic African humanism, personalism, hospitality, wholesome personal relations, and the overwhelming sense of the sacred, have been infested and obscured by the cankerworm of western materialism and individualism.

Granted that Africans have a lot to learn and borrow from western civilization, the decline of that civilization suggests that the salvation of Africa however, or indeed the entire world does not lie in the indiscriminate appropriation of the values of such a civilization. To absorb uncritically the values of a derailing civilization is to embark on a suicidal course; hence, the significance of Iroegbu's ohacratic invitation for all Africans to go back to their communal roots.

Furthermore, authentic socio-political changes in the society are effective and lasting only to the extent that they are based on resolute changes in personal conduct. Iroegbu's ohacratic solution to the extant African problems depicted as that which must begin with the individual members of the *oha-umunna*, is indeed not without credit to his political thought.

However, Iroegbu in some cases seems to presume the mind of his readers in their understanding of certain technical terms employed in his analysis. For instance, he calls his ohacratic community "*oha-umunna*" (Iroegbu, 1994, 5), without any anterior or posterior explication of the term *"umunna"*. Here, a reader not familiar with this Igbo term simply throws a guess at it at best and at worst, get confused. The work thus faces the risk of multiple interpretations by readers, or even a "toss-aside" by an impatient reader.

Again, Iroegbu seems to engage so much in cultural nostalgia in this century of hyper-technological breakthroughs and scientific development. Perhaps, he needs to be reminded here that culture is dynamic and not static, and so it may be unproductive to engage in deep cultural nostalgia or romanticize traditional household values when the world is advancing on the wings of science and technology. It would seem that Iroegbu is taking us backward. What Africa urgently needs today is the knowledge and power that come from technology, so as to enjoy competitive advantage in the global community.

Furthermore, as Nwankwo pointed out, Iroegbu did not establish relationship of man and divinity especially in socio-political and ethical practices; his theological background would have bearing on this point, in order to set things right concerning man's action in the society.

Conclusion

Iroegbu's ohacratic political thought, notwithstanding the above criticisms, remains relevant in the field of socio-political philosophy. No doubt the crucial and critical nature of the problem of development facing African countries demands that all political theories implemented within the African continent must be adapted

FB 30

Djbouti pecple

to our African contextual realities. The issue of democracy and the need to contextualize it in the African context for positive results is the basis of Iroegbu's ingenious and provocative theory of ohacracy. At the end, one thing stands out for Iroegbu's illimitable reward and credit: He has challenged the African nations in the light of ohacracy either to embrace true democracy that will work for Africa or sacrifice development.

WORKS CITED

Brownie, Ian (Ed). *United Nations International Covenant on Economic, Social and Cultural Rights of 1976 in Basil Documents on Human Rights*. Oxford: Clarendon Press, 1988.

Catechism of the Catholic Church. Kenya: Paulines Publication-Africa, 1995.

Ehusani, G. *An Afro-Christian Vision*. Ibadan: Ambassador Publishers, 1997.

Etuk, A. "Muslim-Christian Relationship in Nigeria: A Historical review" in Sylvanus Nnoruka (Ed). *Christianity, Islam and Salvation Mission*. Owerri: Living Flames Resources, 2011.

Flannery, Austin (Ed). *.Dignitatis Humane in Vatican Council II*. Mumbai: St. Paul's Publishers, 2001.

Gandium et spes in (Ed) Austin Flannery. *Vatican Council* II. Mumbai: St. Paul's Publishers, 2001.

Iroegbu. P. and Izibili M. *Kpim of Democracy: Thematic Introduction to Socio-political Philosophy*. Benin-City. Ever-Blessed Publishers, 2004.

Iroegbu, P. "African Vicious Triangles, A Plea for Ohacracy: The Socio-political Lee-Way". Unpublished Public Lecturer, Delivered at the University of Lonvain, Belgium, Nov. 12, 1994.

John, Elijah Okon. "Ontological Placement in Western, Eastern and African Philosophies: A Contemporary Analysis" in *Uyo Journal of Humanities*. Vol. 11, July, 2006.

John, Elijah Okon. *Man and the State: Issues in Socio-political Philiosophy*. Uyo: Afahaide Publishers, 2009.

John Paul II, "Decalogue of Assisi for peace" in *Letter to Heads of States and Governments*, Feb. 2002.

John Paul II, "Letter for the 1994 Year of the Family" in Samuel Uzoukwu. *The Wise Teacher John Paul II*. Owerri: Martins Continental Publishers, 2002.

Locke, J. *Two Treaties of Government*. London: Everyman's Library, 1986.

Musonda, D. "Life as a Gift and a Task" in *African Christian Studies*. Nairobi, July,1986.

National Policy on Education. Lagos: NERDC, 2004.

Nyerere, J. *Ujamaa: Essay on Socialism*. London: Oxford University Press, 1970.

Nwankwor, I. "Iroegbu on Ohacracy for Integral Socio-political True Existence" in *Integrative Humanism Journal*. Vol. 1, No. 2, 2011.

Odey, J. *Sharia and the Rest of US*. Enugu: Snaap Press, 2000.

Odey, J. *Africa: The Agony of a Continent: Can Liberation Theology offer any Solution?* Enugu: Snaap Press, 1996.

Oyebola, A. *Black Man's Dilemma*. Ibadan: Board Publications, 1982.

Omoregbe, K. *Knowing Philosophy*. Lagos: Joja Educational Research and Publishers, 2001.

Omoregebe, J. *A Philosophical Look at Religion*. Lagos: Joja Educational Research and Publishers, 1993.

Peschke, K. *Christian Ethics: Moral Theology in the Light of Vatican II*. Vol. 2. India: Theological Publications in India, 1992.

Pontifical Connal for Justice Compendium of the Social Doctrine of the Church. Kenya: Paulines Publications in Africa, 2004.

Schaeffer, Francis A. *He is there and He is not Silent*. Wheaton: Tyndale House, 1072.

CPSIA information can be obtained
at www.ICGtesting.com
Printed in the USA
LVOW13s1625220617
539024LV00010B/545/P